CRAZY FOR YOU

CRAZY FOR YOU:
THE MAKING OF WOMEN'S MADNESS

JILL ASTBURY

Melbourne

OXFORD UNIVERSITY PRESS

Oxford   Auckland   New York

OXFORD UNIVERSITY PRESS AUSTRALIA

Oxford   New York
Athens   Auckland   Bangkok   Bombay
Calcutta   Cape Town   Dar es Salaam   Delhi
Florence   Hong Kong   Istanbul   Karachi
Kuala Lumpur   Madras   Madrid   Melbourne
Mexico City   Nairobi   Paris   Singapore
Taipei   Tokyo   Toronto

and associated companies in
Berlin   Ibadan

OXFORD is a trade mark of Oxford University Press

National Library of Australia
Cataloguing-in-Publication data:

Astbury, Jill.
Crazy for you: the making of women's madness.

Includes index.
ISBN 0 19 553768 8.

1. Women — Mental health. 2. Women — Mental
health — Sociological aspects. 3. Sexism in medicine.
4. Women — Health and hygiene — Sociological
aspects. I. Title.

616.890082

Edited by Cathryn Game
Text design by Dita Nance
Cover design by Steve Randles
Typeset by Desktop Concepts P/L, Melbourne
Printed by McPherson's Printing Group
Published by Oxford University Press,
253 Normanby Road, South Melbourne, Australia

CONTENTS

ACKNOWLEDGMENTS

This started out as a book on women and madness but became one on mad, or what I have called, using Alice James's phrase, neurotic science.

The book is based on a postgraduate course I teach, and my first thanks go to all the health professionals — doctors, psychologists, nurses, physiotherapists, pharmacists, scientists, social workers — for their enthusiasm and their incisive comments on the theories and evidence presented here. Knowing that 'neurotic science' continues to exert a toxic effect on the lives and minds of women who seek health care, and has had to be contested emotionally and intellectually by them as it has been by me, was of enormous encouragement in completing this work.

For the chapter on 'Wild women and sex in science', I am grateful to the librarians at the Wellcome Institute of the History of Medicine and Related Sciences in London who alerted me to so many interesting historical sources. Ann Oakley and her colleagues at the Social Science Research Unit at London University made me very welcome during the time I spent on study leave there in 1993 and made valuable comments on this chapter. I want to thank my colleagues at the Key Centre for Women's Health in Society, particularly Jane Fisher for our discussions on psychosomatic research into childbearing, Susan Donath for her interest and comments on the Freud chapters, and Lorraine Dennerstein and Carol Morse, my co-authors on the WHO report, *Psychosocial and Mental Health Aspects of Women's Health*, which prompted me to develop my section into the current book. Cathryn Game has spared no effort in her careful editing of the book, and Mary Panjari provided invaluable assistance with locating relevant research papers on sexual abuse and violence. Judith Lumley, Director of the Centre for the Study of Mothers and Children's Health, has unfailingly provided support and interest over many years of friendship and professional collaboration.

Finally, for the wonderful conversations on neurotic science and so much else, over the years, I want to thank my friends — Jan Epstein, Renata Singer, Martha Macintyre, Susie Hancock, Ann Potter, Diana Burden and Judy Wheaton. And, for her continuous involvement with this project, her original insights and emotional generosity, I am indebted to my daughter, Rebecca McMillan.

1

INTRODUCTION: PRONENESS AND DISORDER

She who does not lose her mind over certain things has no mind to lose.

With apologies to Gotthold Ephraim Lessing,
author of the play *Emilia Galotti* (1772)

She was almost beside herself at the idea of its being supposed that she had merely fancied something on that occasion.

Sigmund Freud, 'Fragment of an analysis of a case of hysteria' (1905)

In writing this book I am attempting not so much to answer a question as to change the kind of question that is asked. Early in 1993, following the publication of a WHO report on women's mental health, which Lorraine Dennerstein, Carol Morse and I wrote,[1] a journalist asked me: 'Why are women more prone to mental health problems than men?' The question was ostensibly based on the finding that twice as many women as men experience depression. By asking about 'proneness' the journalist was implicitly accepting, expressing and reinforcing the long-standing belief that women have an innate tendency to mental disorder. A query about 'proneness' immediately directs one's attention inwards to the intrapsychic, rather than outwards to society and what actually happens to women in their work, family and personal lives or how these experiences impinge on their mental health.

One of the principal aims of this book is to redress this balance. I will argue that there is a need to move away from the idea that women have some essential biologically based proclivity to create their own neurosis and foment their own misery. Most of all, I will show how this notion of proneness, so eagerly taken up in scientific theories and research, has not produced impartial knowledge at all but rather distorted observations and serious misunderstandings of women's emotional distress.

Many of the scientific theories from the nineteenth century onwards that sought to explain women to themselves, and none more so than Freud's revised theory of hysteria, have functioned as a defensive bulwark that prevented the conditions of women's lives from being taken into account in explanations of their mental distress. Indeed, I consider that these theories are themselves psychogenic, being powerful ideological instruments in the creation of neurosis. This book is concerned with the examination of this 'neurotic science', a science that says infinitely more about the psychology of the observer than the observed, and especially about the observer's often malign fantasies of the other.

The question about women's proneness to depression contains an assumption that is rarely made explicit. It has to do with seeing female rates of depression as pathological, too high and a problem. The only vantage point from which such a view is possible is that which assumes male rates of depression constitute a norm, are in themselves completely unproblematic and provide the only reasonable point of departure from which pathology in women can be measured. Males' rates become the unremarked given that requires no explanation. Consequently traditional sociological and psychological theories have been applied in ways that obscure the fact that men's activities are gendered, as opposed to representing the 'human', and have made it difficult to understand women's participation in social life. The implicit adoption of a male norm, where its gendered nature remains obscured, has been called *androcentrism* or *phallocentrism*. It can be found in various guises from supposedly scientific research to the most blatant forms of social control directed to women.

The pervasiveness of the androcentric approach can be appreciated if, instead of asking about the problem of women's depression, the rates of depression in men are positioned instead as problematic, perplexing and in need of clarification. Why, it could be asked, but usually isn't, are male rates so abnormally low? Why do men not become more depressed about the disproportionate amount of physical and sexual violence they commit, the inequitable contribution they make to the work of the household and the care of children, the greatly increased number of murders they perpetrate or the excess number of deaths on the road they cause? Is it hormonally based? Does testosterone interfere with the development of full humanity and emotional sensitivity? Of course, it is precisely with apparently insulting questions like these that scientific investigations on the faulty biology, malignant hormones, inadequate morality and inherent psychopathology of women have been preoccupied in the seemingly tireless search to explain and pinpoint the origins of female 'difference'.

The usual absence of men as the focus of questions of this kind eloquently underlines how gender — and very often class and race too — can silently but nevertheless strenuously determine what is identified as a 'problem' and who gets to decide on what will be seen as one. Although a problem is always a problem for someone, the ubiquitous presence of gender bias in scientific research meant that the fact of its existence was easily overlooked. Because such bias was the norm, it could literally not be seen or engaged with as an epistemological issue.

For very many years, there was thought to be nothing at all odd about the almost universal situation of male researchers investigating female research subjects and proposing more or less complicated solutions to what the researchers themselves had constructed as the problem of female difference. Once this assumption of difference was embedded in the research, it became an easy matter to prove that it existed and that women departed in a pathological way from the ideal of a male norm; in other words, women were deviant by definition. The research stemming from this viewpoint had a systematic blindness. It could literally not see what it was doing as the normative quality of its own pre-suppositions made them invisible. And such research, therefore, could not avoid mirroring and reproducing the broader social and structural inequalities and stereotypes related to gender within the fabric of its own research as in the relationship between the male, active, rational researcher and the female, passive, emotional research subject. Thus the definition and construction of 'problems' and 'knowledge' by science has been primarily man-made. Women, by and large, have been excluded; they have neither been the researchers who investigated problems on the basis of what was problematic for them nor has their experience of the world acted as a basis for constructing theories of their own psychology.

Discussion of the woman question, as it was called in the nineteenth century, was dominated by male opinion. Evidence as opposed to opinion was, and in many ways, still is, lacking altogether or is woefully insufficient. As John Stuart Mill wrote in *The Subjection of Women* published in 1869:

> We may safely assert that the knowledge which men can acquire of women, even as they have been and are, without reference to what they might be, is wretchedly imperfect and superficial, and always will be so, until women themselves have told all that they have to tell. And this time has not come.[2]

We continue to know far more of what scientific 'experts' think about women's nature, and what is needed for the 'normal' functioning of their bodies, minds and lives, than we do about what women think of themselves or what they believe is 'for their own good'. But even more importantly, because of its effect on emotional well-being, is that what women do think of themselves is structured, mediated and shaped through the process of grappling with what is thought of them. If expert opinion stresses pathology, vulnerability and disorder, which it does, then women will be constantly poised to refract themselves through a glass darkly. The impact of androcentric science, its quality and the way it has been used to serve social and ideological aims in the nineteenth century and in this one are considered in different ways in each chapter of this book.

Through their association with science and the legitimacy it confers, medicine and psychiatry especially have been instrumental in forming women's conception of who and what they are. Medical and psychological science has defined and delimited women's mental, physical and emotional abilities for them. At the same time, the theories that positioned women as inherently predisposed to disorder and disease have relied on hermetically sealed categories of explanation and premises about woman's nature that cannot be 'penetrated' because they are designed to preclude the discovery of contrary evidence. The impress of these essentialist theories of woman's nature and woman's madness comprehensively prevented the elicitation of the very information or evidence most needed to test or refute them. In other words, within the dominant discourse on women's mental health, it has been difficult if not impossible for women and any alternative view of them to be heard. I contend that this situation has made for not just poor science but also for neurotic science; this combination is discussed in relation to Freud's theories of women, the case history of Dora and most especially in the way childhood sexual abuse was able to be denied as a pressing social problem for so long.

Sylvia Plath believed that as a woman you are damned anyway; if you are normal you are mad by implication and if you are abnormal you are mad by definition. In the following pages I intend to investigate why the belief in women's inherent proneness to mental disorder has been so tenacious, and want to explore the deleterious effects of living between implication and definition. This is the psychological territory of what might be called the 'razor's edge' of normality for women. It consists of the behaviour, intellectual manoeuvres and emotional adaptations, adjustments and compromises that characterise the experience of surviving within circumscribed boundaries.

Such boundaries are held firm by cultural, social and personal beliefs and practices that collectively reinforce the idea that mental and emotional normality for women demands that they constantly, self-consciously and anxiously appraise their feelings and behaviour to ensure that they remain within that small acceptable zone between deficiency and excess. Science will be revealed to have had no small role in devising and policing this zone. Its involvement in the process began in earnest in the second half of the nineteenth century when its utterances quickly became the gold standard against which women had to measure, or rather mismeasure, their thoughts, feelings and actions to gauge their normalcy.

Today, recognisably similar scientific theories continue to influence conceptions of women's sanity and madness and perform the same normative role. Much of the professional discourse on women's physical and mental health is haunted by nineteenth-century views of biological determinism. Central to the moral force of these views is the threat, uttered overtly or covertly, that to trangress what is 'natural' and 'normal', as defined by the scientific experts, is to invite madness.

Women have been endlessly exhorted to change themselves and have had little choice but to comply. But as Amy Tan has written in *The Joy Luck Club*, 'no matter how much she changed her life, she could not change the world that surrounded her'.[3] Compliance has operated on two levels; first, compliance or acceptance of what their medical, social and psychological problems were and why they were problems and, second, compliance with the range of solutions offered to these problems. From the nineteenth century, medical treatments, including psychological ones, have increasingly offered useful techniques for the social control of women.

Sometimes the medical solutions to women's 'problems' have been obviously invasive, like the clitoridectomies and ovariectomies performed on thousands of women in both the UK and the USA in the late nineteenth century. Clitoridectomy, for example, was pioneered in the 1860s by Dr Isaac Baker Brown as a solution to masturbation, nymphomania, depression and marital dissatis-faction. Elaine Showalter relates that Brown performed five cli-toridectomies on women whose only 'madness' consisted of wanting a divorce and 'in each case the woman returned to her husband subdued'.[4]

While such blatant surgical genital mutilation is rarer in West-ern countries now than in the nineteenth century, it continues to occur. Worldwide some 70–100 million women are affected by female genital mutilation (FGM). It is practised in more than forty northern and Central African, Middle Eastern, southern and Cen-tral American countries as well as by some groups in Indonesia and Malaysia. It is also arguable whether the thousands of oper-ations that annually take place in the USA and elsewhere to 'aug-ment' or reduce women's breasts, tighten their vaginas or redesign their faces and other body parts arise from a qualitatively differ-ent kind of cultural motivation from that which encourages female genital mutilation. Although FGM is roundly condemned in Western countries with thriving cosmetic surgery industries, these same countries also routinely practise the cutting of the per-ineum in labour, even though episiotomy has no proven benefit. Is the husband who asks the doctor doing an episiotomy on his wife to 'Make sure you sew her up tight for me' expressing such a dif-ferent attitude from that which supports FGM? All the surgical practices designed to fillet, fill out and reorder women's bodies participate in the same continuum of belief that creates and then caters to an anxiety in women that their bodies, in their original form, are neither well made nor readily acceptable.

Until 1989, when he surrendered his licence following charges of grossly unprofessional conduct, an American doctor, James C. Burt, was busily rearranging women's genitalia to make them bet-ter wives. Dr Burt believed that women were anatomically defec-tive and 'structurally inadequate for intercourse'. His surgical remedy was to remove the hood of the clitoris, reposition the vagina, move the urethra and alter the walls between the rectum and the vagina. He was convinced that his 'love surgery' would turn frigid wives into 'horny little mice'.[5]

The ever-growing range of diagnostic, pharmacological and surgical techniques related to women's sexual and reproductive lives demonstrates that this tradition of interference for women's 'own good' continues to thrive. Pregnancy is a good example of the medicalisation of what is for most women a normal and unproblematic state. It has been defined in terms of its risk, and the best that can be hoped for within the medical model that ascribes risk is to be classified as 'low risk'. All medically supervised pregnancies receive intensive surveillance, ranging from a plethora of foetal diagnostic techniques — chorionic villus sampling, amniocentesis and ultrasound — to the use in labour of interventions including induction, foetal monitoring, forceps delivery or Caesarean section. Similarly, there are numerous medical and chemical treatments for menstruation and pre-menstrual syndrome.

The language of inadequacy and failure is readily attached to the female body and its functioning. In pregnancy, there is the risk posed by the 'incompetent cervix', and in labour there is the spectre of obstetric intervention brought about by 'failure to progress'. The lifelong use of hormone replacement therapy, from middle age onwards, has been advocated for the 'oestrogen deficiency disease' of menopause. Indeed, 'failing' ovaries seem to be a growth industry, and their treatment has resulted in prescriptions for hormone replacement therapy outstripping those for other drugs. By 1992, Premarin, an oestrogen product, had overtaken Amoxil, a brand of amoxycillin, as the most widely prescribed drug in the USA. The age at which ovaries begin to fail and are in need of outside hormonal help seems to be getting earlier and earlier; even women in their thirties are thought to be at risk and in need of treatment. At this rate of decline, one is bound to wonder whether women's ovaries ever work properly! Acceptance of the 'normality' of women's bodies, let alone their minds, unaided by medical assistance, seems, if anything, further away than ever.

Often the most deeply internalised beliefs, the ones that exert most control over our minds and our lives, are hardest to articulate. Even when they are conscious and able to be spoken about, questioning and contesting them is difficult. This is particularly true for women attempting to challenge internalised beliefs about the characteristics of their 'nature'. In Jane Austen's novel, *Persuasion*, when Anne Elliot attempts to argue against Captain Harville's view that women are inconstant, he points to all the evidence against her:

> 'But let me observe that all histories are against you, all stories, prose and verse. If I had such a memory as Benwick, I could bring you fifty quotations in a moment, and I do not think I ever opened a book in my life which had not something to say upon woman's inconstancy. Songs and proverbs, all talk of woman's fickleness. But perhaps you will say, these were all written by men.'
>
> 'Perhaps I shall. Yes, yes, if you please, no reference to examples in books. Men have had every advantage of us in telling their own story. Education has been theirs in so much higher a degree; the pen has been in their hands.'[6]

Feminist critiques of knowledge in the sciences and social sciences make basically the same point albeit in a somewhat different form. One of the givens of these critiques is that previous social, psychological and scientific theories purporting to explain women and the world have been constructed by and based on the experiences and ideas of men in their own interests, never by or for women themselves. And if men and women occupy different positions in the social structure and this situation, in turn, is associated with different experiences of the world, then recourse to only one set of criteria to explain their behaviour and understanding will necessarily produce incomplete and inadequate knowledge. Moreover, if only one gender influences the criteria adopted for use in scientific research, then any findings that flow from those criteria cannot support claims to universal knowledge and will cause data to be misinterpreted.

At least three main forms of feminist approach can be adopted when doing research. They include, first, feminist empiricism, which takes the position that there is nothing fundamentally wrong with current methods of scientific enquiry once androcentric biases are removed; second, a feminist standpoint to research based on

Hegel's thinking about the relationship of master and slave, which asserts that men's dominant position in social life and in science necessarily and inevitably leads to partial and perverse understanding of both social life and science which only ever presents the master's view, never the slave's; and third, feminist poststructuralism, which seeks to deconstruct dominant views of reality so as to reveal the unarticulated presuppositions and intense partiality of what is usually presented as being completely impartial.

Benjamin, among others, has argued that the concept of gender, because it embodies that of difference and serves as a basis for power relations, is able to problematise and at the same time clarify the way science and research have been practised.[7] Without the concept of gender, it is not possible to begin to ask questions about how the different social categories occupied by women and men differentially affect how they see and understand the world.

As a feminist psychologist — if that is not an oxymoron — I find myself in a dilemma. On the one hand, I am often aware of the continuing androcentric bias in published research and therefore am not entirely convinced that the reforms to science sought by feminist empiricism are likely to work. On the other hand, while poststructuralist analysis works well as a critical tool for revealing androcentric bias in non-feminist discourses and research, it has less to offer as a constructive methodology for undertaking new feminist research. Indeed, the whole issue of what, if anything, can be called a 'fact' or 'empirical evidence' in poststructuralist analysis is uncertain.

In this book I will be examining the empirical research published in medical and social science research journals. In doing this a point is quickly reached at which one has to decide how to treat the 'facts' contained therein. Although I realise that even apparently 'hard' data, such as rates of disease, are socially constructed to various extents, I accept that empirical evidence, despite its susceptibility to various sources of bias, does exist and is worth seeking. I also consider that some views have better evidence and are more tenable than others, and that androcentric bias is inconsistent with good research.

Sandra Harding's arguments regarding the need for 'strong objectivism' that incorporates feminist critiques of science seem to offer a viable framework for feminist empirical research.[8] This position is very different from the old neutrality ideal. It rejects the notion that evidence or data 'speak for themselves' and does not concur with the universalising claims of science to understand all existence.

Cultural influences and other values invariably determine the origin of problems that prompt the search for empirical evidence. This is true in the sense of the broader culture and what it conceives to be worth enquiring about and, perhaps more importantly, what it deems does not merit 'scientific' enquiry, as well as in the specific sense of the values that vivify the culture of a particular discipline. Data is always interpreted — published papers do not end with the results section. The interpretation of results and the choice of statistical treatments or other analytic treatments are also subject to a variety of influences beyond the stated hypotheses and the particular research paradigm underpinning the research. These influences include unstated beliefs of the researcher and his or her personal, cultural and ideological values, which powerfully affect the way data is interpreted.[9]

As Stephen Jay Gould points out, an iconography of expectation operates even with visual material. Photographs and pictures can be profoundly ideological in content and do not necessarily function as mere reflective mirrors of nature. 'Few scientists would view an image itself as intrinsically ideological in content. Pictures, as accurate mirrors of nature, just are.' Numerous opportunities exist for the subtle manipulation of photographs of objects and even more present themselves in the representation of animate beings. Gould argues that

> many of our pictures are incarnations of concepts masquerading as neutral descriptions of nature. These are the most potent sources of conformity, since ideas passing as descriptions lead us to equate the tentative with the unambiguously factual. Suggestions for the organization of thought are transformed to established patterns in nature. Guesses and hunches become things.[10]

Certainly, Jean Martin Charcot, the French doctor with whom Freud studied in the 1880s, was indignant at the possibility that his photographs of 'mad' women were anything other than accurate representations of their mental states. Charcot made more use of photography than anyone else engaged in psychiatric practice in the nineteenth century, and his photographic *oeuvre* occupied a three-volume work, *Nouvelle iconographie photographique de la Salpêtrière*. Showalter has written that 'Charcot's hospital became an environment in which female hysteria was perpetually presented, represented and reproduced.'[11] Charcot could not believe that he in any way affected what he saw and reproduced. As far as he was concerned mental illness resided in the person; it was an independent entity: 'It would be truly marvellous if I were thus able to create illnesses at the pleasure of my whim and my caprice. But as for the truth, I am absolutely only the photographer; I register what I see'.[12]

Any research methodology can, in one sense, be seen as forming a more or less coherent set of suggestions for the organisation of research, and feminist approaches to research are no exception. At different times all three forms of feminist approach to research may be seen to have influenced this book. While there might be different modes of analysing the theories and evidence, the discourse of medical science on women's emotional well-being tends towards the monolithic and is heavily overburdened by nineteenth-century essentialist assumptions about woman's 'nature'. Moreover, the published empirical research is underpinned by a positivist model of science, which originally helped to construct and authenticate the same essentialist view, making reform from within the model extremely unlikely. In what follows, I will examine this discourse, its dictates and its neurotic impress on women's sensibilities. I intend to show how the unexamined androcentrism of much that has passed for science is incompatible with science's own espousal of neutrality, objectivity and impartiality. And, to paraphrase Gould, I want to explore the way in which ideological concepts and malignant fantasies of woman as the other have for too long masqueraded as neutral descriptions of her nature.

2

THE RAZOR'S EDGE: IDEOLOGY AND SELF-LIMITATION

The history of women and madness, or what Elaine Showalter calls the 'female malady',[1] has often been confounded with the belief that, for women, history is synonymous with nature. The dominance of the essentialist view that woman's 'nature' was unmediated by culture undermined the possibility of asking questions about how culture fashioned the lineaments of this very 'nature'. In the past, woman's nature has been seen to exist as a separate and independent entity untouched by and unresponsive to any cultural imprinting. The unquestioned belief that woman's nature was more prone to mental illness meant that the cultural and historical specificity of the images, behaviour, symptoms and attributes assigned to women could be conveniently ignored or dismissed as irrelevant. Only with an acknowledgement of the social construction of gender does it become possible to examine the psychological impact of growing up female in a society that historically has defined 'female' as less than fully human.

How the concept of 'woman' is socially constructed, and what it expresses about the values and expectations cultures assign to being female, is something that has to be investigated rather than assumed. Anthropological research, beginning in the 1920s with Margaret Mead's work with adolescent girls in Samoa, challenged the idea of the universal woman with static and immutable characteristics. In her book *Coming of Age in Samoa* Mead provided empirical evidence that becoming a woman in Samoa was not the same thing as becoming one in America and that the concept of 'woman' could therefore not be regarded as having a fixed meaning that was uniform throughout different cultures.[2] On the contrary, her work showed that what is involved in being a woman varies considerably between cultures. It can also change within the same culture along with changing social mores. Likewise gender experiences can and do vary between categories of class, sexual preference and race. Postmodernist feminists have argued that just as there is no universal woman, there is no single, coherent form of feminism that can speak for all women or all feminists; rather there are 'feminisms'.[3] Nevertheless, these 'feminisms' agree that phallocentrism or androcentrism inheres in all our dominant mainstream (or what has been dubbed 'malestream') Western ways of thinking about the world.

The social philosopher, George Simmel, also writing in the 1920s, was one of the first to draw attention to the great but unnoticed bias associated with the fact that 'our whole civilization is a masculine civilization'. Simmel, anticipating the arguments of later feminists, asserted that the difficulty of recognising masculine bias arose because the standards used to estimate the values of male and female nature were not neutral but essentially masculine. He went on to note how this brought about the 'naive identification of the concept "human being" and the concept "man" which in many languages even causes the same word to be used for the two concepts'.[4] This same equation resulted in inadequate achievements being seen as feminine and distinguished ones as masculine.

The use of contrast and opposition, together with the attribution of positive value to only one of the two contrasting qualities, defines a dualistic style of making sense of the world. It is a way of thinking characterised by a representational construction of the world in binary terms where one term is always privileged in relation to the other. A self-sustaining system is created in which the privileged term is regarded as the norm and its opposite is defined only in relation or reaction to it and is devalued accordingly. It is a familiar list: rational/irrational, objective/subjective, thinking/feeling, culture/nature, science/art, mind/body, masculine/feminine.

It is from this list that sex-role stereotypes derive. In the early 1970s research by Broverman and co-workers revealed that psychotherapists accepted sex-role stereotypes to the same extent as everyone else.[5] Therapists displayed the full play of dualistic thinking in the beliefs that informed their clinical practice. The research found that therapists not only endorsed characteristics which defined stereotypic notions of femininity but also saw them as the opposite of the qualities associated with masculinity. In addition, feminine characteristics carried a heavy load of negative connotations.

> Our research demonstrates the contemporary existence of clearly defined sex role stereotypes for men and women contrary to the phenomenon of 'unisex' currently touted in the media. Women are perceived as relatively less competent, less independent, less objective and less logical than men. Men are perceived as lacking interpersonal sensitivity, warmth and expressiveness in comparison to women. Moreover, stereotypically masculine traits are more often perceived to be desirable than are the stereotypically feminine characteristics. Most importantly, both men and women incorporate both the positive and negative traits of the appropriate stereotype in their self concepts.[6]

Women looking to therapy for 'help' were almost invariably going to encounter from their therapist more of the same attitudes that had formed their own presenting symptoms of low self-esteem, a lack of confidence and a distressingly high level of anxiety.

Two years after Broverman and his colleagues, Benjamin Fabrikant did a replication of their study and asked therapists to rate (positively or negatively) the characteristics associated with femininity and masculinity. Fabrikant found that male therapists rated 70 per cent of the 'female' words as negative while they rated 71 per cent of 'male' words as positive. Despite being well-educated, high-achieving women practising a profession, 68 per cent of female therapists also rated the female words as negative and 67 per cent of the male words as positive.[7]

This finding points up the difficulty women face in being able to resist or contest the highly negative view of the qualities seen to be intrinsic to their identity. In what almost reads like a caricature of negative femininity, both male and female therapists agreed that women could be described as: 'chatterer, decorative, dependent, dizzy, domestic, fearful, flighty, fragile, generous, irrational, nurturing, overemotional, passive, subordinate, temperamental, virtuous'. Male therapists added 'manipulative' and 'perplexing' while female therapists included some positive characteristics as well as some additional negative ones. The female therapists added 'devoted, empathic, gentle, kind, sentimental, slave, yielding'.[8]

If these dualisms always and only exist in relation to one another, the question becomes one of asking whether and in what way it is possible to speak, write or think outside them — or inside them, for that matter. For women, any attempt to be heard will first have to overcome the view that what they are saying is *prima facie* likely to lack reason, objectivity, impartiality and power. Surmounting this credibility hurdle will be difficult enough when the content of what is being said relates to easily verifiable matters of reason or fact. It will be almost impossible, however, if a woman is attempting to claim importance for any qualities on the devalued side of the long string of binary oppositions. In this instance, she will be attempting to have difference, so long imbued with connotations of negativity and inferiority, seen differently. The Descartian split between body and mind has been especially detrimental to the possibility of women being heard. Reason and mind has been identified not only with masculinity but also with independence, objectivity, impartiality, authority and power. Body, mind's despised opposite, has been linked with femininity, dependence, subjectivity, partiality and an inherent lack of authority and power.

Even the apparently neutral presentation of data in scientific journals is affected by this split. Health statistics typically show data for males first, in the left-hand column, and that for women, second, in the right-hand column, or present data for men in an upper line and that for women in a lower line. The meaning being conveyed is like subliminal advertising. It is not necessarily obvious that 'top' is better than 'bottom', but such an interpretation is suggested when other variables are presented in the same way, for example when 'employed' is above 'unemployed' or when 'literate' precedes 'illiterate'.[9]

Another instance of how this split operates can be seen in the difficulty experienced by pregnant women looking for an obstetrician sympathetic to 'natural' childbirth. In Victoria, Australia, almost one in three women have some kind of operative delivery, including Caesarean section, forceps and vacuum extraction, and in all Western countries rates of obstetric procedures have increased markedly since the 1960s.[10] This increase has coexisted with the rise of 'natural' childbirth, birth plans and childbirth education that prepares women to give birth rather than be delivered. Yet despite the fact that women, through consumer groups, have clearly voiced their preference to give birth with as much autonomy and as little obstetric intervention as possible, the figures on the rising tide of Caesarean sections indicate that they have had a singular lack of success in being heard. The evidence on obstetric intervention would seem to suggest that their wishes, beliefs and feelings have been accorded little validity and have had no impact on professional practice. If anything there is an inverse relationship between women's expressed preferences and obstetric practice.

In the following pages I will argue that the problem of being heard is one that crucially impinges on women and their mental health. Dualistic thinking configures women's emotional lives as much as their intellectual ones and is instrumental in creating the conditions for the anxiety, depression and low self-esteem so often documented in psychiatric research and clinical treatment of women. In the past, women's higher rates of certain mental disorders have been interpreted as deriving from innate, immutable and 'natural' features of their psyches. Clarifying the connection between dualistic thinking, psychological theories and the emotional well-being of those, who because of their gender, are positioned on the devalued side of the series of oppositions has not been high on the agenda of previous research in women's mental health. Earlier work typically sought the likely causes of women's higher rates of distress and disorder in the reproductive, intrapsychic and hormonal sphere.

Not surprisingly, given the devaluing of the body, femininity and subjectivity in dualistic thinking, the tendency to pathologise women's minds and bodies is most strikingly apparent in research concerned with women's reproductive functioning. A voluminous research literature proceeds from the assumption that existing personality disorders in women are the cause of all manner of reproductive difficulties. Research carried out from the 1950s through to the 1980s shows an obsession with searching for and finding psychological pathology in women to account for everything from infertility, premature rupture of the membranes, pre-eclampsia and premature delivery to an excessively long labour, uterine dysfunction, high levels of analgesia and anaesthesia and obstetric complications, including operative delivery. In this research, the cause of all these difficulties was invariably attributed, after the event, to some psychological shortcoming in the mother. Methodologically this is inadequate. The only way to test meaningfully whether the theorised connection between personality and obstetric complication exists is to establish the psychological status of the mother *before* the complication or obstetric difficulty occurs. Concentrating on the woman's psychological state *after* an obstetric complication has occurred means that it is impossible to disentangle whether her emotional state caused the complication or whether the complication caused her emotional state. Moreover, an assessment of a woman's personality or emotional state made when she is depressed suggesting she has a 'dysfunctional' personality might bear no relationship to how she would score on the same measure when she was feeling well.

To read earlier research in this vein is to confront a veritable cornucopia of psychopathology in the mother. It suggests that obstetrical difficulties of one sort or another can be triggered by anything from latent homosexuality, 'repressed [masculine] striving', guilt about masturbation, repression and suspicion;[11] personality abnormalities such as being a 'manic ... psychopathic deviate';[12] to being narcissistic, immature, less feminine and less desirous of the pregnancy.[13] In a similar vein, the research sought to prove that women who experienced obstetrical difficulties were socially introverted, hypochrondiacal and users of pathological defences;[14] had high levels of anxiety,[15] exhibited hostility and psychoneurosis[16] or had a negative or complicated relationship with their own mother, who herself was likely to have shown difficulties in adjusting to motherhood.[17]

Research of this kind was underpinned by the unshakeable belief that every physical outcome of pregnancy and birth could be confidently traced back to a psychological cause. The research took place within a theoretical context that assumed the truth of its central hypothesis. Considerable effort was therefore poured into the task of confirming the belief that the workings of a woman's mind and psyche always affected the workings of her body and little or none into querying whether such a cause and effect relationship really did exist. Factors outside the woman's own psyche that could affect the progress and outcome of labour and delivery were simply not investigated.

Of course the dominance of a psychosomatic model of obstetric complication made it extremely unlikely that any alternative explanation would be considered. The culture of medicine and the rising rate of obstetric intervention, which saw the incidence of Caesarean section rise from around 4 per cent in the 1960s to 17 per cent today in Australia and 25 per cent in the USA, remained outside the critical gaze of psychosomatically inclined researchers.

Not surprisingly, the intellectual position that informed the psychosomatic view of obstetric complication derived from psychoanalytic theories regarding women. Of seminal importance were the neo-Freudian ideas enthusiastically taken up and elaborated by psychoanalyst Helene Deutsch in her two-volume work, *The Psychology of Women*. This work was first published in the

USA in 1945 and was reprinted some thirteen times. It was crucial in the way its view of women shaped and informed much of the psychosomatic research in obstetrics and gynaecology over the next forty years. Through its adoption by Herbert Thoms, a professor of obstetrics and gynaecology, who pioneered natural childbirth programs at Grace-New Haven Hospital in 1947, the psychoanalytic model also influenced the kind of ante-natal education American women received. Deutsch never deviated from her belief that:

> Every single physiological gesture, every labour pain, as it were, testifies not only to the mutual dependence of the somatic and psychic factors, but also to the fact that in all the biologic functions of reproduction, the woman's whole psychic development and her whole emotional past play a decisive part.[18]

Indeed, twenty years before the publication of *The Psychology of Women*, Deutsch had written a paper with Freud that stated a set of psychoanalytic axioms from which she never departed. It was called 'The psychology of woman in relation to the functions of reproduction'. Deutsch read it at the Eighth International Psycho-Analytic Congress in Salzburg in 1924. The paper, like the later book, is remarkable for its strict adherence to Freud's beliefs. All the physical symptoms of pregnancy are interpreted as reflecting earlier unresolved conflicts. For example, morning sickness and food cravings, both common occurrences in pregnancy, are confidently stated to be the expression of the later part of the oral phase of development, whereby there is a tendency to expel again — orally — the object that has been incorporated. Similarly, the prime psychological meaning of giving birth, in keeping with the tenets of Freud's thinking, is seen to be masochistic. 'In actual fact parturition is for the woman an orgy of masochistic pleasure'.[19]

The Freudian view of childbirth also stressed the importance of penis envy as the woman's main motivation in becoming a mother. This assertion did not go unchallenged by Karen Horney, who was one of the most outspoken and ablest critics of Freud and Deutsch. Superficially, Horney had much in common with Helene Deutsch.

They were born within a year of one another, Deutsch in 1884, Horney in 1885. Both became doctors and then psychiatrists at a time when very few women did; both undertook psychoanalytic training; both married, had children and ultimately both left Europe and emigrated to the USA because of Nazism.

Theoretically, however, their views diverged quite early on. By the 1920s Horney was questioning the biological basis of the difference between the sexes and was becomingly increasingly interested in the influence of culture and the relationship between women's psyches and their social subordination. In her move away from the biological account of gender difference, Horney was influenced by the ideas of George Simmel, mentioned earlier, and she quotes Simmel approvingly in her critical review of Deutsch's work, 'Psychoanalysis of the sexual functions of women', published in the *International Psychoanalytic Journal* in 1926.

In this review, Horney could barely conceal how absurd she thought Deutsch's psychoanalytically inspired views of childbirth and motherhood were: 'We must give expression, from a sober clinical point of view, to some criticism of the extraordinary view [expressed by Deutsch] that the actual orgasm of the woman takes place during childbirth'. Horney rejected Deutsch and Freud's belief that motherhood had only a secondhand meaning and was a mere by-product of penis envy. She insisted that motherhood was an independently meaningful and joyful event: 'At this point I, as a woman, ask in amazement, and what about motherhood? And the blissful consciousness of bearing a new life within oneself?'[20]

Yet Horney's contrary views were not heard for very long. As she grew more critical of orthodox Freudian views, Horney became something of a pariah. Her ideas were effectively censored. None of her papers was accepted for publication in the *International Journal of Psychoanalysis* after the mid 1930s.

The theories that dominated subsequent research and clinical practice were clearly those of Freud and Deutsch. Their beliefs on the psychological meaning of motherhood are discernible almost immediately in the empirical research that took place from the

1920s onwards. For example, between 1925 and 1930, Dr Gregory Zilboorg published two descriptive studies on pregnancy and childbirth and their psychological effects. The 1928 paper was called 'Malignant psychoses related to childbirth',[21] and it was followed in 1929 by 'The dynamics of schizophrenic reactions related to pregnancy and childbirth'.[22]

The imprint of Freudian thinking in Zilboorg's reference to his postpartum schizophrenic patients is unmistakable. 'The child, it appears, has for these women more the value of a lost male organ than anything else ... Childbirth being a castration, the psychotic reaction to it is a recrudescence of the penis envy'. Zilboorg's observations of his patients communicate far more about his Freudian preconceptions and how they determine what he sees than they do about the patients themselves, let alone offering any insight into how they experience the world.

Zilboorg's research in the 1920s was the first to adopt a Freudian lens in 'explaining' the causal link between women's psychological and reproductive functioning. As we have seen, research underpinned by the same Freudian ideas, begun in the 1920s, continued to flourish for many years after World War II. The overriding preoccupation of these studies on pregnancy and childbirth was to prove that the psychological state of the mother was the cause of any obstetric difficulties she experienced. Psychosomatic theory ordained that physiological pathology in pregnancy and birth had a counterpart in, and was dependent on, psychological pathology.

Evidence from more recent research seriously contests this hypothesis. It has become obvious that obstetrical interventions themselves are significant in the development of emotional disorders, including depression, after the birth of an infant. In a reversal of the earlier idea, it now seems likely that obstetric interventions and complications are just as likely to be a cause of later psychological problems, as an effect of earlier ones.[24] A corollary of recent findings on the psychogenic potential of interventionist obstetric practice is that much of what takes place during the course of pregnancy, labour and delivery is not under women's control. What happens in the labour ward is more likely to be an expression of the professional enculturation of their doctors than a reflection of women's psychological functioning.

Nevertheless, therapeutic and research effort continues to look for intrinsic biological, hormonal or endogenous causes to explain women's psychological distress. The published literature on the relationship between women's reproductive processes, from menarche to menopause, and their mental health and well-being is immense. It is not one where quantity bears much resemblance to quality.

Michael Gitlin and Robert Pasnau in their paper, 'Psychiatric syndromes linked to reproductive function in women', published in the *American Journal of Psychiatry* in 1989, assess the status of current knowledge on this topic.[25] They consider the evidence relating to four psychiatric syndromes specifically linked to women's reproductive functions, namely postpartum depression, premenstrual syndrome, post-hysterectomy depression and involutional melancholia. They conclude that postpartum depression comprises three separate syndromes; that the effective study of premenstrual syndrome depends on improved methodology; and that there is no evidence for post-hysterectomy depression and involutional melancholia.

These researchers argue that the reason for the current poor level of understanding is that it rests on unwarranted assumptions and conclusions based on old, poorly conducted studies and a mixture of myths and culturally biased attitudes towards women. Such attitudes have contaminated supposedly objective observations and implied etiological links, with the result that observations more often and more accurately reflect the psychology of the observer, usually a man, than the observed. Acquiring knowledge, they conclude, will depend on designing better quality studies using data-based research. Progress in this direction is still in its early stages.

The long ascendancy of the belief that women's psyches created their own distress, unmediated by the conditions of their lives or what happened to them, has formed an almost insuperable obstacle against which women have had to struggle in attempting to have their perceptions and experiences taken into account in clinical practice and in the explanatory models that inform psychiatric practice.

It could be argued that women's obstetric experiences, to take but one example, could be overlooked for so long precisely because of the influence of the dualistic thinking referred to earlier. Women's feelings and subjective knowledge about their bodies must, within this framework, be devalued compared with men's thinking, and objective knowledge informed and legitimated by medical science. The problem is that this objectivity has been more apparent than real. Far from being untainted by bias, scientific theories on women have been suffused with androcentrism. Observer bias in the form of culturally accepted but erroneous beliefs and expectations regarding women can affect both the initial theoretical adequacy of the kind of research likely to be undertaken and the status of the observations and evidence that such research seeks to amass.

Dualistic thinking ensures that women will encounter frustration in trying to communicate, because in the dominant discourse they are positioned as other, different and deviant. By definition, what they say can never achieve appropriate male authority. Although they do not specifically address the impact of dualistic thinking on women's mental health, a number of theoretical approaches have something to offer in exploring this question.

Sander Gilman's writings on stereotyping, for example, apply equally to women and to groups discriminated against or stereotyped because of religious, racial or ethnic differences.[26] Gilman asserts that all forms of stereotyping depend on the existence of dualistic thinking, which construes difference from the dominant group's notion of 'normal' in a negative and quite often punitive manner.

He considers that the dualisms themselves have a psychological underpinning, which explains why they survive so tenaciously. Dualistic thinking, according to Gilman, is a by-product or consequence of a childhood conflict between the 'good' and 'bad' self.

This conflict occurs at an early stage in the development of the child when notions of the good and bad self are first formed. Relying on psychoanalytic theory, Gilman asserts that, at this time, a split occurs between the good and bad self, which is accompanied by a projection of elements of the bad self on to the external world and other people. The psychological purpose of this splitting and consequent projection is to maintain relative emotional safety and coherence within the self. Splitting and denial of elements of the 'bad' self from within the self and projection of them on to others, Gilman argues, underlie all forms of stereotyping.

The object of stereotyping, whether the person is seen as this 'bad' 'other', on racial, class, ethnic, religious or gender grounds, becomes the repository for all that is perceived to be threatening, aberrant and despised, and all that one wishes to expunge from the self to make it pristine and perfect. Gilman's argument thus provides a workable explanation of why the dualisms underlying gender stereotyping come about initially and what psychological needs they continue to meet in people's lives.

Nonetheless, Gilman's argument is fundamentally conservative. It replaces the usual biological reductionism with a psychological variant. And because this psychological reductionism relies on psychodynamic theories of development, which are themselves biologically based, his argument never sheds its biological foundations. As such, its effect, when applied to gender, is to reinforce rather than challenge existing notions of women. Difference, in Gilman's account, remains as unassailable and stigmatised as it is in the arguments of any conservative sociobiologist. Indeed, by suggesting that stereotyping serves a psychological need, which is deeply embedded in the process of normal human development, Gilman's argument seems to imply that stereotyping and the discriminatory practices that stem from it are unavoidable.

Another way of considering how these dualisms might set boundaries for expression and dissent for women, and one that posits a social rather than biological basis, has been articulated by the anthropologist, Edwin Ardener, in his theory of the relationship of dominant to subdominant groups.[27] Ardener's views are pertinent because they illuminate the process whereby the dominant group's model of reality stifles and frustrates the attempts of subdominant groups to structure a different or competing model of reality that better reflects their experience. Subdominant groups such as women, Ardener argues, are compelled to transform, or in a sense translate, their own models in terms of the received, dominant one that expresses a male world view. In doing this, they are only ever able to achieve an approximate, never a perfect, fit with the dominant model. Effectively, subdominant groups become what Charlotte Hardman has termed 'muted groups',[28] whose members become muted or are relatively less articulate compared with the dominant group because they have to express themselves through the structures and idioms of that group. It is not that muted groups can't speak but rather that they can't be heard.

In many ways the theory of muted groups is related to Foucault's ideas regarding 'subjugated knowledges'. Like the expression of muted groups, subjugated knowledges cannot be acknowledged or heard. According to Foucault, they are present 'but disguised within the body of functionalist and systematising theory'. These knowledges are devalued 'as inadequate to their task or insufficiently elaborated: naive knowledges, located low down on the hierarchy, beneath the required level of cognition or scientificity'.[29] Like the inherent frustrations of communication for those in muted groups, subjugated knowledges also lack the conceptual space in the dominant discourse that would allow for their recognition. Significantly, muted groups are rendered most inarticulate and most frustrated when it comes to expressing matters of special concern to them because the dominant model has no place for their concerns.

The absence of a conceptual space in which the concerns and experience of a muted group might be heard has the effect of making the experiences, needs and wishes of the group invisible and incomprehensible. By applying the idea of muted groups to psychoanalytic theorising on women, it is easy to see why Freud's final essay, 'Femininity', includes no awareness that women themselves might have something to offer in understanding this subject. 'If you want to know more about femininity,' he wrote to his students, 'you must interrogate your own experience or turn to the poets, or else wait until science can give you more profound and more coherent information.'[30]

The same inability of the dominant group to hear, let alone comprehend, what members of subdominant group might be saying, feeling or wanting obviously applies to race as well. Toni Morrison, winner of the 1993 Nobel prize for literature, made this clear in an interview when she talked about the dominant white society's inability to perceive black people and black things.

> Black people and black things and Africa-type things are understood to be a blank space for white imagination. It's the 'Heart of Darkness'. No Africans talk in there. It's just some place to go, it's like Isak Dinesen said: the Africans were like forms of nature. We're this fantasy world of otherness.[31]

In a society that is culturally defined by white men based on their experience of the world, it is inevitable that some features relating to women and their experience will not fit into the model. This lack of fit, or what might be termed the cultural and psychological dissonance betwen the two models, cannot be remedied while the structural inequalities and relative positions of the two groups persist. Consequently, any attempts to modify the dominant model using its own terms are bound to fail. Ardener describes how: 'The ultimate negativity of attempts to modify dominant structures by their own "rules" derives from the totally reality-defining nature of such structures'.[32] The effect of futile attempts to modify dominant structures will usually be to reinforce the muting process. Those who feel muted might decide to say no more. This process might not be conscious, and indeed a subdominant or subordinate group that is already muted might further reinforce the effect of the process by quelling its own internal 'voice'. As a result of transforming and forcibly fitting perceptions of an alternative reality into terms acknowledged by the dominant structure, this voice might effectively disappear into silence or, if expressed, might be positioned by the dominant group and/or subjectively experienced as 'mad' or 'bad'.

One example of how the muting process can be helped along by the opinions of the dominant group is found in the language used to refer to expressions of grievance or dissatisfaction by women. Interestingly, these words are typically used to refer to women's complaints. Women who complain are said to 'nag', 'moan', 'whinge' or 'bitch'. All these words simultaneously register irritation at the grievance and dismiss it as unimportant. They belong to a special class of complaint words, whose use serves to denigrate the grievance and deny that any 'real' injustice is occurring. For women, the use of such denigratory words, especially by men with whom they have intimate relationships, actively fosters the process of self-silencing. Not wanting to be seen as a 'nag', a woman might opt to silence her feelings of anger or injustice. Silence might be seen as preferable emotionally to the censure and 'put down' conveyed by this class of words. Silence might also feel preferable to voicing a sense of injustice knowing that it is going to be trivialised.

The frustrated communication that members of a muted group are especially likely to experience, I would argue, leads not just to frustration and muting but also to serious emotional distress, including deep depression.

In Dana Crowley Jack's book, *Silencing the Self*, the comments of most of the depressed women she interviewed confirm the importance of self-silencing in the development of depression. Jack believes that depression in women largely stems from the cumulative effect of self-censorship and that 'inequality stifles a woman's direct communication'. In responding to this inequality, Jack contends that women often first try to accomplish change by an inner revolt against the outer structures that feel so confining. She theorises that self-censorhip is a reaction to the unavoidable frustration of being unable to modify dominant structures using their own rules.[33]

Jack also describes the pointless and ultimately self-destructive efforts many women will make to avoid conflict and suppress anger in order to preserve a relationship. Depressed women, she notes, will often appear outwardly compliant and passive. However, their efforts to maintain harmony come at the cost of retaining an authentic sense of self and often conceal anger and despair — the 'roar which lies on the other side of silence'.

Instead of women being 'prone' to depression or other forms of mental illness because of some innate, biologically based tendency to mental pathology, I believe there is a better explanation, which is more consistent with the theories just described. It seems more feasible and more consistent with emerging evidence to regard much of women's depression and 'madness' as a manifestation of the emotional frustration and sense of futility and failure arising out of unsuccessful attempts to fit forcibly into an unaccommodating structure of culturally constructed meaning that claims to define and understand them. From this perspective, depression might be regarded as a potent social metaphor that directs attention to an emotional state in which it feels impossible for one's unhappiness ever to be transformed, acted on or acknowledged within the dominant discourse. The boundaries of meaning acceptable within this discourse are felt to be impermeable to one's experience or view of reality and are designed to ignore the psychogenic potential of many of the gendered events that impact on women, like sexual, emotional and physical violence, particularly violence by those with whom one is intimately connected.

Shirley Ardener, in another context, writes that sometimes the effort of adjustment can become overstrained to the degree that orderly conduct is impossible.[34] Disorderly conduct by women has typically been seen as evidence of their hysteria, but Ardener's ideas offer another way of understanding why such hysterical behaviour might come about. Her account has the added advantage of providing an explanation that does not depend on appeals to reproductive pathology of one kind or another.

If a fictional illustration of the psychological damage deriving from frustrated communication and muting were required, none could be more compelling than the one contained in the late nineteenth-century autobiographical novel, *The Yellow Wallpaper*, written by Charlotte Perkins Gilman.[35]

Gilman was the name of her second husband, and her changes of name attest to the contingent quality of this and other aspects of a woman's identity during her lifetime. She was born Charlotte Anna Perkins in 1860. Her father left soon after she was born, and she grew up living in poverty with her mother and brother. They moved constantly. By the time she was 18 and already supporting herself as a commercial artist and governess, Charlotte Perkins had shifted nineteen times, and fourteen of these moves were to another city. In 1884, she married Walter Stetson, an artist, and their daughter, Katharine Beecher, was born a year later. Following the birth, Charlotte suffered from a 'nervous disorder', or what would today be called postnatal depression, and consulted Dr Silas Weir Mitchell, the foremost American neurologist and neuropsychiatrist of his day.

Weir Mitchell belonged to Philadelphia's élite and seemed predestined to become a doctor, being the seventh physician in three generations of medical men. Besides being a doctor Mitchell wrote and published short stories and novels, including *Constance Trescot*, *The Waters of Oblivion* and *Hephzibah Guinness*. Most significantly, Mitchell was held in great esteem for his expertise in the treatment of women's nervous disorders.

His famous rest cure for women consisted of sensory deprivation, isolation, massage and weight gain to restore depleted energy stores. Most of all, for the cure to be effective, a woman had to acknowledge the necessity of accepting her domestic and wifely role. The cure was originally devised by Mitchell when he was a contract surgeon during the American Civil War and developed therapeutic techniques with soldiers who had suffered gunshot wounds and other traumatic injuries of nerves. Although Mitchell thought the cure was suitable for the treatment of women with nervous disorders, he did not consider that they, too, might have experienced violent or traumatic events. Rather, Mitchell relied on the then fashionable view that women had run down or overspent their energy reserves and consequently needed to have them topped up.

The apparent need to separate the causes of mental illness in men and women, whereby the causes of women's madness are regarded as natural and internal and men's are considered as unnatural and external, can also be recognised in the treatment of soldiers during World War I. Although manifesting all the signs of hysteria, they were given a new and different diagnosis — 'shell shock' — so that no opprobrium, by virtue of association to the most characteristic of all forms of female madness, would attach to them.

Another example can be found in the differentiation Charcot made in the causes of hysteria in women compared with men. Charcot preserved traditional gender identities for hysterics of both sexes. He referred to 'virile' hysteria in men and stressed the importance of real events in triggering hysteria, such as marital turmoil, the death of a family member and physical trauma, such as accidents at work. Women, by contrast, become hysterical as a consequence of their proclivity to do so. It is in their nature to be emotional, and hysterics have this nature in an exaggerated form and cannot control their emotions at all.

In Gilman's case, Dr Mitchell told her to live as domestic a life as possible. In practice this meant that she had to rest after every meal, have her child with her all the time, even though simply dressing her baby left her shaking and crying, and, most crushing of all, she was instructed to 'never touch pen, brush or pencil as long as you live'.[36] Following this regime, Gilman found she 'came perilously close to losing my mind. The mental agony grew so unbearable that I would sit blankly moving my head from side to side'.[37] But in a 'moment of clear vision' Gilman saw the cause of her illness. Unlike the majority of women suffering the same circumscribed existence and the same nervous disorder, she was able to articulate her frustration and act on it.

Gilman understood the implications of her experience and changed her life. Somehow she had the confidence and self-belief to reject Mitchell's view and embrace her own. She abandoned domesticity, her husband and the prescribed role of being 'the angel in the house' and went to California with the express intention of doing exactly what she had been told not to — she took up the pen — and continued to use it for the rest of her life. After efforts to achieve a reconciliation with her husband failed, Gilman moved with her daughter to live permanently in California.

During this time of severe economic hardship, in which she supported herself, her daughter and then her mother by running a boarding house, she initiated her writing and lecturing career.

And once she started, Gilman wrote prolifically. Her books included *Women and Economics: A Study of the Economic Relation Between Men and Women* (1898), *Concerning Children* (1900), *The Home: Its Work and Influence* (1902), *Human Work* (1904) and *Man-made World: Or Our Androcentric Culture* (1911). Besides her autobiographical novel, *The Yellow Wallpaper*, Gilman later wrote three utopian novels, *Moving the Mountain* (1911), *Herland* (1915) and *With Her in Ourland* (1916). They were all published in serial form in Gilman's own monthly magazine, the *Forerunner*, which ran from November 1909 to December 1916. Gilman wrote every line of the thirty-two-page magazine, amounting in the end to twenty-eight full-length books. She once remarked that her mental capital was the only kind invested in the venture.

Seven years after Gilman suffered Mitchell's rest cure, *The Yellow Wallpaper* was published in the *New England Magazine* in May 1892. It had been rejected earlier by Horace Scudder, editor of the *Atlantic Monthly*, who wrote to Gilman saying: 'I could not forgive myself if I made others as miserable as I have made myself!'[38] Certainly, it is a terrifying and curiously lucid tale of madness.

Gilman wrote *The Yellow Wallpaper* with the express purpose of persuading Mitchell to change his mind about the efficacy of his 'cure' and of showing him the emotional damage he and his rest cure had inflicted on her and so many other women. *The Yellow Wallpaper* testifies to Gilman's cold rage at her treatment and the smugness and stupidity of a profession that was wreaking havoc in the minds of women under the guise of helping them and making them better.

The narrator of *The Yellow Wallpaper* recounts how she has been brought by her husband John, a physician just like Mitchell, to a colonial mansion for the summer so that she can recover from her 'temporary nervous depression — [her] slight hysterical tendency'. She has to take 'phosphates or phospites — whichever it is, and tonics, and journeys, and air, and exercise, and am absolutely forbidden to "work" until I am well again'.

In a few economical sentences, Gilman sets out the position of the wife who knows she cannot make her ideas or her reality count in any conflict of opinion either with her husband or her doctor. The narrator has learned to keep silent about her recalcitrant ideas and any behaviour of which her husband disapproves. She is well aware that her disagreement and the evasive manoeuvres and transformations undertaken to hide her opposition carry a high psychological cost. Her analysis pinpoints the psychological and social causes of female exhaustion and why it was such a widespread problem.

> Personally, I disagree with their ideas.
>
> Personally, I believe that congenial work, with excitement and change, would do me good.
>
> But what is one to do?
>
> I did write for a while in spite of them; but it does exhaust me a good deal — having to be so sly about it, or else meet with heavy opposition.[39]

This emphasis on her unexpressed personal and private thoughts continues throughout the book, at once giving them voice and silencing them. Her opinions remain suffocatingly, self-destructively private.

In *The Madwoman in the Attic* Gilbert and Gubar enumerate how obsessive images of enclosure and confinement and the desire to escape, so conspicuous in Gilman's autobiographical novel, featured time and again in the nineteenth-century literature created by women.[40] They argue, quoting Virginia Woolf, that the female writer was locked into a double bind wherein she had to choose between admitting she was 'only a woman' or protesting she was 'as good as a man'.

The 'choice' arising from these alternatives and the culture that created them caused many women, writers or not, to feel trapped and sickened. The psychic state induced by this razor's edge of normality, whereby women were 'warned that if they do not behave like angels they must be monsters', had characteristic somatic forms. They included agoraphobia, claustrophobia, anorexia, headaches, tiredness, depression and, of course, hysteria. Moreover, the same symptoms, the same narrow margin of 'choice' and the same ferocious disapproval of transgression remain observable despite the undoubtedly positive changes in women's social position.

Long-standing domestic confinement and the much-valued cultural product of its transformation — privacy — together ensured that the experiences of women like Gilman's narrator would continue to go unseen and unheard in the public sphere, otherwise known as the world, and that they would play no part, for a very long time, in informing psychiatric theories about them. The unacceptable, contesting thoughts Gilman's narrator registers can never exist outside herself; there is simply nowhere for them to go and no one who can hear her. Certainly her husband's construction of what causes and cures female madness cannot even contemplate the thoughts and feelings she is having. If she does write, it has to be done clandestinely, in spite of her husband and her brother, another doctor. Her husband infantilises and patronises his 'little girl'. He bullies her into conforming to his view of what will make her well, and she is left in no doubt about how guilty and responsible she should feel for what he is doing for her.

> He is very careful and loving, and hardly lets me stir without special direction.
>
> I have a schedule prescription for each hour in the day; he takes all care from me, and so I feel basely ungrateful not to value it more.
>
> He said we came here solely on my account, that I was to have perfect rest and all the air I could get.[41]

She is made to inhabit the upstairs room, formerly a nursery, with its barred windows and hideous yellow wallpaper — 'I never saw a worse paper in my life'.

John's understanding of his wife's illness, dutifully echoing the received wisdom of Weir Mitchell, compels him to believe that anything she wants and expresses a desire for she must, on no account, be given. 'I don't like our room a bit. I wanted one downstairs that opened on the piazza and had roses all over the window, and such pretty old-fashioned chintz hangings! John would not hear of it.'[42]

Denied the right to work openly, the narrator creates her own secret work in an increasingly pathological parody of the real thing. She sets her mind to making sense of the layers of pattern in the yellow wallpaper, a mental task that progressively and desperately obsesses her.

> I lie here on this great immovable bed — it is nailed down, I believe — and follow that pattern about by the hour. It is as good as gymnastics, I assure you. I start, we'll say, at the bottom, down in the corner over there where it has not been touched, and I determine for the thousandth time that I will follow that pointless pattern to some sort of a conclusion.[43]

She comes to believe that there is a woman imprisoned behind the wallpaper who creeps about and shakes the front pattern trying to get out. But escape is impossible. 'And she is all the time trying to climb through. But nobody could climb through that pattern — it strangles so.'[44] The narrator cannot climb through the pattern set for her life, either. By the end of the book she is floridly psychotic.

But the madness felt by the narrator has a very different aetiology from that proposed by her physician husband. His model of female madness, imprinted with the pattern of the dominant androcentric discourse, is culturally proofed against admitting any alternative psychiatric aetiology. Yet Gilman makes it quite clear that the blindness of John's model of his wife's illness and the cure that flows from this model guarantee that her initial distress will be exacerbated and transformed into true madness.

In *The Yellow Wallpaper*, the cure is definitely worse than the disease. More than this, Gilman shows that the cure, in enacting society's cramped judgement of woman's nature and place in the world, potentiates another even more pathological form of the 'disease'. Gilman, unlike the narrator in her book, did not go mad, although, as she admitted, she did come perilously close to doing so. She saw and understood the pattern, and refused to silence and immure herself within it. Nevertheless, she was affected by the stress of living as someone in constant opposition to the status quo, and experienced bouts of depression throughout her life. Patricia Vertinsky has written that Charlotte Perkins Gilman achieved 'emancipation without joy'.[44] While Gilman's clear insight and subsequent action was rare, the experiences that prompted her unusual actions were endemic to middle- and upper-middle-class women in the nineteenth century. For most, no alternative to the dominant model of reality that Gilman managed to repudiate could be conceived.

One of the strongest forces operating at the time to strengthen the dominant model, and to disarm women's overt and covert misgivings about their place in society, was the power of science. The science of the late nineteenth century exerted an impeccable and unparalleled authority. Science believed that it made its researches and based its conclusions about woman's nature on the bedrock of incontrovertible biological fact. But, as we shall see in the next chapter, the context of scientific discovery about women in the second half of the nineteenth century imbibed more heavily from its own fantasy world of otherness than from any other source.

3

WILD WOMEN AND SEX IN SCIENCE

In 1891, Mrs Eliza Lynn Linton wrote a three-part denunciation of feminism and the 'wild women' who espoused it for the periodical, the *Nineteenth Century*. The matter of women's rights, she opined, was one for science to decide:

> The question of women's political power is from beginning to end a question of sex, and all that depends on sex — its moral and intellectual limitations, its emotional excesses, its personal disabilities, its social conditions. It is a question of science, as purely as the best hygienic conditions or the accurate understanding of physiology. And science is dead set against it.[1]

By the second half of the nineteenth century, science had attained its position of ascendancy over religion and politics as a source of authority.[2] As Elizabeth Fee has noted, it was 'science' in general, as it was referred to in the periodical press, that was mystified and held in awe, rather than any particular science or any specific scientific law or concept. Fee writes:

> In many debates, Science played a role equivalent to that of God or nature: the role of the ultimate law-giver, providing the basic rules by which the individual and society must abide. Science was given the task of identifying the laws of nature, so that these could then be

applied to society. Society and the state as much as the individual had a responsibility to live by natural law.[3]

The success of science in understanding the natural world provided the rationale for believing that it could extend its intellectual territory to understanding man and his place in nature. Contained within this study of man was an important but troublesome subsection, the study of woman, otherwise referred to as the 'woman question'.

It was now considered possible and desirable to establish woman's proper place in culture 'scientifically', as dictated by a scientific understanding of her nature and the limits her biology imposed on her participation in social life. Consequently women's bodies, their constitution and their control, were central to the cultural struggles of those opposed to as well as those in favour of an expanded role for women in society.

Science, with its special truth status, was invoked as the ultimate authority in these struggles. Benjamin has argued that the lack of attention accorded to the relationship between women and science in the nineteenth century was inevitable until recently.[4] The two could not be disentangled because of the scientific construction of gender on the one hand and the gendered construction of science on the other, and the naturalness of science as a manly calling was reinforced by the absence of women as members of the scientific academies. There were no women in the British Royal Society until 1946, and none in the French Académie des Sciences until 1979. Benjamin considers that the lack of attention was not 'a simple oversight, a blind dismissal or a case of premeditated trivialisation, this neglect is of a more fundamental nature. It is rooted in the fact that scientific practice has, since its origins, been almost exclusively male'.[5]

Unfortunately, nearly all the information needed to discuss sex differences usefully did not exist in the nineteenth century.[6] This included data derived from genetics, endocrinology and neurophysiology, to say nothing of evidence needed from a non-androcentric form of sociology, anthropology and psychology, which certainly did not exist then and barely does now. According to Bram Dijkstra, the scientists of the late nineteenth century, the biologists, sociologists and anthropologists who focused on the sex roles of the human species — these early 'sexologists', who might actually best be given the generic title of 'bio-sexists', were of crucial importance in building a pseudo-scientific foundation for the anti-feminine attitudes prevalent around 1900.[7]

The paucity of relevant evidence did absolutely nothing to inhibit the luxuriant growth of pseudoscientific theorising on the 'woman question'.

In 1883 Leslie Stephen, the father of Virginia Woolf, the writer, and Vanessa Bell, the painter, defined science as 'that body of truths which may be held to as definitely established, so that no reasonable person doubts them'.[8] Science promised to deliver truth of an impeccably impartial, disinterested kind; a truth uncontaminated by political or personal self-interest and with which it was impossible to argue without being unreasonable.

For women especially, this positioning of opposition as unreasonable was an efficient means of maintaining the authority of science and in a sense 'shoehorning' — or should that be 'corseting'? — debate to remain within its self-created boundaries. It is an illustrative example of a dominant ideology (as discussed in the previous chapter) whose model of reality and whose language, arguments and idioms must be utilised regardless of how well or how badly they serve the interests of those in 'muted groups'. To be heard at all, women had to use the model of reason and reality science created; but, where it was not a good fit for what they wanted to say, they, not it, were perceived as unreasonable.

Moreover, the ideology of the 'science of man' was so virulently misogynistic that reading its many offerings on the 'natural' relationship between the sexes and woman's 'proper' place in nature and culture has been likened to 'entering into an insane asylum in which the inmates have written all the rules'.[9] Yet in an exquisite irony, the authority of science was such that the biosexists who invoked it could dismiss the arguments of those who disagreed with its pronouncements and label them as the mad ones. Feminists, particularly, were liable to be seen as deranged and degenerate. Any attempt to achieve equality was represented as signalling a return to an earlier, more primitive stage of evolutionary development. For Mrs Linton, feminists were 'wild women', degenerates in the arc of evolutionary progress. Relying on the theories of Charles Darwin and Carl Vogt, she equated feminists' aspirations for equality with 'the translation into the cultured classes of certain qualities and practices hitherto confined to the uncultured and savages'.

The curious idea that equality between the sexes was primitive rested on a somewhat tortuous piece of logic. In 1871, Charles Darwin expressed this as clearly as anyone in *The Descent of Man*. Beginning with the premise that woman had certain characteristics, such as intuition, rapid perception and imitation, in greater quantities than man, Darwin quickly grasped the essential similarity between these characteristics and those 'known' to distinguish the 'lower races'.[10] Once this similarity was accepted, it led to the conclusion that woman partook of 'a past and lower state of civilization'.

Furthermore, standard scientific doctrine held that the distance and difference between men and women became more rather than less marked as a function of evolutionary progress. With evolutionary progress it was deemed that woman's lower state of civilisation accelerated relative to man's. As man rose, woman sank. According to Darwin, man had become more intelligent than woman as a result of selective evolutionary pressures, and the continuous nature of these pressures led him to conclude that 'man has ultimately become superior to woman'. On account of this biological, scientific reason and no other, 'the present inequality between the sexes' had come about.[11]

From this perspective, the matter of women's rights was terribly misguided. For woman, the pursuit of her rights was wrong. Her efforts to seek equality were futile from a biological standpoint. They merely confirmed the biological standpoint by demonstrating just how ignorant feminists were of the facts of biology and evolutionary theory and how uncivilised and degenerate they were in desiring a revival of the more primitive state of equality between the sexes.

Of course, biologically based arguments against equality coincided with and were a predictable reaction to the strengthening of demands by women for the vote, property rights, higher education and professions. The more women challenged traditional sex roles, the more science in general and medical science in particular were called upon to justify and preserve rigidly demarcated sexual divisions of labour in society. Science was believed to offer the empirical, rational means by which it could be shown that nothing could alter the natural difference between man and woman; in short, science provided proof that the current social hierarchy rested on immutable laws of nature. As Thomas Huxley so pompously and succinctly put it: 'What has been decided among prehistoric protozoa cannot be annulled by an act of Parliament.'[12]

Pursuing her rights was a retrograde step for woman. Moreover, it was fraught with dangers to her femininity and threatened to remove the one role, that of being a wife and mother, for which she received male approbation. Seeking her rights inevitably transformed woman in a civilised society from the 'gentle mother' nature designed her to be into the 'Amazonian brawler' of her primitive past.[13]

When it came to divining the social meanings of living by natural law, there were diverse, not to say contradictory, interpretations. Both the opponents and supporters of women's rights felt compelled to couch their arguments in the terms dictated by science, thus attesting to the dominance of the scientific model. For the opponents of women's rights this obligation was accompanied by an almost seamless fusion of their own most deeply felt beliefs with the dictates of science. Anti-suffragists, for example, appealed to the authority of science in their arguments about the biological imperative, which called out for strict limits on women's participation in social, educational and political institutions.

Women were entreated to endorse, even demand, their own social limitation. The editor of the *Nineteenth Century* magazine, James Knowles, asked his female readers in 1889 to sign An Appeal Against Female Suffrage. The appeal was cast in scientific language. It declared that 'the emancipating process has now reached the limits fixed by the physical constitution of women'.[14]

On the other hand, supporters of female suffrage argued that there was no need for artificial constraints on women because competition alone would be enough to ensure the operation of the law of survival of the fittest. Setting up or maintaining prohibitions against women studying in universities, for example, was said to interfere with the natural selection of the fittest and was therefore claimed by supporters of women's rights to be antithetical to evolutionary progress.

In 1875, Dr Frances White, responding to eugenic calls for women from the educated classes to have large numbers of children, couched her argument within the framework of evolutionary theory, saying that further human evolution required a decline rather than an increase in fertility. 'Evolution is thus seen to provide for the intellectual elevation of woman by constantly decreasing demands upon her for the performance of those functions which are purely physical.'[15]

In contrast with the comfortable synchrony between personal belief and science enjoyed by anti-suffragists, their opponents had to contend with the consciousness of their transgression. Suffragists and feminists could not fail to be aware that their belief about woman's fundamental equality with man was in conflict with much of what passed for scientific truth and in which endless variations on the theme of woman's natural inferiority were played.

Opposition meant always being in reaction, always working against the grain and always being locked into searching, somewhat fruitlessly, to find an alternative interpretation to the remarkably consistent results of a misogynistic science. No matter what branch of science was involved, the results invariably pointed to the same conclusion about woman's place in nature, thereby creating a network of mutually supportive and interlocking scientific 'facts'.

Some advocates of women's rights were not downcast — in print at least — at the weight of scientific opinion ranged against them. Charlotte Perkins Gilman, for example, perfected a method in her writings of apparently accepting the premises of orthodox science and then subverting them to come to the kind of radical social solutions designed to horrify those with whom she was seeming to agree.

The special truth status accorded to science placed it in a privileged relationship to both truth and nature. And while this chapter is more concerned with the scientific writings of the time, the images of women that science produced express even more forcefully than words its power and ideological underpinnings. Jordanova makes a similar point to Gould concerning the ideological possibilities of imagery. By adopting a tradition of realism, whose paradigm is the 'supposedly unmediated eye of the camera', medical imagery of women was presented as an unaltered, unqualified record of the objective natural world.[16] In effect, these images embodied the gendered relationship of knower to known, with the knower focusing the 'male gaze' of the scientist on what was to be known and penetrated, namely, the nature of woman.

Perhaps the clearest statement of this relationship is found in the sculpture Louis Ernest Barrias made for the Conservatoire National des Arts et Métiers in 1899. Entitled 'Nature unveiling herself before science', it depicts a woman undressing herself, her breasts already showing, the rest of her body waiting to be revealed. Just as nature is personified as a woman, science is personified as a man and one, moreover, who in time will undoubtedly complete the unveiling he has begun and gain from nature the full 'picture' he desires.

Opening up the woman's body to the male gaze was further facilitated by the availability of wax models. These models began to be made in northern Italy towards the end of the eighteenth century and were sold all over Europe to aid anatomical study. Although both male and female models were made, the 'Venuses', as the female models were called, differed in a number of significant ways from the models of men. Jordanova comments: 'I know of no male models which show the complete body either covered with flesh or recumbent. Instead there are either upright muscle men, with no flesh at all, or severely truncated

male torsos'. The 'Venuses', by contrast, often lay on 'silk or vel-
vet cushions, in passive, yet sexually inviting poses' and were
adorned with 'flowing hair, pearl necklaces, removable parts and
small foetuses'.[17]

By the 1880s, the metaphorical significance of Darwin's evolutionary theories first expressed in *On the Origin of Species* (1859)
and followed up in *The Descent of Man* (1871) was ubiquitous.
As Ehrenreich and English discovered, it was difficult by this time
'to find a popular tract or article on any subject — education, suffrage, immigration, foreign relations — which [was] not embellished with Darwinian metaphors'.[18]

While those looking for scientific justification for the superior
development of the white European middle-class male and the
inherent inferiority of everyone else relied primarily on evolutionary theories, they also borrowed from many other contemporary
scientific sources. In the second half of the nineteenth century,
craniology was just as important as evolutionary theory as a
source of scientific authority, and both came into being at very
much the same time. Carl Vogt's *Lectures on Man* were published
in 1864, some five years after the appearance of Darwin's *On the
Origin of Species*. The evidence and arguments of each were freely
borrowed from and used to support one another, and they were
regarded as equally scientific.

Vogt, the Professor of Natural History at the University of
Geneva, beginning with the craniological evidence that women's
head size was smaller than men's, went on to insist that 'the skulls
of man and woman are to be separated as if they belonged to two
different species'. Not reticent about placing female cranial capacity in the scheme of things, Vogt suggested to other (male) scientists that

we may, therefore, say that the type of the female skull approaches, in
many respects, that of the infant, and in a still greater degree that of
the lower races; and with this is connected the remarkable circum-
stance, that the difference between the sexes, as regards cranial cavity, increases with the development of the race, so that the male
European excels much more the female than the Negro the Negress.[19]

To allow women the same rights as men was considered by many to invite social disaster; neither women's bodies or minds were adequate for such rights or the responsibilities they entailed. The idea that there were no differences in the mental abilities of the sexes was an absurdity, according to McGrigor Allan of the London Anthropological Society, who believed this 'doctrine' had a 'most baneful effect in unsettling society'. He fulminated against this claim, asserting: 'No distinction in the minds of men and women! Nature flatly contradicts this absurd assertion, and warns against encouraging this foolish and mischievous flattery of women'.[20] For McGrigor Allan and many others following Vogt's lead, a woman was a kind of adult child, while 'Man' was the head of creation.

Fear over the social unrest likely to result from giving women the vote, or in any other way expanding their role beyond that of wife, mother and angel of the house, was also voiced by the French anthropologist, Paul Broca. Broca, another enthusiastic craniologist, had made thousands of head measurements, which proved, to his complete satisfaction, the biological inferiority of women's brains based on their smaller size and weight. In a paper 'On anthropology' (1868) for the *Anthropological Review*, Broca ventilated his concern that any disturbance or change in the traditional division of labour between the sexes could produce a 'perturbation of the races' that would seriously interfere with the orderly progress of evolution.[21]

Fears about interference with evolution were directed towards 'negroes' in the same way they were directed towards women. Virulently racist papers, like the one by James Hunt on 'On the Negro's place in Nature', also enlisted 'nature' and the dictates of the evolutionary process to disbar blacks from claiming equality.[22] Earlier, Vogt had placed the adult black man in his correct evolutionary position: 'the grown-up Negro partakes, as regards his intellectual faculties, of the nature of the child, the female, and the senile White'.[23]

Within this discourse on difference in late nineteenth-century culture in England, Germany, France and the USA, women and blacks shared a position of biologically based inferiority and pathology. Gilman believes that this means one cannot consider one without considering the other: 'The image of the woman [thus] haunts the reading of the black'.[24] Other groups positioned as aberrant and diseased in this discourse included Jews (see chapter 4) and other 'degenerates', such as criminals. Black women and black children were presumably even lower than black men, although a discernible and fitting distance from white women, white children and senile white men, but they did not merit separate mention and remained a blind category.

The belief that women came behind men in evolutionary development rested on the notion that ontogeny recapitulates phylogeny; that is, it embraced the idea that the individual organism repeats in its own development and life history the development and life history of the race.

WHAT IS, SHOULD BE

'Science', relying on a social interpretation of Darwin's theory of evolution, was particularly useful in shoring up the doctrine of a natural hierarchy, with white men at the top and black men at the bottom, and providing 'evidence' of the necessity for men and women to inhabit completely separate spheres. As we have seen, this use of Darwinian theory was by no means secondhand. Darwin himself forcibly expressed the idea that woman's evolutionary growth was inferior compared with man's in *The Descent of Man*. Just as Vogt and Schopenhauer saw woman as perennially undeveloped, both a child and a savage, Darwin agreed that 'the female somewhat resembles her young offspring throughout life', thus lending his inestimable scientific authority to the ideas of Vogt.[25] Scientists carefully charted woman's evolutionary progress. On the basis of the very best scientific evidence they had created, men of science found themselves forced to conclude that woman was stuck in an eternal adolescence.

The equation of maleness with science was one that could not be inspected at the time. According to Benjamin, 'Science is male in the dual sense that the natural sciences have been associated with men's work, and, moreover, with manly work'.[26] Until the concept of gender as an analytical tool emerged, science and gender remained indivisible, which served to obscure the self-serving aspects of male science that excluded, exploited and marginalised women and their interests.

Nineteenth-century science conceded that woman had passed through a number of lower forms, but had not and could never expect to reach the pinnacle of human development and maturity, which was exclusively male. In fact, as we have seen, it was proposed that, as civilisation and evolution advanced, the differences and the mental and emotional distances between the sexes grew greater.

Schopenhauer was one of the earliest biosexists to describe woman's inferior development. Even before Darwin had published his ideas on evolution, Schopenhauer, in his essay 'Of women' (1851), knew that woman was fixed at 'a kind of intermediate stage between the child and the full grown man, who is man in the strict sense of the word'.[27]

If 'hard' physical evidence were needed to explain woman's position halfway between the child and the man, whom Schopenhauer obviously regarded as the true human being, Paul Topinard, another French anthropologist, could see it unerringly in her skeleton. As so often with the writings of the time, Topinard's observations possess a strange surface rationality. They employ the precise, apparently value-neutral language of scientific discourse, but the whole force of the observations and descriptions is to ventilate virulent fantasies of female otherness and inferiority. Topinard wrote:

> The outlines of the adult female cranium are intermediate between those of the child and the adult man: they are softer, more graceful and delicate — the forehead is more perpendicular — the superciliary ridges and the gabella are far less developed, often not at all; the crown is higher and more horizontal, the brain weight and cranial capacity are less.[28]

Other advocates of 'brain sex', like Paul Mobius, were quite explicit in drawing out the political and social implications of woman's difference. His influential essay on woman's biological inferiority was uncompromisingly entitled 'On the physiological debility of woman'. Woman's intellectual debility, Mobius argued, was both natural and desirable because it was consistent with her primary role of being a successful breeder:

> If we wish to have women who fulfil their responsibilities as mothers, we cannot expect them to have a masculine brain. If it were possible for the feminine abilities to develop in a parallel fashion to those of a male, the organs of motherhood would shrivel, and we would have a hateful and useless hybrid creature on our hands.[29]

Mobius was at pains to prove that woman had accomplished little in the arts and sciences not because of her subjection but because of her inferiority. He saw a great danger in the emancipation movement. Female brains were argued to be inferior from infancy, having simpler convolutions about the Sylvian fissures, a smaller, less convex island of Keil and frontal gyrus and an inferior parietal lobe. Thought and education for women was useless and wrong and made them ill, Mobius believed. His writings leave no doubt that the thought of intellectual women made him ill, too. 'Excessive use of the brain does not just confuse woman, it makes her ill.'[30] Mobius was sure that schools and higher education for women only made them nervous and weak. They should therefore be protected against intellectual activity.

A pathologist by training, Mobius was intensely interested in analysing neurasthenia and hysteria, and his work was of interest to Joseph Breuer and Sigmund Freud, who quoted him favourably in their book, *Studies in Hysteria*. Mobius was also referred to in the immensely influential two-volume work, *Adolescence*, written by the American psychologist and academic, George Stanley Hall. Hall, who was president of Clark University in the USA from 1888 to 1920, was responsible for inviting Freud to America.

Even as adults women remained childlike, never growing to the same height as men or developing other traits, like beards, which indicated true biological maturity in 'human beings'.[31] The same process that selected certain male body parts or secondary sex characteristics as necessary signs of the adult human being, and thus made the definition of *man* synonymous with that for *human being*, simultaneously excluded woman. Psychologically, too, woman was said to be closer to child than man, being weak-willed, impulsive, perceptive, imitative, timid and dependent. Primarily a reproducer of the race, nothing in the way of intellectual or creative originality could be expected of her. She was 'animal like' and 'dependent', according to Mobius, and 'just like the animals, since time immemorial, has done nothing but ceaselessly repeat herself'.[32]

In addition to evolutionary theory, which was the crowning glory of scientific argument against women, much use was made of the first law of thermodynamics. The law stated that energy could be transformed but never destroyed. When applied to human beings it was taken to mean that the body and mind were closed energy systems with a finite amount of usable energy for which all functions had to compete. Freud relied on this law in formulating his theory of a 'dynamic' psychology.

With little effort, the law of thermodynamics could be applied in explaining the 'problem' functioning of the female body. It was the basis for the discovery, from first principles, that the uterus and ovaries were in competition with the brain for a fixed amount of vital energy. Women who ignored the energy needs of their reproductive systems did so at their own peril and to their own detriment. Ill health for women and their unborn children surely followed if energy was spent on mental effort rather than nourishing physical functions like menstruation. In fitting deference to the idea that her biology should rule her life, a menstruating woman should rest and cut down all mental work to a minimum, including, in adolescence, staying home from school.

Often the writings on menstruation were couched in the language of solicitous concern. Hall's prose was suffused with a tone of reverent admiration for female reproductive functions:

> Periodicity, perhaps the deepest law of the cosmos, celebrates its highest triumphs in woman's life. For years everything must give way to its thorough and settled establishment. In the monthly Sabbaths of

rest, the ideal school should revert to the meaning of the word leisure. The paradise of stated rest should be revisited, idleness be actively cultivated; reverie, in which the soul, which needs these seasons of withdrawal for its own development, expatiates over the whole life of the race, should be provided for and encouraged in every legitimate way, for in rest the whole momentum of heredity is felt in ways most favorable to full and complete development.[33]

But the concern and respect for womanly functions was part of an altruism that had a solid self-serving basis in maintaining the status quo. Giving proper attention to menstruation meant withdrawing from work and study, and proved that woman was not biologically fitted for what was called 'sex competition' in the public world. There was no real choice here; woman was required to heed 'Lord Nature':

> Then woman should realize that to be is greater than to do; should step reverently aside from her daily routine and let Lord Nature work. In this time of sensitiveness and perturbation, when anaemia and chlorosis are so peculiarly immanent to her sex, remission of toil should not only be permitted, but required.[34]

What happened to 'Mother Nature' in Hall's science is a mystery. Perhaps, in deference to that science, she too had reverently stepped aside, as Hall wished all women to do, so that 'Lord Nature' could prevail.

Science and nature together decreed that the primary purpose of a woman's life was reproduction, and in this way 'proved' that the doctrine of 'separate spheres' had a biological rather than a social or political basis. Acceptance of this premise meant it was unarguable that woman should conserve and concentrate all her energies in the work of the home, regulating her bodily functions in the service of reproductive success. The opposite was taken to be true for men, who were urged to direct their energies towards the work of the mind, 'higher functions' and pursuits outside the home.

Banking and economic metaphors were handy in expressing the cost or benefit of these 'deposits' and 'withdrawals' of energy capital: spending in one area was seen to deplete savings in another. Men had to be careful about 'spending their seed' too recklessly, whether that spending occurred during sexual relations within or outside marriage or through masturbation, which was thought to be the cause of many physical and psychological ills, or in dreams. Male essence — sperm — should be saved for properly male activities, and there was no more manly calling than science.

Men of science took it for granted that great achievements in one sphere of activity necessarily meant poorer achievements in other spheres. A great deal of scientific energy was dedicated to proving that intellectual women became sterile. *Evidence* and *proof* were conveniently synonymous with theoretical expectation. Women who tried to engage in demanding academic pursuits were confidently and spitefully forewarned that they would ruin their reproductive systems, which would languish through energy starvation. Hall spent many pages of his chapter on the adolescent girl quoting statistics that demonstrated the infertility of the college-educated woman. His excessive concern, however, has to be understood in terms of the very marked demographic trend to declining marriage and birth rates, which had become evident in the late nineteenth century, especially among the middle classes. He did not waste any time on considering that the smaller family size of college-educated women, which he saw as evidence of infertility, might be due to choice rather than atrophic ovaries. Hall lamented that other universities and colleges did not do more research like his, which brought out so well the 'psycho-physiological differences between the sexes'.[35]

Menstruation, pregnancy, labour, the puerperium and menopause were all considered to be times of critical vulnerability when appropriate energy conservation for women was essential. No other pursuits should be allowed to compete for the woman's energies during these danger periods. The more some aspect of her reproductive functioning could be shown as casting a blight over her whole lifespan, the more important it became to limit woman's participation in society. Intellectual pursuits, particularly higher education, were undoubtedly perilous undertakings, and women who foolishly engaged in them were likely to 'unsex' themselves and go mad in the process. One 'scientific' study undertaken in

1902, shortly before Hall's *magnum opus* appeared, came to the conclusion that higher education caused insanity. It announced that 42 per cent of women admitted to insane asylums were well educated compared with 16 per cent of men.[36] Social factors governing the diagnosis of mental illness and admission rates to asylums were not, of course, considered in this argument, which assumed that there was a causal link between female biology, education and madness. Neither was it possible, given the gendered nature of science, to consider the adverse psychological effects of this kind of science on women's mental health.

Science was awash with premonitions of disaster for women who transgressed the pitifully narrow boundaries it mapped out for their lives. By threatening women who undertook university study with the prospect of insanity, science made no small contribution to the psychic strain it was ostensibly seeking to avoid. In his belief that higher education for women caused infertility, Hall was in perfect sympathy with Herbert Spencer's view that: 'Absolute or relative infertility in women is generally produced by mental labour carried to excess'.[37]

Hall's preoccupation with fertility was overtly eugenic. He believed that if the educated classes had fewer children then the population would be kept up by the 'lowest', with 'old families being ploughed under' and 'retrogressive evolution' and race extermination resulting. He railed at the biological immorality and selfishness of women who sought to develop their brains at the expense of their descendants. 'She has taken up and utilized in her own life all that was meant for her descendants.' Such a course of action was the 'very apotheosis of selfishness from the standpoint of every biological ethics'.[38]

Probably the most cloying expression of the absolute need for female selflessness was formulated by the English art critic, John Ruskin, in *Sesame and Lilies*, his paean of praise to the desirability of men and women occupying completely separate spheres. Certainly women, as the lilies, should not be out in the fields or anywhere else but must occupy the 'vestal temple' of the home. Here, then, was woman's 'true place' where, in 'true wifely subjection', she should exercise 'her great function' for praise. All woman needed to do in this domestic temple, watched over by the 'Household Gods', was acquit herself as a paragon of selflessness. 'She should be enduringly, incorruptibly good; instinctively, infallibly wise — wise, not for self-development, but for self-renunciation.'[39]

Unlike Charlotte Perkins Gilman, most women found it difficult to resist these ideas, dutifully internalising them and living lives pinched by their strictures. Some, like Margaret Cleaves, herself a doctor, publically admitted the foolishness of their intellectual ambitions. In her book, *The Autobiography of a Neurasthene*, Cleaves regards her neurasthenia as the consequence of too much intellectual work, which overdrew the reserves of her energy and produced the sorry state of affairs she likened to having a 'sprained brain'. She accepted absolutely the views of Weir Mitchell and others, that 'girls and women are unfit to bear the continued labor of mind because of the disqualifications existing in their physiological life'.[40]

Apart from shrunken, atrophic ovaries, intellectual women were believed to have shrunken breasts or no breasts at all, loud voices, masculine movements and muscular physiques. In the intellectual atmosphere of suffocating dualism then extant, mind was masculine, just as body was feminine. This logic determined that a woman with a mind could not exist as anything but an aberration. She was a defective woman because of the damage she inflicted on her reproductive functioning and a defective man, fatally disqualified by her female biology, albeit damaged, and her tendency to break down and go mad as a result of her unnatural activities.

Other immutable biologically based differences between women and men concerned the possession of anabolic and katabolic cells. According to Geddes and Thomson, anabolic cells were of large size, placid and conservative and were typified by the ovum, whereas katabolic cells were characterised by their small size, activity and variability and were best exemplified by sperm.[41] The supposed mental differences between the sexes derived from this scientific fact. Women and their placid, conservative, anabolic nature were in the middle range for intelligence while men, with their greater innate activity and variability, produced more idiots but also more, if not all, the geniuses in a society. The question why have there been no great women artists (or whatever) could now, thanks to science, be answered without venturing beyond the cellular level.

Questions regarding the impact of current social arrangements on the development of talent in women were unnecessary. More than that, they could be dismissed and derided as misinformed and unscientific because they ignored the all-important fact that biology and biologically based differences between the sexes were the logical antecedents and immutable causes of current social arrangements. Innate, unchangeable biological differences between men and women constituted an insuperable impediment to heeding any call for improving women's position in society.

Hall took advantage of all these prevailing scientific ideas in order to lend the most scientific gloss to his psychological theories of women and their 'natural' place in society. He argued that the biological difference between men and women was total, and wholeheartedly endorsed recapitulation theory, which placed women at the level of child or youth on the evolutionary scale. He also saw women's nature as conservative rather than variable and anabolic rather than katabolic. At the outset of his chapter on adolescent girls and their education in *Adolescence*, he sets out the 'biological and anthropological standpoint' as follows:

> Our modern knowlege of woman represents her as having characteristic differences from man in every organ and tissue, as conservative in body and mind, fulfilling the function of seeing to it that no acquired good be lost to mankind, as anabolic rather than katabolic, or disposed to assimilate or digest on a higher plane, as normally representing childhood and youth in the full meridian of its glory in all her dimensions and nature ... She is by nature more typical and a better representative of the race and less prone to specialization.[42]

Conveniently, she is also less sensitive to pain than man, 'more often insane' and as superior to man in altruism as she is behind him in 'truth telling, being more prone to ruse and deception'. He informs us that woman's vasomotor system is more excitable and that she is more emotional, hypnotisable and suggestible, and blushes and cries more easily than man.

Hall was convinced that woman's position on the 'phyletic scale' was nearer to childhood than man's, and consequently she was more primitive than man. Such a belief was easily proven. It was literally written on her body, which was more often mutilated in 'savage and civilized life', her long hair, her choice of covering for her body, namely, feathers, skins, furs and flowing garments, and her preference for 'partial exposure of her person'.[43]

Hall imbued his conservative and confining beliefs about women with sentimental hyperbole. Being stunted and fixated at an intermediate point on the phyletic scale, Hall enthused, was 'glorious' for women. However, woman's glorious position was precarious and could easily be lost if she stepped out of line and did not comply with the laws of her soul, itself a 'magnificent organ of heredity'. Compliance with these laws was essential if her psychic activities were to remain 'unperverted'. By contrast, thinking, consciousness and deliberation were mistaken, even perverted, activities for woman, who was constituted to work by intuition and feeling. Hall was convinced that if woman 'abandons her natural naiveté and takes up the burden of guiding and accounting for her life by consciousness, she is likely to lose more than she gains, according to the old saw that she who deliberates is lost'.[44]

On the other hand, if woman accepted her nature and lived by its laws, Hall promised her that 'biological psychology' was already dreaming of 'a new philosophy of sex', which would place the wife and mother at 'the heart of a new world and make her the object of a new religion and almost of a new worship'.[45] The *Kinde*, *Kirche* and *Kuche* of Nazi Germany were not far away and would find emotional and intellectual nourishment from ideas such as these.

Courteously, this new biological psychology and philosophy of sex, which, naturally, woman could take no part in devising, would grant her 'reverent exemption from sex competition and reconsecrate her to the higher responsibilities of the human race'. Whether she wanted this reconsecration was immaterial. Woman's only assigned role in this process was to play the role of grateful recipient of the honour bestowed upon her. Woman would be sealed up within the separate sphere of the home undertaking the higher responsibilities of the human race, far removed from 'sex competition' in the world. There, she would occupy a place where no room existed for the 'blind worship of mere mental illumination'. Forcibly protected in this way, woman would not be able to overdraw her reserves or lose her 'mammary function', and she would realise that 'to be is greater than to do'.[46]

Above all, she would obey what Hall calls 'Lord Nature', in an unwitting but entirely accurate underlining of science's androcentric construction of woman's 'nature'. Hall's laudatory endorsement of 'Lord Nature' imbibes none of the critical insight of John Stuart Mill. How little Hall was aware of the cultural preconceptions that formed his ideas becomes readily apparent when his turgid assertions are compared with Mill's thinking on woman's nature. Mill realised that there was nothing natural about the 'nature' of woman:

> What is now called the nature of women is an eminently artificial thing — the result of forced repression in some directions, unnatural stimulation in others. It may be asserted without scruple, that no other class of dependants have had their character so entirely distorted from its natural proportions by their relation with their masters.[47]

Hall did not find any problem with this master–servant relationship that worried Mill. For Hall, men's right to decide what women should be like was 'inalienable and eternal'.[48] In Hall's thinking, men's preferences were identical with those of 'Lord Nature'; thus what men wanted and what Nature decreed amounted to the same thing.

More recently, Sander Gilman in his book, *Inscribing the Other*, has echoed Mill's views in asserting that woman's 'nature' is socially constructed and therefore unnatural. According to Gilman, what was previously taken as woman's nature might be nothing more than male projections about the fantasy world of otherness that woman signifies for men fused with woman's response to this creation of herself through a phallocentric world.[49]

MEDICAL SCIENCE

It was on the basis of this kind of 'science' and the indivisible relationship between biology and society, science and gender, just described that doctors increasingly assumed their right to pronounce on how girls and women should lead their lives. Both determined by her nature but tragically estranged from it, women were instructed to rely on the pronouncements of doctors in order to know themselves and to learn how to live their lives. Medical advice and authority was ideally suited to this monitoring and policing task because of its role in constructing the precarious razor's edge of normal functioning open to women.

Women were at double jeopardy. It was inherent in woman's biological, reproductive nature to become ill. And if they stepped outside the boundaries of that nature, as prescribed for them by medical science, they were told that this transgression would bring with it a further heavy burden of ill health. Thus women were sick because they were female, and if they were currently well, women were cautioned, hectored and threatened that they would become sick if they did anything that was not female.

Dr James Crichton Browne, in a series of ten articles for the *Educational Review* in 1892, expanded at length on the woeful effects of education for girls and was especially scathing about what he saw as the relentless zeal of 'intersexual' competition. Like Hall, Browne held that difference between the sexes occurred in every organ and tissue. The results of intersexual competition were appalling from a medical point of view. Career ambitions in girls, according to Dr Browne, led to all manner of physical and mental illnesses, including headaches, gastric troubles, anorexia scholastica, neurasthenia and functional nerve troubles.[50]

The process of medicalisation of the normal biological events of the female life span depended on creating the view that these events — menarche, menstruation, pregnancy, childbirth and menopause — were more correctly seen as medical problems and therefore the rightful province of the doctor. Dr J.T. Wilson believed that American girls had hereditary tendencies towards functional disorders and therefore, in order to achieve 'healthy and vigorous womanhood', nothing less than medical supervision was required in most cases.[51]

Sickness, actual or potential, was synonymous with femininity. Weir Mitchell, with his immense authority as an expert in the nervous disorders of women, decreed that no one knew a woman who did not know a sick woman. Fortunately for his line of business, Mitchell was confident that education could do nothing to alter this state of affairs. In a similar vein, Dr Engelmann, in the presidential address to the American Gynaecology Society in 1900, was convinced that gynaecological problems were associated with mental strain. He saw the entire span of women's reproductive lives in the calamitous terms of impending or actual shipwreck:

> Many a young life is battered and forever crippled in the breakers of puberty; if it cross these unharmed and is not dashed to pieces on the rock of childbirth, it may still ground on the ever-recurring shallows of menstruation, and, lastly, upon the final bar of the menopause ere protection is found in the unruffled waters of the harbor beyond the reach of sexual storms.[52]

Doctors' views were accorded extra cachet over those of other professionals. Hall, for example, in rejecting the work of researchers (often women) who produced empirical evidence that higher education had no deleterious effect on women's health, did so on the basis that this evidence contradicted the opinion of doctors like Weir Mitchell and refuted the theory of conservation of energy. In his eighty-six-page chapter on adolescent girls and their education Hall frequently cited and deferred to medical opinion. At the same time, he bolstered his own views by corroborating them with the opinions of medical science and doctors. His many references to the books and papers written by male doctors on women's education, exercise, behaviour during menstruation, age at marriage and desirable number of children, to name but a few, serve to highlight the breadth of the territory presided over by medicine.

Some of the medical sources Hall referred to include Dr Clarke on *Sex in Education, or a Fair Chance for Girls* (1873), which promised to provide anything but; Dr Clouston's 'Female education from a medical point of view'(1884); Dr Thorburn's book of the same title (1884); Dr Weir Mitchell's *Doctor and Patient* (1888); Dr Browne's 'Sex in education' (1892); Dr Storer's 'Female hygiene' (1871); Dr Beard's *American Nervousness: Its Causes and Consequences* (1881); Dr Wilson's 'Menstrual disorders in schoolgirls' (1885); Dr Preston's 'Influence of college life on health' (1895); Dr Taylor's 'Puberty in girls and certain of its disturbances' (1896); and Dr Smith's 'Menstruation and some of its effects upon the normal mentalization of woman' (1896).

Doctors' views, for Hall, simply had greater credibility than those expressed by other professionals. He thought it 'more probable that the doctor's objective and personal tests and opinions are nearer the truth'. Ideally, these opinions should be those of men, who 'because of their sex must of necessity always remain objective'.[53] Hall's explicit preference for medical opinion, and his unquestioned belief that truth and objectivity were a function of male gender, is just one example of the widespread acceptance that men were inherently more knowledgeable than women.

Henry Finck, writing in the *Independent* in 1901, had also declared that men's right to decide what women should be like was 'inalienable and eternal'.[54] It was taken to follow that the biological events of women's reproductive lives were bound to require treatment unless the most careful consideration was paid to the dictates of 'Lord Nature' duly interpreted by her doctor.

Almost every aspect of a woman's behaviour could come under scrutiny in determining that she lived as 'nature' intended. Woman's theorised place on the phyletic scale was meant to prove she was closer to nature than culture, but this by no means equipped her to express her nature unassisted. Indeed, she was upbraided to make extensive changes to what she might otherwise wish to do, and these changes were set out for her in voluminous detail by her doctor. Generally speaking, the most important rule was to regulate her life according to the demands of her body. Her appropriate life goal was therefore to use her body for its approved, designated purpose — that of reproducing the race or, as Mobius said, of endlessly repeating herself. The mind should be held back or else both mind and body would suffer disease.

Dr Clouston expressed his familiarity with the theory of finite energy when developing this topic in 1884. Women, he believed, had a peculiar power of taking out of themselves more than they could bear and therefore it was crucial to check mental effort by them so as to not 'spoil a good mother to make a grammarian'.[55] Dr Beard, author of *American Nervousness: Its Causes and Consequences*, who coined the term *neurasthenia*, believed that schools for girls were 'unphysiological' and violated nature at every step.[56]

Hall believed implicitly in the notion that there was sex in mind and in science. To deny this proposition, he asserted, was like saying there was no age in the mind and therefore it was possible to use the same teaching methods regardless of the age of the child. Hall, with his appeal to Lord Nature and his insistence on sex in mind, illustrates perfectly Benjamin's point about the gendered nature of science and the scientific construction of gender. Men, for Hall, were more suited to science and all work of the mind. By contrast women should aspire towards the ideal of the body, so perfectly captured in Hall's mind in his preferred model of the 'lawn tennis girl'. The lawn tennis girl was the epitome of youthful, feminine health and vigour. She was an outdoor girl, whose natural preference was for physical rather than mental activity. 'Bookishness' was a very bad thing in a girl and, if playing tennis, obviously she could not have her head buried in books. Bookishness for Hall denoted 'artificiality, pedantry, [and] the lugging of dead knowledge'.[57] He concurred with Oliver Wendell Holmes' suggestion that 'girls' brains should be put out to grass for a few generations'.[58]

Once these steps of converting the normal as well as the pathological functions of women's bodies into medical problems had been made, it was a relatively simple matter to reinforce and legitimise this view. By incorporating both normal and pathological as parts of the same spectrum, the division between them could become increasingly blurred, so that the normal quickly became seen as precarious and potentially pathological, as the quote from Dr Engelmann shows. As a result, the whole of women's lives, when they were healthy just as much as when they were ill, came under the scrutiny of doctors. Women and their management became a seemingly rightful province of an increasingly large medical jurisdiction.

In both the nineteenth century and the current one, part of this jurisdiction has been concerned with defining the limits of movement and healthy exercise for women. The range of activity within these limits, in keeping with the reproductive imperative, can be remarkably narrow and confining. One nineteenth-century example, cited by Vertinsky, concerned bicycle riding. Advice on bicycle riding captures the tone of thinly veiled threat associated with much medical advice and the way it sought to curtail women's freedom, in this case through affecting their mobility and fitness.

No sooner were the freedom-conferring possibilities of bicycle riding for women far beyond the confines of the home realised than it became known, almost like a medical counterreflex, that bicycle riding was detrimental to women's health. Bicycle riding, doctors pointed out, was easily overdone and could cause damage to women's health. Indeed, a medical condition quickly appeared requiring the attention of vigilant physicians who perceptively recognised the alarming and unmistakable physical signs. Too much cycling caused the condition doctors termed 'bicycle face'. The terms used to describe this new medical condition were couched in the language of strict scientific rigour and spoke of careful observation. Bicycle face was said to be recognisable by such telltale features as wild staring eyes, a strained expression and a projecting jaw and a 'general focusing of all the features toward the centre, a sort of physiognomic implosion'.[59]

Predictably, the greatest medical concern was focused on the damage cycling could do to female reproductive health. The risks were deemed to be so great that many doctors believed no woman should become a habitual cyclist without medical authorisation. Dr E. B. Turner wrote 'A report on cycling in health and disease' for the *British Medical Journal* in 1896, in which he enumerated the 'physiological crimes' caused by cycling during menstruation, pregnancy or in the three months post partum. Cycling could also cause uterine displacement and hardening of the pelvic organs, and some doctors were concerned about women using the friction from their bicycle seats to masturbate.[60]

The coming of the scientific age in the nineteenth century, rather than bringing an increased understanding of women, provided a brand-new source of legitimation for their social and medical control. Women's 'difference' was now elevated to the status of a scientific fact. Although feminists and other supporters of an expanded role for women in society attempted to counter this notion of inherent difference and intrinsic inferiority, they did so within a scientific framework that itself was gendered. The innate difference between men and women was attested to by anthropology, biology, physics, psychology, sociology and zoology as well as history and religion. Science could now be added to the sources Captain Harville cited in *Persuasion*. There was an interlocking network of scientific authority in which each branch of misogynistic science, in a self-referential manner, invoked and confirmed the authority of all other branches and amassed a huge weight of scientific opinion in the process. For example, Carl Vogt's 1864 *Lectures on Man* were edited, endorsed and made available to an English-speaking audience by the anthropologist, James Hunt. In turn, Vogt's views stongly influenced Darwin, whose reiteration of them in *The Descent of Man* probably influenced everyone.

Those who did not accept that women were inherently inferior had to argue from a fundamentally reactive position. To borrow the language from the theory on the conservation of energy, this reactive position was expensive, emotionally and intellectually. It used up a necessarily finite amount of energy in what was a doomed exercise. The dominant scientific discourse naturally decided what counted as reason and what counted as evidence, and this was done in a way that was preordained to prove its own premises and reasonableness and to demonstrate the unreasonableness of its opponents and their views. And, as we have seen, within the scientific framework of the second half of the nineteenth century, women's views could always be explained away, their interests marginalised and their research findings dismissed as flawed science or pseudoscience by men in positions of preeminence, like Stanley Hall. Hall was even able to disregard Karl Pearson, the psychometrician.

Pearson had argued against the prevailing belief of man's greater variability than woman, but Hall, rather cheekily, in that he had no great claim as a statistician, decided that Pearson's biometric method did not work because he had selected the wrong facts to analyse. Of course, precisely the same objection could be levelled at Hall, who never considered the possibility that his facts were little more than artificial by-products of his fears and fantasies about women.

In an important sense, women could not be 'knowers' — their nature decreed that they were incapable of objectivity and impartiality. Science, as Mrs Linton so succinctly put it, was 'dead set' against them.

The positivistic ideology of science as essentially male, value-neutral and uncontaminated by human influence, advanced by so many of the scientists mentioned in this chapter, has been relegated by recent historians of science to the realm of mythology.[61] However, evolutionist arguments about the emancipatory process having reached its limits continue to thrive. Admittedly, dire warnings about atrophic ovaries are less common, but arguments designed to warn women of the truly adverse consequences that await them if they overstep the mark of men's tolerance and acceptance still abound. All these arguments deliver the threat that, if women persist in pursuing social change, men will become enraged and exact vengeance. Susan Faludi has termed such arguments the 'backlash'.[62]

These warnings and outright threats have been voiced again by Dr Ben Greenstein, author of *The Fragile Male*. Dr Greenstein, head of the lupus endocrine research unit at St Thomas's Hospital in London, puts forward the 'scientific' argument that man inevitably responds to woman's increased power by violence. Predictably, this violence is argued to have a solid evolutionary basis. Greenstein cites the actions of mass murderers — Marc Lepine, who shot dead fourteen women at Montreal University, and George Hennard, who committed a similar crime in Texas — in support of his belief:

> Neither he nor Lepine could know that they were responding in an extreme way to one of the most powerful of biological imperatives in the human male: the need to kill. Both were frustrated males: both believed their roles had been usurped by women, and both did something about it.[63]

How the scientific theories outlined here became incorporated into Freud's new science of psychoanalysis and how they contributed to his understanding female psychosexual development will be described in the next chapter. The new experts said women were susceptible to madness because it was now a scientifically proven fact that their biological constitution was weak and their mental health necessarily precarious as a result. Freud's theories on femininity would lend further weight to this view by revealing hitherto unappreciated facts about women's minds and bodies and the all-too-familiar and pathological conjunction between them.

4
FREUD'S SCIENCE

Nineteenth-century men of science like Hall devoted prodigious intellectual energy to proving 'scientifically' that woman's unequal place in society derived from her inferiority rather than from her subjection. Nature and science agreed that woman was and should only be body, not mind.

Hall believed that woman's essentially physical nature dictated that her energies were best directed into becoming the ideal of the 'lawn tennis girl'. The glowing good health that would result from all this tennis would then assist woman to reproduce the race in a suitably abundant fashion. Hall sought to amass incontrovertible evidence that thinking in general and tertiary education in particular had a detrimental effect on female fertility. Thinking was the enemy of reproduction because it reduced fertility through atrophying woman's ovaries and shrinking her mammary glands.

Of course, Hall's ideas no longer exercise the influence they had at the turn of the century; their language and tone is dated, and Hall's views can be easily caricatured for their sentimental and muddle-headed misogyny and their eugenic fervour. At best, his writings retain a certain historical interest. They do not figure in contemporary reading lists for students of psychology or cultural theory, as Freud's continue to do. One possible reason for this might lie in the difference in the literary abilities of the two men.

Freud was a fine writer, who has been recognised as a great stylist. Thomas Mann, referring to one of Freud's books, wrote that 'in structure and form it is related to all great German essay writing, of which it is a masterpiece'.[1] His case studies and theoretical writing have a freshness, lucidity and seeming modernity that is totally lacking in Hall's turgid two-volume tome, *Adolescence*. But the apparent modernity of Freud's tone tends to deflect attention from the same scientific theories on women that saturate Hall's work and might partly explain why Freud's reliance on these theories has not received much attention.

The links between the two men were strong. Hall referred to Freud's views on sexuality in *Adolescence*, and it was at his instigation that Freud was invited to Clark University to give a series of lectures there in 1909. The occasion was the twentieth anniversary of Clark's founding, and on his visit Freud was awarded the degree of Doctor of Laws. The lectures enabled Freud to present his views personally to an interested American audience. His visit to Clark was memorable as the 'first time I was permitted to speak publicly about psychoanalysis'.[2] The lectures, which were given in German, are dedicated to Hall: 'To Dr G. Stanley Hall, Ph.D., LL.D. President of Clark University, Professor of Psychology and Pedagogics, This Work is Gratefully Dedicated'.

Hall is also acknowledged affectionately by Freud in one of the lectures. In setting out to explain the way in which repression operates, Freud analogises the psychic pressure of repression to that of a noisy person in a lecture room who has to be expelled from the room, but proceeds to make even more of a ruckus outside. At this point, Freud deferentially refers to Hall and suggests that he would have to go out and get the man to promise to behave himself, thereby acknowledging both Hall's authority as president of the university and his powers of persuasion. Freud then tells his audience that this description 'presents what is really no bad picture of the physician's task in the psycho-analytic treatment of the neuroses'.

Although Hall's views appear anachronistic and irrelevant, the continuing impact of Freud's theories on the causes of mental ill health in women demands that his reliance on the same contemporary science is scrutinised.

As we have seen, science was eagerly pressed into service to provide additional confirmation of women's age-old susceptibility to hysteria and other mental illnesses. The secular authority of late nineteenth-century science supplanted all that had preceded it. Once the authority of science was established, there was no need to enlist early Greek beliefs relating to the wandering womb or the religious ideas of the Middle Ages expressed in the *Malleus Maleficarum*, which invoked woman's predisposition to evil, carnal lust and madness.[3] Science could elevate long-held cultural and religious beliefs about woman's proneness to mental disease and disorder to the status of scientifically proven fact. Men of science were now able to prove to their unconcealed satisfaction that woman was biologically programmed for hysteria and other mental disorders. They asserted that woman's physical and mental constitution was weak and lacking in energy, due to the drain of constant uterine activity, and her emotional state intrinsically unstable. Treatments for hysteria and other forms of nervous disorder in women were advanced on the basis of their scientific status. Weir Mitchell's rest cure, for example, was put forward as a therapeutic application of the laws regarding the restoration and conservation of energy. Dire mental consequences were predicted to await women who overdrew their limited energy stores.

In his theories on the human personality and the psychosexual development of women, Sigmund Freud (1856–1939) made a particularly thoroughgoing use of the range of scientific theories mentioned in the previous chapter. Freud considered himself as a scientist first and foremost. He insisted that his therapeutic approach was qualitatively different from existing treatments precisely because he claimed that his intellectual creation — psychoanalysis — was a science.

His early work, *Project for a Scientific Psychology* (1895), is at pains to establish the scientific basis of his psychological ideas. Its language clearly signals this intent with headings such as 'First principal thesis', 'The quantitative line of approach', 'The biological standpoint', 'The functioning of the apparatus' and 'The psychological paths of conduction'. Augmenting this scientific language, Freud employs formulae and diagrams to further expound his ideas.

By coupling psychoanalysis with science, Freud could imbue his approach to the treatment of mental illness with science's credibility and prestige. In the *New Introductory Lectures on Psychoanalysis*, Freud claimed: 'Psychoanalysis ... is a part of science and can adhere to the scientific *Weltanschaung*'.[5] An important part of this scientific world view concerned the biological basis of women's 'difference' and its necessary implications for education, employment and culture.

ADVISABILITY OF SEPARATE SPHERES

Freud embraced the conservative opinions of his time, and they guided the way he wanted to live his own life and the way he theorised all female development. He was an unabashed supporter of separate spheres. In this preference, he can be seen to be following the lead of the French mathematician and philosopher Auguste Comte. Comte is known as the 'father of positivism', a term he coined to describe the scientific methodology that Freud, like many of his contemporaries, was to take up with such enthusiasm.

No one was more convinced of the necessity of separate spheres than Comte, except perhaps John Ruskin. As his liking for sexual apartheid would predict, Comte was a thoroughgoing dualist, and in his *System of Positive Polity* (1851) he reiterated all the age-old oppositions meant to separate and contrast woman's nature from man's. Woman, according to Comte, was the affective sex while man was the active one. Woman was also the originator of spiritual power; it was her 'peculiar vocation' to offer sympathy and sacrifice and to purify and vivify the objective (male) element. Towards this end, she was meant give up all her active impulses and serve, in perfect passivity, as man's spiritual filling station. It was essential that she should 'abstain altogether from the practical pursuits of the stronger sex'.[6]

For Comte, an ideal state of affairs obtained when woman conducted 'the moral education of Humanity'. She was enjoined to do so 'free in the sacred retirement' of the home. Like Hall, the sentimental hyperbole of Comte's worship of woman, while claiming high regard for woman, actually reinforced a social status quo that aimed to exclude her ruthlessly. In Comte's sociology, it was convenient, to say the least, to uncover the scientific truth that 'equality in the position of the two sexes is contrary to their nature'. And woman's freedom to serve in the sacred retirement of the home had the added benefit that man was 'in no danger of rivalry in the affairs of life'.[7]

Comte's distaste at the prospect of woman's participation in the affairs of life was shared by Freud and underlay his enthusiasm for separate spheres. Freud made his preference clear in a letter to his fiancée, Martha Bernays, on 15 November 1883, in which he told her he had been translating John Stuart Mill and thought Mill's views on the emancipation of women showed that he lacked a sense of the absurd. In his letter, Freud asserted his opposition to the possibility of married women working and assumed his fiancée would be of the same mind:

> I dare say we agree that housekeeping and the care and education of children claim the whole person and practically rule out any profession … It seems a completely unrealistic notion to send women into the struggle for existence in the same way as men. Am I to think of my delicate sweet girl as a competitor?[8]

More than forty years after writing this letter, Freud's views had not changed. In the essay 'Some psychical consequences of the anatomical distinction between the sexes' Freud cautions his readers that: 'We must not allow ourselves to be deflected from such conclusions by the denials of feminists, who are anxious to force us to regard the two sexes as completely equal in position and worth.'[9] It appears that, for Freud, the chief impediment to women going into the struggle for existence with men issued from their inequality. Mill, like the feminists Freud takes to task, believed women were men's equals and, for Freud, his real absurdity lay in this belief.

Freud's conventional notions of women's nature and proper position in society extended far beyond his own domestic arrangements. His writings on women show how readily he accepted prevailing 'scientific' views on women and how thoroughly they informed the explanatory framework of his theorising. In his views on women, if nothing else, Freud remained in curiously complete sympathy with his former friend, Wilhelm Fliess.

Writing in *The Course of Life* Fliess, too, reiterated late nineteenth-century scientific clichés that never tired of pointing out the biological basis of woman's nature and her difference from man. While man was naturally innovative, woman was conservative: 'woman opposes change: she receives passively and adds nothing of her own'. Furthermore, her life was dominated by her sexual, that is, reproductive, function: 'The truly characteristic [*sic*] in the life of the healthy woman is that her sexual task forms the center to which everything is referred back ... Love of children is the distinctive mark of the healthy woman.'[10]

The scientific world view to which Freud subscribed was characterised by advances in several different areas of knowledge. During his childhood and youth there occurred the publication of Charles Darwin's many writings, beginning with *On the Origin of Species* in 1859, Louis Pasteur's germ theory of disease, Gregor Mendel's work on genetics and Hermann von Helmholtz's work in physics. The physiologist Ernst Brucke, who was a university teacher and an early, revered mentor of Freud's, had transferred von Helmholtz's principle of conservation of energy from physics to physiology. Brucke argued that the living organism was a dynamic system to which the laws of physics and chemistry applied. Advocates of positivism, like Brucke, believed its style of inquiry in the natural sciences should be extended into the investigation of all human thought and behaviour. Freud eagerly accepted this proposition and made it a goal of his own work.

'DYNAMIC' PSYCHOLOGY

The centrepoint of Freud's scientific psychology was the idea of a dynamic theory of personality, which he adapted from physics and chemistry. In his theory, we find 'man' conceptualised as an energy system that has only a given amount of energy at its disposal. Freud posited that the energising of one part of the personality was necessarily accompanied by the depletion of another part. Following the model of dynamic energy established in the natural sciences, Freud theorised the human psyche as a closed system in which energy could be transformed but never destroyed. Consequently, the transformations and exchanges of energy within the system had the utmost importance for emotional well-being.

Late in his his life, Freud attested to the significance of this dynamic perspective as a linchpin to his entire theory and the goal of his life's work: 'My life has been aimed at one goal only; to infer or to guess how the mental apparatus is constructed and what forces interplay and counteract in it.'[11] Freud's 'dynamic' psychology thus asserted that human behaviour should be understood as the product of mutually interacting urging and checking forces within the individual. He created psychoanalytic terms *cathexes* and *decathexes* to name these instinctual and counter-instinctual forces.

THE DESCENT AND DESCENT OF WOMEN

However, the ideas of Darwin, especially the application of evolutionary theory to society and the prescription of social roles in it, are most evident in Freud's psychological theories regarding women. The impact of Darwin's thinking on Freud's has been discussed by Ritvo, but she does not deal specifically with how it vivifies Freud's theories on women.[12]

Like many late nineteenth-century thinkers, Freud was enamoured of recapitulation theory and elaborated its defining notion, that ontogeny recapitulated phylogeny, in his theory of psychosexual development. In his *Introductory Lectures on Psychoanalysis* Freud plainly expressed his belief in recapitulation theory: 'Each individual somehow recapitulated in an abbreviated form the entire development of the human race.'[13]

In the 1919 edition of *The Interpretation of Dreams* (originally published in 1900) it is obvious that recapitulation theory still retained a strong explanatory power in his theorising:

Dreaming is on the whole an example of regression to the dreamer's earliest condition, a revival of his childhood ... Behind this childhood of the individual we are promised a picture of a phylogenetic childhood — a picture of the human race, of which the individual's development is in fact an abbreviated recapitulation influenced by the chance circumstances of life.[14]

Freud also accepted the standard view that children and people from primitive races had parallel levels of development: 'There is a great deal of resemblance between the relations of children and of primitive man towards animals.'[15]

Of course, women were explicitly linked with children and those from the 'lower races' in nineteenth-century evolutionary theory, and Freud does not depart conspicuously from this position. Indeed, he stated the parallel development of the 'uncultivated' woman and the child in a widely quoted passage from *Three Essays on the Theory of Sexuality*, commenting: '... children behave in the same kind of way as an average uncultivated woman in whom the same polymorphous perverse disposition persists.'[16] Freud set out from the same cultural norm and arrived at the same 'scientific' conclusion as Stanley Hall and the numerous anthropologists who were convinced that women occupied a lower position than men on the 'phyletic scale' because of their biology. Indeed, his entire theory of psychosexual development depends to a large extent on the notion of recapitulation.

In the short journey between assumption and conclusion, Freud hit upon a universal law. He called it the Oedipus complex. It is Freud's particular contribution to the Darwinian project of fixing woman a position on the phyletic scale that accurately reflected her nature. The process through which Freud established the Oedipus complex and proved that it was a universal law of human behaviour is interesting in what it reveals about his interpretation of positivist methodology and in its far-reaching consequences for the psychoanalytic treatment of women. Freud was unabashedly in search of universal laws of human nature and behaviour. His way of establishing these laws, an aim held in common with natural scientists, diverged rather sharply from the usual scientific methodology. Like the natural scientists with whom he aligned himself, Freud believed experiments were capable of testing hypotheses and leading to predictable outcomes. With sufficient replication they would lead to the establishment of universal laws. Freud's approach to replication, a necessity given his determination to establish universal laws, was decidedly idiosyncratic. To check the workings of the unconscious and his simultaneous premise and proof of the dynamic forces at work, he had to show that his findings with a small number of mentally ill 'patients' could be replicated more broadly.

Rather than extending and replicating his findings with a large number of normal people, Freud chose a different path. He analysed himself. This self-analysis went on through the 1890s. His efforts were aimed at checking the findings gained from patients by analysing his own dreams and free associations until he believed he understood the inner dynamic processes at work. Freud thought he could shed all his preconceptions, knowledge and personal beliefs for the purposes of his own analysis. He was convinced he could allow his mind to become a *tabula rasa* on which psychoanalytic insights would accurately inscribe themselves.

The ultimate 'proof' and verification of the existence of the Oedipus complex, for example, came from Freud's self-analysis. He wrote to his friend Fliess in 1897 with the news. 'I have found, in my own case too, being in love with the mother and jealous of the father, and I now consider it a universal event of early childhood.'[17]

Freud used his own experience as the norm against which his patients' experiences were measured. If there was concurrence between the two, a law could be posited. As chief discoverer of the laws of human behaviour, Freud became the arbiter who decided on the credibility, reliability and validity of his patients' experiences according to these laws. But if concurrence with Freud's own male experience of the world is evidence of the 'truth' of universal laws of behaviour, then what of non-concurrence? Might it be taken to constitute 'lies', 'resistance', 'denial' or 'fantasy'?

The non-concurrence of patients' experiences with Freud's own is a highly significant issue. It has far-reaching implications for his ability to hear and believe what his female patients said to him. According to the theory of dominant and muted groups, Freud's theoretical tenets would preclude him from hearing his female patients in an undistorted way. As we shall see later, this criticism seems particularly pertinent when we examine the case history of Dora, the 18-year-old girl brought by her father to Freud so that he would get her to see 'reason'. The psychological distress Dora experienced when faced with Freud's apparent disbelief of her account of what happened with Herr K is a poignant example of frustrated communication: 'She was almost beside herself at the idea of its being supposed that she had merely fancied something on that occasion.'[18]

Many critics have understandably baulked at Freud's self-analysis as proof of his own theories. It has problems from a standard positivist viewpoint of extreme selection bias, inadequate sample size for inferring anything about the general population, and a very large expectancy effect. One critic, Ernest Gellner, in his book, *The Psychoanalytic Movement*, finds the use of self-analysis as proof decidedly unconvincing. Gellner writes:

> It is not entirely clear why this particular piece of introspection should not be doomed, like that of other men, to self-deception, but instead be classed as heroic and veridical — unless the reason is that its findings are valid, which to outsiders seems somewhat circular reasoning.[19]

In one way, Freud's commitment to the scientific *Weltanschaung* coexisted with a methodology that contravened its most basic principles. On the other hand, his acceptance of recapitulation theory makes it unsurprising that Freud accepted a developmental view of the personality. In fact, the word *development* was convertible with the term *evolution* in the nineteenth century.[20]

Development was theorised by Freud, in keeping with the phyletic model, to proceed in a predictable sequence with set tasks at each stage. Each of these stages was given a different name, such as the oral, anal, phallic or oedipal stage. Abnormal behaviour was seen as the outcome of an interaction between environmental experiences, and biologically based features of psychosexual development and different kinds of mental illness were graded hierarchically, according to their level of maturity, and assigned to specific stages of development using a phylogenetic model.

Current behaviour, from this developmental perspective, can only be understood in terms of what has preceded it, and current psychological crises invariably reactivate past crises. The individual's emotional well-being seems to hover precariously, poised between the present and the past, always under the pull of some kind of recapitulationary pressure. For women, this recapitulationary pull was particularly strong and is related, it seems, to their biologically determined lower level of development. Women were always in danger of being pulled back, developmentally speaking, to an earlier level of psychosexual maturity.

Freud's theories on 'femininity' make it abundantly clear that he believed they experienced a particularly fraught interaction between the present and the past. Resolving the developmental crises of childhood so as to ensure sustainable psychological growth was extremely problematic for most women. The all-important Oedipus complex not only occurred at a different and later time in the development of women compared with men but also might never be satisfactorily resolved. Freud puts it this way in *Female Sexuality*:

> Thus in women the Oedipus complex is the end result of a fairly lengthy development. It is not destroyed, but created by the influence of castration; it escapes the strongly hostile influences which, in the male, have a destructive effect on it, and indeed it is all too often not surmounted by the female at all. For this reason, too, the cultural consequences of its break up are smaller and of less importance in her.[21]

For Freud, woman's biology serves to exclude her from culture, just as his beliefs about her biology and its influence on her place in culture prevent him from being able to create a complete and coherent theory of femininity. His interpretive framework can be seen to filter and distort his observations to such an extent that his beliefs about penis envy are always substantiated and confirmed.

The overriding influence of the lack of a penis in women's development can be gauged from a memorable passage in Freud's essay,

'Femininity'. In this passage Freud abandoned his stance of the impartial, scientific observer merely recording factual observations, and freely admitted that he was engaging in speculation. His speculations accorded so closely with his 'observed facts' about the nature of female sexuality that the two are indistinguishable.

> People say that women contributed but little to the discoveries and inventions of civilisation, but perhaps after all they did discover one technical process, that of plaiting and weaving. If this is so, one is tempted to guess at the unconscious motive at the back of this achievement. Nature herself might be regarded as having provided a model for imitation, by causing pubic hair to grow at the period of sexual maturity so as to veil the genitals. The step that remained to be taken was to attach the hairs permanently together, whereas in the body they are fixed in the skin and only tangled with one another. If you repudiate this idea as being fantastic, and accuse me of have an *idée fixe* on the subject of the influence exercised by the lack of a penis upon the development of femininity, I cannot of course defend myself.[22]

The ideas expressed in this passage exemplify how closely Freud identified woman with nature. The impress of nature on women is so great that it is almost as if they exist outside culture and are inherently disqualified from contributing to it. Their sole contribution, plaiting and weaving — and even this modest achievement is not wholly conceded ('perhaps, after all') — is reactive and compensatory, arising from shame and wearily, but predictably, from penis envy. The *idée fixe*, which Freud knows he cannot defend himself against, issues from a dualist double bind. He experienced marked and continuing difficulty in saying what it was to be a woman. All along Freud was dominated and hemmed in by what woman was not when he was attempting to say what she was. Woman was not a man; she did not possess a penis. The task Freud set himself, and which he admitted he never succeeded in completing, was an impossible one: that of transforming a negation — 'the little creature without a penis'.[23]

Culture, far from creating the nature of women, is positioned as a consequence of it; a necessary reflection of immutable biological differences between men and women. While boys can and do go on to become men in Freud's theory, girls go on to become, well, girls. They are marooned in an intermediate stage of human development just as surely as they were in Hall's theory. Hall stated quite explicitly that women were nature's adolescents, and Freud, although his theories are more complex, basically asserts the same view.

Recalling and restating recapitulation theory, Freud embellished the usual set of biological reasons in a more novel way. Craniologists could cite smaller head measurements, and anthropologists could lament that women couldn't grow beards, but Freud appreciated that the true reason why little girls could never hope to attain the pinnacle of masculine maturity was their awareness that they lacked a penis.

Penis envy cast a pall over a girl's entire development. As Freud wrote in the essay, 'Some psychical consequences of the anatomical distinction between the sexes':

> [Girls] notice the penis ... strikingly visible and of large proportions [and] at once recognise it as the superior counterpart of their own small and inconspicuous organ, and from that time forward fall a victim to envy for the penis ... she makes her judgement and her decision in a flash. She has seen it and knows that she is without it and wants to have it.[24]

Her experience of penis envy is such a blow to her narcissism that it causes the little girl to stop masturbating. 'After a woman has become aware of the wound to her narcissism, she develops, like a scar, a sense of inferiority.' And because masturbation is seen as an active, masculine form of activity, the giving up of masturbation is at the same time a turning towards femininity and passivity, in Freud's eyes.

The effect of recapitulation theory is strikingly evident in the inference Freud drew about the shift women were meant to make from relying on the infantile, primitive clitoris as a source of masturbatory and therefore pathological stimulation to the mature, adult sexuality assigned to vaginal orgasm. 'You will see that a step in development, such as this one, which gets rid of phallic activity, *must* smooth the path for femininity.'[25] Of course, it was

Freud who first determined that clitoral orgasm was infantile and primitive and in this way pathologised its continued occurrence in the lives of adult women. Privileging a male norm, he preordained the requisite steps in development and then 'discovered' that women's biology meant they could not complete these steps nor attain full — masculine — maturity.

The equation of passivity with femininity and activity with masculinity recalls the theory of anabolic and katabolic cells, referred to in the previous chapter, which saw the female ovum as the exemplar of the passive, placid anabolic cell. Both Freud's theory and that of Geddes and Thomson, whose book *Evolution* was in Freud's library at his London home, sought to yoke female biological difference to arrested human development, which in turn legitimated her social subjection.

The significance of the phyletic scale is bolstered in Freudian theory by the supposed reaction of a woman to her physical difference from man. Chiefly, it is her disappointment with her female genitalia, rather than any real constraints imposed by external social reality, that Freud posits as the main impediment to woman's ability to effect a successful transfer from earlier, more primitive to later, more mature stages in development.

The girl's discovery of her own castration, according to Freud, exercised a crucial role in her development. It gave 'its special stamp to the character of woman as a member of society'. As this discovery of her genital deprivation occurred in early childhood, it is easy to see why Freud was able to view the social influences acting on the girl after the oedipal stage as being of decidedly marginal importance.

Aware that she has nothing worthwhile to lose means that the girl, according to Freud, can stay in the oedipal phase for life. Strong repression, which ended the phase for the boy, only took place because of his fear of castration. For Freud it was a 'fact', which 'must' be believed, that the girl's indeterminate stay in the oedipal phase resulted in impaired super-ego development. 'The formation of the super-ego must suffer in these circumstances.'[26]

SURROGATE MOTHERHOOD

The centrality of motherhood in female development in Freud's theory is also identical with that prescribed by so many scientists mentioned in the preceding chapter. But in Freudian theory, even motherhood is not a uniquely female achievement. It, too, becomes another form of behaviour the pursuit of which is fuelled by penis envy.

> But now the girl's libido slips into position by means — there is no other way of putting it — of the equation 'penis = child'. She gives up her wish for a penis and puts in place of it a wish for a child: and with this purpose in view she takes her father as a love object. Her mother becomes the object of her jealousy.[27]

Freud routinely expressed his opinions in the imperative form as logically necessary truths. He was comfortable in the role of the impartialist, the man of science who neutrally transmitted observed facts to the public. Thus he claims that his 1933 essay, 'Femininity', 'contains nothing but observed facts with hardly any speculative additions'.[28] These observed facts are given force by being expressed in the imperative form, as propositions that cannot be denied.

In describing the initiation of the castration complex in the girl, Freud wrote:

> The castration complex in the girl, as well, is started by the sight of the genital organs of the other sex. She immediately notices the difference and — it must be admitted — its significance. She feels herself at a great disadvantage, and often declares that she would 'like to have something like that too', and falls a victim to penis envy, which leaves ineradicable traces on her development and character formation, and even, in the most favourable instances, is not overcome without a great expenditure of mental energy.[29]

Freud's conclusions about female psychosexual development flow smoothly from his premises. It is the truth of these premises and what Sandra Harding calls the 'context of discovery', or where problems are generated from and why, that is problematic. If, as Freud believed, penis envy is the major characteristic of the girl's psyche, then of course this will leave 'ineradicable traces on her development'. The main problem with all these formulations is that Freud always seems to assume what he sets out to prove, creating an irrefutable, hermetically sealed system of belief.

Freud was committed to the same scientific goal mentioned in the previous chapter, namely to confirm that woman's nature depends on her innate, biological difference from man's. Like his contemporaries in other fields, Freud was keen to prove that female biology was the primary determinant of woman's inferior level of psychosexual development; once again, nature not culture was privileged in explaining woman's social subjection.

> I cannot evade the notion (though I hesitate to give it expression) that for women the level of what is ethically normal is different from what it is for men [Freud wrote in 'Some psychical consequences of the anatomical distinction between the sexes']. Their super-ego is never so inexorable, so impersonal, so independent of its emotional origins as we require it to be in men. Character traits which critics of every epoch have brought up against women — that they show less sense of justice than men, that they are less ready to submit to the great exigencies of life, that they are more often influenced in their judgement by feelings of affection or hostility — all these would be amply accounted for by the modification in the formation of the super-ego which we have inferred above.[30]

Accepting the received wisdom, the prejudice of 'every epoch' as unimpeachable truth, Freud then looks to his own psychoanalytic concepts to shed new and superior light on why woman has such poor character traits.

In his inability to evade the notion of woman's ethical inferiority and his *a posteriori* psychoanalytic interpretation of the true basis of this inferiority, Freud demonstrates how effortlessly the history of a prejudice could be transmuted into a scientific truth, an abiding fact of nature. In what now reads like a parody of scientific impartiality, the gender of the 'we' who sets the requirement that men will have inexorable super-egos or are the 'critics' of 'every epoch' goes unremarked. It cannot be otherwise. The objectivity and neutrality of the scientist Freud believed himself to be was sacrosanct. There was no way in which gender or race could emerge as conspicuous figures from this supposedly neutral ground and be recognised as powerful determinants of what science saw as a problem. How the scientist and his values and prejudices contributed to the construction of 'the problem of the woman', 'the problem of the Jew' or the 'problem of slavery' was simply not open to investigation. The scientific method itself was supposed to transcend the subjective, the idiosyncratic and the personal, and guarantee that all of its findings were impeccably fair, objective and reasonable.

It is noticeable again and again in Freud's writing how he adopts a tone of pained but unswerving honesty when seeking to transform his own opinions and the cultural clichés of the day concerning women into psychic laws: 'I cannot evade the notion (though I hesitate to give it expression)'. He makes a split between the personal, subjective 'I' and the impersonal, objective 'notion'. The notion is presented as existing outside Freud's mind rather than being a product of it. At the same time, Freud places himself in the flattering position of the fearless seeker after truth who is prepared to utter the unpalatable but essential notions others cannot face. This habit of endowing his subjective beliefs with the impartial, logically necessary quality of self-evident truth is not confined to his writings on women but is perhaps most apparent in them. And it is because his views on the nature of women diverge so little from those repeated by the critics of every epoch that Freud's claims to scientific objectivity and originality are less sustainable on this subject than on any other.

Yet it would be inaccurate to present Freud as an unswerving, convinced biological determinist. Freud's attitude to psychosexual development in women was, in fact, quite complex and vacillated between closed-minded conviction on the role played by biology compared with culture and open-minded puzzlement. All his writings reflect this ambivalence, namely *Three Essays on the Theory of Sexuality* (1905), 'Some psychical consequences of the anatomical distinction between the sexes' (1925), 'Female sexuality' (1931) and 'Femininity' (1933). For Freud, women were the 'dark continent', and he was quite prepared to admit that female analysts might be in a better position to work effectively with female patients.

When Freud expressed uncertainty about the causal factors in female sexuality, this uncertainty focused on the same matters about which he could be utterly dogmatic. For instance, he realised that any theory of female sexuality must be based to some extent on biological knowledge, and was well aware that this knowledge was not available when he was trying to construct his own theory of female sexuality. Thus in an essay, one of three on sexuality, 'The transformations of puberty', which was concerned with the way in which girls supposedly exchanged one area of genital excitement (the clitoral–masculine) for another (the vaginal–feminine) at puberty, Freud deliberately concluded his essay in the most tentative way. He admitted: 'we know far too little of the biological processes constituting the essence of sexuality to be able to construct from our fragmentary information a theory adequate to the understanding alike of normal and of pathological conditions'.[31]

A similar attitude of caution informs a discussion of passivity in a later essay, 'Femininity'. Here too Freud makes hypothetical statements and considers alternative possibilities to the proposition that passivity in women is innate.

> It may be that the part played by women in the sexual function leads them to incline towards passive behaviour and passive aims, and that this inclination extends into their ordinary life to a greater or lesser degree, according to whether the influence of their sexual life as a model is limited or far-reaching. But we must take care not to underestimate the influence of social conventions, which also force women into passive situations. The whole thing is still very obscure.[32]

Despite the whole thing still being 'very obscure', Freud claimed that this particular essay 'contains nothing but observed facts, with hardly any speculative additions'.[33] These observed facts are so far at variance with the tentative tone of the passage just quoted that they tend to obliterate the fact that Freud ever admitted uncertainty regarding the determinants of female sexuality.

Obviously, there is a very wide discrepancy between Freud's expressions of doubt concerning female sexuality and his convictions on the same subject. On the one hand, he is able to empha-sise the possible influence of culture and social conventions in the development of female personality, and on the other to claim that social conventions are unimportant in determining the way women develop. Freud's early doubts about the determinants of the female psyche, particularly his consideration of the part played by culture and socialisation, were later replaced by the opinion that women were almost completely created by biology and sexuality, which was innate and immutable.

Even so, his much-quoted last words on femininity expressed neither ambivalence nor certainty but more a feeling of helpless-ness. 'If you want to know more about femininity', he instructed his students, 'you must interrogate your own experience or turn to the poets, or else wait until science can give you more profound and more coherent information.'[34] Significantly, Freud does not canvass the possibility that women themselves might possess knowledge about femininity and should therefore be questioned by the presumably male seeker after truth to whom these com-ments were addressed.

The foregoing discussion has concentrated on the derivative sci-entific framework of Freud's theories on women. This is a sepa-rate issue from considering the efficacy of psychoanalysis or its effect on twentieth-century thinking. Notions such as the uncon-scious, infantile sexuality, the use of repression as a defence mech-anism of the psyche, penis envy, the death wish, the importance of our earliest experiences — have all pervaded our cultural con-sciousness. Psychoanalysis has also produced directly, or as a reaction, a huge number of psychotherapies. As far back as 1977, the number of distinct psychotherapies was put at two hundred.[35]

Its growth since its beginnings in Vienna a hundred years ago is analogous to the spread of a new religion. Of course, this is exactly what its critics accuse it of being. Karl Popper has called the unfalsifiability of its central beliefs, indeed the transformation of any criticism into further confirmatory evidence for these very beliefs, 'self-reinforcing dogmatism'. Such dogmatism and unfalsifiability is antithetical to the principles of positivistic science that Freud himself espoused.

There is no doubt that the psychoanalytic perspective has left an indelible mark on how we see ourselves. Psychoanalysis has influenced the theory and practice of art, education, literature, anthropology and medicine, especially psychiatry. It has also enduringly affected the field of psychosomatic research and the theorised connection between the workings of women's bodies and their minds. Its theories on what constitutes normal femininity have affected the psychiatric treatment of several generations of women. Perhaps, most importantly, these theories made it a precondition of recovery from neurosis and hysteria that women's sense of what happened in their lives should be reshaped and redefined through the prism of Freudian orthodoxy.

In the next chapter, the impact of Freud's theoretical revisions of the so-called 'seduction' theory of hysteria on the treatment of women in therapy will be discussed. The effect of psychoanalytic theories and therapy extended far beyond clinical practice, and I will argue that they have had a profound influence on women's sense of themselves as authentic witnesses to their own lives.

5

A SCIENTIFIC FAIRY TALE

When Freud began to treat hysteria in the 1890s, it was again regarded, in the way the Greeks did, as an affliction, a mental disorder that required the attention of physicians, rather than a sin in need of punishment or a proof of bewitchment by the devil.

Hysteria was chief among the 'nervous disorders' to which women were believed to be peculiarly susceptible. By the latter half of the nineteenth century, the cult of invalidism was in full swing among educated, middle-class women and functioned as the polar star of the claustrophobic doctrine that condemned these women to be angels of the house and idols of self-renunciation. As Bram Dijkstra amply illustrates in his book, *Idols of Perversity* (1986), illness and even death were considered aesthetic, *haute couture* physical states for women. Images of frail, fainting and defenceless women were produced and reproduced by a multitude of British, US and European (male) painters in the second half of the nineteenth century.[1]

Alice James, the sister of Henry, the novelist, and William, the philosopher, was the youngest child and only girl in a family of five children. She passed her life in the apparently perverse role of an invalid but died in 1892, of an entirely real disease — breast cancer — at the age of 42. Alice had a shrewd understanding of what ailed her. In the privacy of her diary she wrote of the emotional ill effects of self-abnegation: 'How sick one gets of being "good", how much I should respect myself if I could burst out and make everyone wretched for 24 hours ...'[2] Privately, Alice was able intellectually to contest the dictates of 'good' womanhood that cramped and sickened her, but she never managed to free herself from their power, and lived her life within their narrow margins.

Unlike her compatriot, Charlotte Perkins Gilman, who refused the role of invalid, Alice James's invalidism almost constituted her identity. Alice in her actual diary and Charlotte in her fictional one, *The Yellow Wallpaper*, expressed feelings and ideas totally at odds with the mores of the social and medical milieu that defined and pathologised them. It is as if the disjunction between their private thoughts and the ones they knew were publically acceptable was so great that they acceded to the futility of trying to express themselves outside their diaries.

The pattern of the yellow wallpaper, as Gilman symbolised the dominant discourse that silenced, sickened and frustrated her character to the point of psychosis, is impenetrable even to the most strenuous effort. From this perspective, women's madness consists of language and ideas endlessly driven back on themselves, of irrevocably private speech. Thoughts are confined to diaries not so that no one will see them but because no one would understand or accept them.

Gilman's feminist analysis of her social position prompted her to change her life. Alice James's insights never amounted to a convincing critique of her assigned role. Hers was a frustrated, partial rebellion. No matter how much she wished to 'burst out' and make others wretched, albeit briefly, the only person she ever made really wretched and sick was herself.

Alice, for all her intelligence, largely believed and assimilated the prevailing views about woman's nature. Her own lived experience served as a constant proof of woman's innate propensity for mental and physical fraility. She believed that women had fewer emotional needs than men, and she accepted that she was neurotic. Nevertheless, she warned her brother William against feeling her life was wasted:

> You must remember that a woman, by nature, needs much less to feed upon than a man, a few emotions and she is satisfied; so when I am gone, pray don't think of me simply as a creature who might have been something else, had *neurotic science* [my emphasis] been born. Notwithstanding the poverty of my outside experience, I have always had a significance for myself —[3]

In common with the oppressive need to be 'good', Alice was aware of and had a distaste for the passivity demanded of women. She told William of the feelings aroused by a humiliating medical examination in a letter written in 1886: 'I think the difficulty is my inability to assume the receptive attitude, that cardinal virtue in woman, the absence of which has always made me so uncharming to and uncharmed by the male sex.'[4] Thus an invalid could be prostrated but determinedly unreceptive. There were two ways a woman might regard this unreceptiveness, if she were aware of it in the first place. She could attribute it to an inborn inability, a mistake of nature beyond her control, or she could claim her unreceptiveness as a conscious refusal — a rebellion against the intent of the social order. Perhaps the first possibility, accepted by Alice James and most of her ailing peers, was an intrinsic ingredient of their chronic invalidism and the second, adopted by Charlotte Perkins Gilman, a prerequisite for recovery and a modicum of health.

When Alice James wrote this letter, she was by no means unusual in her experience of invalidism and nervous disorder. She was one of many thousands of white, middle-class women in Europe and the USA caught up in a rising tide of distress and disorder. Some sense of the proportions of this epidemic is provided by Edward Shorter in his 1989 paper, 'Women and Jews in a private nervous clinic in late nineteenth-century Vienna'. Shorter notes that the number of patients in public asylums in Prussia alone rose from 14 500 in 1875 to 59 000 in 1900, an increase of more than 400 per cent. In private profit-making clinics, the number of patients increased from 320 in 1852 to 8500 by 1906, an increase of more than 2500 per cent. Shorter, a medical historian, documents how Jews and women were 'objects of particular curiosity in neurology and psychiatry in the nineteenth century'.[5] And in the evolutionary debate Jews, because of their supposed degeneracy, were consigned, like women and blacks, to a lower position on the phyletic scale.

The perceived liability of Jews and women to nervous disorder, and in particular to hysteria, was a matter that could not fail to engage the emotions of Sigmund Freud, a Jewish doctor specialising in the treatment of these same disorders. Indeed Freud's first theory of hysteria can be understood as a strenuous rebuttal of the belief that doubly linked women and Jews through a shared proneness to hysteria and a low position on the phyletic scale. Freud's alternative explanation of hysteria stressed the aetiological significance of actual events in the early lives of distressed individuals over the influence of evolutionary retardation and inborn taints.

It is now well known that, in his first theory on hysteria, Freud argued that traumatic childhood sexual experiences were causal. His seminal paper, 'The aetiology of hysteria', presented to the Society for Psychiatry and Neurology in Vienna on 21 April 1896, expressed this belief in a completely unequivocal manner:

> I therefore put forward the thesis that at the bottom of every case of hysteria there are one or more occurrences of premature sexual experience, occurrences which belong to the earliest years of childhood but which can be reproduced through the work of psycho-analysis in spite of the intervening decades.[6]

The assertions made in this paper, as we shall see, are sharply at variance with the beliefs that informed his final view of the causes of hysteria. What is perhaps more significant, because ultimately it is of more enduring value in understanding the characteristic forms of emotional distress and disorder experienced by women, is the predictive accuracy of his first formulations. Increasingly, these early assertions are being supported by findings from contemporary research on childhood sexual abuse.

He was clear, for example, about the type of sexual experience in childhood that produced long-term emotional disorder: 'Sexual experiences in childhood consisting in stimulation of the genitals, coitus-like acts and so on, must therefore be recognized, in the last analysis, as being the traumas which lead to a hysterical reaction …' Freud was also aware of the importance of the child's age when the abuse occurred. He realised that the younger and more immature the child was, physically and psychologically, the more terribly would forced sexual experiences interfere with subsequent development: 'Injuries sustained by an organ which is as yet immature, or by a function which is in the process of developing, often cause more severe and lasting effects than they could do in maturer years.'[7]

One of the more conspicuous ironies of Freud's retraction of his original ideas was that their theoretical replacement was primarily responsible for the protracted delay in uncovering the true magnitude of the 'severe and lasting effects' he described. The legacy of this retraction on psychiatric practice and research will be discussed in the following chapter. In 'The aetiology of hysteria', however, Freud was not only able to identify a range of factors that determined the severity of the psychological outcome experienced by sexualised children but also was aware of the arguments that would be used to discredit his claims. Referring to his assertion that there was a relationship between early age of abuse and the severity and duration of its effects, Freud correctly predicted that:

> This statement is certain to be met from different directions by two mutually contradictory objections. Some people will say that sexual abuses of this kind, whether practised upon children or between them, happen too seldom for it to be possible to regard them as the determinant of such a common neurosis as hysteria. Others will perhaps argue that, on the contrary, such experiences are very frequent — much too frequent for us to be able to attribute an aetiological significance to the fact of their occurrence. They will further maintain that it is easy, by making a few enquiries, to find people who remember scenes of sexual seduction and sexual abuse in their childhood years, and yet who have never been hysterical.[8]

He countered the argument about the infrequency and therefore unimportance of childhood experience with evidence from a number of different sources. They included the recently published article by Dr Stekel in 1895 entitled 'Coitus in childhood', the reports of colleagues and publications by paediatricians. Masson has also documented Freud's familiarity with the findings of forensic psychiatry involving the criminal abuse of small children. During his time in Paris between 1885 and 1886 Freud reported that he 'rarely missed' the autopsies and lectures of the professor of legal medicine, Paul Camille Hippolyte Brouardel, at the Paris morgue. Perhaps his experience there prompted Freud to point out in his 1896 lecture on hysteria that even if the published evidence on which he had to rely was scanty, 'it is to be expected that increased attention to the subject will very soon confirm the great frequency of sexual experiences and sexual activity in childhood'.[9]

This last point has a continuing relevance. As feminists continue to emphasise in relation to the many 'silences' in women's lives, claims dismissing the importance of a subject on the grounds that there is 'no evidence' for its existence are meaningless if, in fact, no evidence has ever been sought. Many of these 'silences', such as the experience of childhood sexual abuse and the emotional impact of physical and sexual violence in adult life, are now being broached. Nevertheless a good deal of caution is still warranted for assertions that rely on the lack of evidence about an issue as a 'reason' for dismissing it. It is almost axiomatic that an absence of enquiry and a lack of investigation will obtain when what is of interest to women is not shared by those responsible for deciding the research agenda and even more so when it has been decided in advance that these interests and concerns are inconsequential or lie outside the parameters of 'proper' scientific inquiry. As Freud predicted nearly a hundred years ago, once the subject of child sexual abuse began to receive serious attention from clinicians and researchers, from the 1980s onwards, evidence regarding its existence and prevalence began to accumulate at a rapid rate.

Freud displayed similar prescience regarding the counterarguments directed towards his assertions concerning the traumatic force of early abuse and the part played by the psychological defense of repression. Here he articulated exactly the arguments used by fathers belonging to the False Memory Syndrome Foundation. This American organisation was formed in response to allegations of sexual abuse by adult children, usually daughters against their fathers. In the much publicised case of Holly Ramona, who had sought counselling for depression and bulimia, her father contended that her 'repressed memory syndrome' of his abuse was manufactured by her counsellor and that she was duped into believing in abuse that had never happened. Gary Ramona successfully sued his daughter's counsellor, her psychiatrist and the Western Medical Centre of Anaheim. Some expert witnesses, like the San Francisco psychiatrist, Lenore Terr, supported the view that repressed memories do exist and that repression comes into being because children who experience terror and repeated abuse survive by dissociating and putting themselves into trance states during the rapes or beatings. However, other experts argued against the whole notion of repression and 'repressed memory syndrome' as defying common sense.

The Ramona case provides a contemporary illustration of the arguments regarding memory distortion and repression with which Freud was so familiar. Whether a therapist accepts or rejects claims concerning repressed memory will vary according to the conditions under which the memory or memories are elicited, the philosophical stance of the therapist regarding the likely validity of memory, his or her attitudes towards the whole idea that the psyche has such things as mechanisms of defense including repression, the weight and significance placed on the concurrent presence of other symptoms or conditions that might indicate prior abuse, such as depression or bulimia, and the believability of the woman making the claims as judged by her listener.

As the differences in the expert opinion expressed in the Ramona case underline, all these issues are far from being resolved among contemporary psychologists and psychiatrists. In particular, the Ramona case illustrates the difficulty that a young, 'sick' woman is likely to encounter in being believed when she makes claims of incest that rely on her testimony and on her memory of past events, which have remained repressed and unarticulated until they have come out or been brought out by therapy. The difference between these two is crucial. Therapists can easily be charged with implanting suggestions of abuse in the mind of a distressed and suggestible client. The issue is further complicated by evidence (to be discussed in the final chapter) that attests to links between early, severe abuse, hypnotisability, dissociative symptoms and suggestibility. Moreover, while the charge of manipulation is ostensibly directed towards the therapist, it also functions to undermine the client's credibility as a witness because, if she wasn't so suggestible and therefore unreliable, she wouldn't be so manipulable.

An additional factor that can influence a legal outcome is the financial standing of the litigant. Typically, a young woman will be severely disadvantaged in this way compared with her father. Gary Ramona, for example, spent more than a million dollars on his case. An important part of this case was provided by expert witnesses who testified that Holly was delusional — a dupe of members of the same 'helping professions' to which they themselves belonged.

Before discussing recent evidence relating to the occurrence of childhood sexual abuse and its psychological outcomes in proper detail, it is necessary to return to the change Freud made in his theory of hysteria and what might have motivated it.

In 1896, Freud, building on the initial insights of Breuer, with whom he had published *Studies in Hysteria* the year before, argued that psychoanalytic techniques were uniquely able to gain access to the content of what had been repressed. The defining characteristic of psychoanalytic technique was said to be its ability to make conscious events and processes of thought that Breuer asserted were otherwise 'inadmissible to consciousness'.[10]

In describing the predictive value of childhood sexual experience for hysteria Freud maintained that 'it does not matter if many people experience infantile sexual scenes without becoming hysterics, provided only that all the people who become hysterics have experienced scenes of that kind'.[11] This line of thinking is well accepted in other areas of medicine. For example, not everyone who comes into contact with the flu virus develops influenza, but all those with influenza have necessarily had contact with the virus. The signs or symptoms of hysteria were, of course, somewhat more complicated than those associated with a physical illness like influenza. Further, with hysteria Freud was theorising a lag time between the alleged cause in childhood and its effect in adult life of years rather than days.

Retrospective inference is always open to criticism. Certainty about past causes of current events is complicated and undermined by the interpolation of many other possible causative factors in the intervening period. Other plausible explanations can be put forward to account for the existence of problems such as anxiety or depression, somatic disorders, eating disorders or drug and alcohol problems that have been related to childhood sexual abuse. Before researchers interested themselves in the association between childhood abuse and these common problems in the lives of adult women, there was no shortage of theory calling on everything from intrapsychic pathology, hormonal derangement, constitutional proneness to chemical imbalance and reproductive abnormality to account for their existence.

Freud divided the eighteen patients on whom he based his initial theory into three groups according to whom he reported was responsible for inflicting the sexual trauma on the child, which brought about 'severe neurotic illness which threatened to make life impossible'. The first group consisted of assaults, 'mostly practised on female children, by adults who were strangers'. The second was composed of the 'much more numerous cases' committed by 'some adult looking after the child — a nursery maid or governess or tutor, or, unhappily all too often, a close relative'. It was only in the 1920s that Freud could bring himself to name fathers as the main perpetrators of abuse in this most numerous group of cases. The third group comprised relationships between children usually of different sexes and usually between a brother and sister. Freud believed these relationships were often prolonged beyond puberty and had far-reaching consequences for both parties.[12]

For a couple of years then, leading up to and including *Studies in Hysteria* (1895) and 'The aetiology of hysteria' (1896), there existed a theory of hysteria and a form of psychotherapy grounded in an acceptance of what women were telling Freud about their lives. At the time Freud accorded these women's stories an unequivocal truth status. It is impossible to overstate what a radical step this was. Even psychologically normal women were considered incapable of possessing knowledge, either of themselves or anything else. But women with hysteria made up another order of unbelievability entirely. Hysterical women were taken to be commensurate with hysterical liars. Yet it was on the basis of what these women said that Freud predicated his first theory of hysteria.

How far Freud's reliance on his patients' accounts diverged from the practice of his contemporaries becomes clear if he is compared with his contemporary, Emil Kraepilin. Kraepilin was Professor of Psychiatry at Heidelberg between 1890 and 1904, when he left to take up the same post in Munich. He is probably best known today for being the first psychiatrist to distinguish between 'circular insanity' (currently called bipolar disorder) and dementia praecox (now known as schizophrenia). Kraepilin was so convinced of the pointlessness of talking to his patients that no rooms were set aside for this purpose in his hospital clinic.[13] When he did question patients, their utterances were largely redundant. All they could do was prove their own insanity, something Kraepilin was sure of before they said anything. His diagnoses were impervious to disproof, as one anecdote makes clear. On one of his rounds, Kraepilin presented a male 'psychopath' to his colleagues. He asked the man what he thought the point of marriage was. 'The patient answered smartly: "In order to have a life companion." Kraepilin then turned to his listeners: "You see even from this answer that we're dealing with a psychopath here."'[14]

For a time, at least, Freud did listen to and believe what his female patients told him. Moreover, their accounts provided the evidence on which Freud based his first theory of hysteria and informed his belief in the unconscious and the mechanisms of defense. But the tenure of this first theory stressing real and traumatic events of childhood, or what Freud later called 'material reality', was to be short lived.

By 1897, Freud had retracted this theory, resiled from the proposition that actual experiences were all that significant and contended instead that universal childhood fantasies were crucial. This was the view he retained and insisted on for the rest of his life. He did not deny that sexual abuse in childhood ever occurred but rather that it was relatively unimportant aetiologically in most cases of hysteria. The shift in emphasis from real events to fantasised wishes was so seismic that psychiatric concern about the existence, extent and consequences of real abuse was effectively obliterated for nearly a hundred years.

In the 1920s, Freud wrote about his change of mind in his 'Autobiographical study'. By this time, the earlier theory had long since been repudiated. Interestingly, in an act of retrospective identification with his first detractors, he has now adopted the same tone of almost patronising incredulity towards his earlier ideas that they expressed in 1896 and against which he argued so vigorously at the time. In the 'Autobiographical study', we also learn how Freud censored his first findings and omitted to say that fathers were mentioned most often as the abusers of their daughters.

> Under the influence of the technical procedure which I used at that time, the majority of my patients reproduced from their childhood scenes in which they were sexually seduced by some grown-up person. With female patients the part of seducer was almost always assigned to their father. I believed these stories, and consequently supposed that I had discovered the roots of the subsequent neurosis in these experiences of sexual seduction in childhood. My confidence was strengthened by a few cases in which relations of this kind with a father, uncle, or elder brother had continued to an age at which memory was to be trusted. If the reader feels inclined to shake his head at my credulity, I cannot altogether blame him ... I was at last obliged to recognize that these scenes of seduction had never taken place, and that they were only phantasies which my patients had made up or which I myself had forced on them ... neurotic symptoms were not related directly to actual events but to wishful phantasies, and that as far as neurosis was concerned psychical reality was of more importance than material reality ... I had in fact stumbled for the first time

upon the Oedipus Complex, which was later to assume such an over-whelming importance, but which I did not recognize as yet in its dis-guise of phantasy. Morevover, seduction during childhood retained a certain share, though a humbler one, in the aetiology of neuroses. But the seducers turned out as a rule to have been older children.[15]

Furthermore, it is only in a 1924 edition of *Studies in Hysteria* that Freud admitted Katharina, one of the case histories discussed, had been sexually assaulted by her father. In retrospect, he said he regretted not including this fact: 'The girl fell ill, therefore, as a result of the sexual attempts on the part of her own father. Dis-tortions like the one which I introduced in the present instance should be altogether avoided in reporting a case history.'[16]

At worst, his admissions of tampering with the evidence con-vict Freud of scientific fraud; at best, they show him to be an unre-liable narrator with an impressive capacity for transforming unpleasant and inconvenient facts. Even his belated admission of censoring what was meant to be straightforward reporting of facts in 'The aetiology of hysteria' proceeds under the cover of dis-missing his early findings. In this way, when he admits that his female patients told him all along that it was their fathers who abused them, not, as he misleadingly reported at the time, their governesses or other unrelated adults, it is as if this is an inconse-quential, even amusing detail from an earlier, more gullible stage of his development. What is more, it is made to appear a trivial admission because now Freud is telling us that, when real abuse does occur, 'as a rule' it is carried out by older children, thus dis-placing, distancing and exonerating fathers even more.

This extended quotation also reveals how energetically Freud propounded the idea that his change of theory was the result of an entirely pristine scientific insight into the importance of children's sexual fantasies. He valorised this realisation as a theoretical breakthrough crucial to the development of psychoanalytic theory and the proof of the 'overwhelming importance' of the Oedipus complex.

Freud's estimation of why he changed his theory was accepted uncritically for the most part up until the 1980s. Janet Malcolm, for example, in referring to this change from actual sexual abuse in childhood to fantasies about such abuse, comments in the following laudatory terms: 'By 1897, Freud had undergone the intellectual revolution that took him from this dour but unremarkable social view of sexual malaise to his radical psychological theories regarding infantile sexuality and the Oedipus complex.'[17] Freud's own estimation of his first theory was on a rather more grandiose scale than 'dour but unremarkable'. After he had given his lecture he wrote to Fliess that he had demonstrated the 'solution to a more than thousand-year-old problem, a "source of the Nile"', even though this estimation was not shared by anyone else at the lecture.[18]

A less flattering interpretation of Freud's change of mind about the basis of hysteria has been argued by Jeffrey Masson, in a series of books beginning with *The Assault on Truth*, first published in 1984.[19] Masson attributes the changes in Freud's thinking more to moral cowardice and self-serving ambition than any higher theoretical imperative. The trenchant, if somewhat polemical, criticisms made by Masson assert that Freud gave up his original ideas that hysterical women became that way because of childhood sexual trauma in response to the 'icy reception' he received from his colleagues when he presented his theory in 1896. In the same letter to Fliess already quoted we learn that Baron Richard von Krafft-Ebing (1840–1902), Professor and head of Department of Psychiatry at University of Vienna, who chaired the meeting at which Freud presented his theory, dismissed it as 'a scientific fairy tale'.

Masson emphasises how Freud's choice of words changes along with his theoretical metamorphosis. In 'The aetiology of hysteria', he used a number of words like *rape*, *abuse*, *attack*, *assault*, *aggression* and *trauma*. The word *seduction* was also included among this list, but the overwhelming sense conveyed by the words in the early work is one of the damage done to the child as a result of the sexual force used against her. Masson charges that in Freud's later theories he largely replaced the longer list of words signifying attack and abuse with the word *seduction*. With its softer connotations, *seduction* implies a sensuous mutuality and the willing participation of the child in the sexual act. In effecting this shift, Masson asserts that Freud was able to foster a sense of ambiguity about what was going on and thereby turned attention away from the damage done to children by adults who sexualised them.

According to Masson, Freud sought to revise his views to make them more palatable. The revision of the 'seduction theory' that followed was less motivated by theoretical compulsion regarding the importance of childhood sexual fantasies than by the realisation that he would not advance professionally if he kept to his initial, socially repugnant view that cast so many men — fathers and well-regarded professionals — in the role of rapist. The idea that the sacred temple of the home might be sullied by acts of rape and incest was clearly sacrilegious in the separate spheres ideology operating at the time. And it was an ideology we know Freud personally endorsed. Before his marriage he was anxious to establish that his own 'sweet, delicate girl' would want no greater contentment than that offered by being a wife and mother.

Certainly, the ostracism Freud experienced after presenting his first version of the theory on the aetiology of hysteria seems to have been total. In an address on his seventieth birthday, he described what took place. However, it is likely that he has mistaken the date, quoting 1895 rather than 1896, which was when his lecture actually received its icy reception:

> It happened that in 1895 I was subjected simultaneously to two powerful convergent influences. On the one hand I had obtained my first glimpses into the depths of the instinctual life of man, and had seen things calculated to sober or even to frighten me. On the other hand the publication of my disagreeable discoveries led to the severance of the greater part of my human contacts: I felt as though I were despised and shunned by everyone. In this loneliness I was seized with a longing for a circle of chosen men of high character who would receive me in a friendly spirit in spite of my temerity. Your society [B'nai B'rith — a Jewish society] was pointed out to me as the place where such men were to be found.[20]

Besides the ostracism and the likely professional consequences its continuance would bring, other factors in the external cultural environment could have motivated Freud to change his theory. Perhaps the most compelling is the possible influence anti-Semitism had on the retraction of the first theory. Anti-Semitic views were so acceptable that the term *anti-Semitism* was considered to refer to a scientific study of Jews.[21] As noted earlier, doctors believed that both Jews and women were especially liable to nervous disease. The susceptibility of Jews was held to derive from hereditary weakness secondary to inbreeding while that of women was linked to the supposed inborn liability of their nervous systems.

It is therefore of considerable interest that when Freud published the 'disagreeable discoveries' that caused 'the severance of the greater part of my human contacts', the only source of support he found was among other Jewish men belonging to the B'nai B'rith. Thus his ostensible 'scientific' ostracism seems to have worked along religious lines. Freud, as a Jewish psychiatrist, occupied a constricted, contradictory social role replete with emotional conflict. He was both a member of the ethnic and religious group considered to be mentally 'sick' and a representative of the professional group supposed to make sick people 'well'.

Besides their shared susceptibility to mental illness, Jews, like women, were believed to be marked by the sign of their sexual difference. From the Middle Ages it had been asserted that Jewish men menstruated. Further, the practice of circumcision was seen to result in mutilated genitalia, which feminised and unmanned the Jew in the process of making him a Jew. Within the discourse on Jewish difference, the stigmata of Jewish degeneration were enumerated, and the fusion of difference and degeneration was believed to be literally inscribed on the Jew's body, to be read off and statistically calibrated by men of science. There was the Jewish voice — it always sounded too Jewish; the Jewish gaze, which English psychologist Francis Galton described as the 'cold, scanning gaze' of the Jew; the Jewish foot — flat and unsuitable for military service; and of course the Jewish nose.[22]

And it was not mental illness in general to which Jews were meant to be vulnerable. Rather, as Gilman has pointed out, 'The

Jew was understood by *fin-de-siècle* medicine as being especially at risk for hysteria, with its roots in seduction and incest.' No less formidable a figure than the French psychiatrist, Jean Martin Charcot, with whom Freud studied for a year, believed in and commented on the 'especially marked predisposition of the Jewish race for hysteria'.[23]

This predisposition was generally understood to derive from perverted sexuality. There was a widespread cultural assumption that Jews engaged in incest and were the carriers of syphilis and responsible for spreading it throughout Europe. How psychologically threatening, then, for Freud to hear from his hysterical female patients, many of whom were Jewish, the identical accusations of incest that dominated the anti-Semitic discourse on Jewish deviance. Surely these accusations were perfectly suited to 'sober and frighten' him and to tax him to find a more sanguine theoretical replacement for his first theory of hysteria.

Jews, like women, could occupy the small, menial place set aside for 'good' Jews. Here they would give no offence to the dominant group but would have to contend with its attitudes towards them, which, if incorporated, would result in self-hatred. If they eschewed this option they could identify with those who reviled them and try to excise every Jewish quality that might identify them. They could even engage in overt anti-Semitism, like Walter Rathenau and Otto Weininger. Walter Rathenau, who went on to become a foreign minister of the Weimar Republic, was one Jewish man who pursued the option of reviling Jews and Jewishness with as much gusto as any anti-Semitic gentile. In an essay written in 1897, he described how identifiably different Jews were from Germans:

> Whoever wishes to hear its language can go any Sunday through the Thiergartenstrasse midday at twelve or evenings glance into the foyer of a Berlin theater. Unique Vision! In the midst of a German life, a separate, strange race ... On the sands of the Mark Brandenburg, an Asiatic horde.[24]

Otto Weininger was a Viennese Jew who denounced his Jewishness, converted to Christianity and fatally shot himself at the age of 23. His extraordinary book, *Sex and Character*, published shortly after his death in 1903, was an immediate sensation partly as a result of his self-inflicted demise.[25] August Strindberg, in a letter to *Die Fackel* on 17 October, described it as 'an awe-inspiring book, which has probably solved the most difficult of all problems'.[26] Actually Weininger believed he had solutions to not one but two of the favourite problems of late nineteenth-century science: the problem of women and the problem of Jews.

Weininger had visited Freud and shown him the manuscript of *Sex and Character*. Freud was not impressed and advised against publication. However, the visit and the book, with its emphasis on bisexuality, caused Fliess to accuse Freud of giving away his ideas to Weininger, either directly or through Hermann Swoboda, who was both a friend of Weininger's and a patient of Freud's. The fact that Weininger favourably cited Freud's ideas in his work while failing to mention those of Fliess presumably added to the latter's ire.

It is hard to say whether Weininger was more misogynistic than anti-Semitic so closely do women and Jews parallel one another in his pseudoscientific-cum-philosophical treatise. For Weininger civilisation was in crisis and decay. He rigidly divided the world and everyone in it into two opposing sides, using a style of dualistic thinking that makes even Comte's seem indecisive by comparison. Decisions had to be made, and the choices were crystal clear for the 'awe inspiring' Weininger:

> The decision must be made between Judaism and Christianity, between business and culture, between male and female, between the race and the individual, between unworthiness and worth, between the earthly and the higher life, between negation and the God-like. Mankind has the choice to make. There are only two poles, and there is no middle way.[27]

Weininger was thoroughly imbued with the sociobiological theories that preoccupied themselves with the correct placement of various groups of people on the phyletic scale. Predictably, he found that the Jewish race 'appears to possess a certain anthropological relationship with both Negroes and Mongolians'.[28]

However, it was in enumerating the similarities between women and Jews that Weininger excelled previous scientists and philosophers. Although his work is primarily devoted to the 'characterology of the sexes', Weininger defends the inclusion of Judaism in his book because 'Judaism is saturated with femininity, with precisely those qualities the essence of which I have shown to be in the strongest opposition to the male nature ... the most manly Jew is more feminine than the least manly Aryan'.[29]

And the qualities women and Jews had in common were legion. The 'homology of the Jew and woman' included a want of personality and a lack of free intelligible ego despite exaggerated egotism. Both were 'devoid of humour but addicted to mockery' and exhibited a complete absence of dignity, genius, greatness and morality. Because they were devoid of individuality, they adhered together in groups 'forming as it were a continuous plasmodium', which nevertheless lacked real solidarity. Like the woman, the Jew required 'the rule of an exterior authority' and was 'devoid of a soul'. Jews and women were 'nothing in themselves'. Not content with depriving the Jew of a soul, Weininger went further and held that the Jewish religion 'has no relation to a true belief in god; it is not a religion of reason, but a belief of old women founded on fear'.[30]

The only course open for a Jew who hated the qualities imputed to Judaism was obvious: 'To defeat Judaism, the Jew must first understand himself and war against himself.'[31] Weininger took his own advice. Shortly after the appearance of *Sex and Character*, he shot himself, becoming the first casualty in his own self-declared holy war.

Being identified as Jewish was clearly no advantage in cultural or scientific circles in late nineteenth-century Vienna if the attitudes Weininger expresses are any guide. Freud and Breuer's consciousness of anti-Semitism might explain why they suppressed any mention of the religious identity of their patients in the published version of *Studies in Hysteria*, although it is obvious from their case notes.

Sander Gilman declares that Freud displaced much of the anxiety about his own racial identity on to his image of woman so that she came to be theorised as embodying many of the despised characteristics attributed to Jews. Such an anxiety, if it existed, cannot have been soothed by another reaction to his theory of hysteria of which he learnt some six months after giving his lecture. On 2 November 1896, just after his father died, Freud wrote to Fliess: 'I recently heard the first reaction to my incursion into psychiatry. "Gruesome, horrible, old wives' psychiatry" were some of the things that were said.'[32] So, even after the religious identity of patients was suppressed, the therapy Freud practised was perceived as female — old wives' psychiatry — with its implicit cultural associations with Jewishness.

By appealing to the very mechanisms of defense Freud discovered, one can argue that he denied and projected on to women the virulent attacks he experienced as a Jew from the ambient anti-Semitic cultural climate. Gilman, for example, asserts that:

> For Freud, the image of the child as sexual being is confused and amalgamated with that of the sexually active female. And that figure serves in Freud's mental universe as the counterrepresentation to the feminized image of the male Jew that haunted the *fin de siècle*.[33]

If this reading is accurate it suggests that Freud's theories on femininity are inherently and doubly stereotypical as they fuse stereotypes of women with those of Jews.

This substitution of woman for (male) Jew is one possible psychological manoeuvre in contesting an otherwise overwhelming psychic threat. But there are others. Refutation could also proceed by showing that the assertions made were not true for Jews as a specific group, true for no one, either Jews or non Jews, or true, in some altered form, for everyone. In this way, the anti-Semitic force of the assertion would be dissolved by being transformed and universalised.

Freud, I believe, pursued the latter option as well as the substitution suggested by Gilman. From this perspective, it becomes easier to understand the attraction some otherwise outlandish theories and practices had for him, including the theory of male periodicity developed by his friend Fliess, his enthusiasm for nasal

surgery, the *idée fixe* quality of his preoccupation with the importance of penis envy and his insistence on the overarching significance of the Oedipus complex. Freud first met Wilhelm Fliess in
1887. According to Ernest Jones, theirs was a 'passionate friendship',[34] which played an important role intellectually, emotionally
and scientifically in Freud's life for the next fifteen years until the
breach over Weininger ended their friendship.

Fliess developed a theory, which held that periodic rhythms
were the key to understanding health, illness and the meaning of
life. Fliess modestly believed his theory of periodicity put him on
a par with the German astronomer Johann Kepler scientifically.
The theory held that both men and women shared a bisexual constitution and were jointly affected by cyclical periodicity. Not only
women with their twenty-eight-day cycles were under the influence of the laws of periodicity but also men had periodic rhythms,
there being a twenty-three-day cycle as well as a twenty-eight-day
one. In other words, all men, not just Jewish men, had periods. As
a universal phenomenon affecting everyone, no stigma can attach
to periodicity and, in particular, the hateful slur directed only at
'feminised' Jewish men is destroyed.

Fliess, a nose and throat specialist, shared Freud's interest in the
problems of human sexuality and asserted that there was a causal
connection between the nose and the genitals. One of his more
arresting scientific 'observations' concerned 'the swelling of the
turbinate bone [of the nose] during menstruation'. This swelling
was so conspicuous, according to Fliess, that it could be 'observed
with the naked eye'.[35]

On the basis of his theorised connection between the nose and
the genitals Fliess, and, for a time, Freud too, believed that neurotic symptoms and hysteria could be successfully treated via
nasal surgery. Freud's friendship with and trust in Fliess led him
to refer one of his first patients, Emma Eckstein, for the surgical
correction of her hysteria. The surgery was carried out in early
February 1895 and went badly wrong. Fliess left half a metre of
surgical gauze in the nasal cavity when he removed the offending
turbinate bone. Emma subsequently experienced persistent

swelling, purulent secretions, fever and bleeding from the nose and mouth. Eventually, another surgeon was called in and discovered a thread of the gauze, which he proceeded to remove.

Freud graphically described what happened in his letter to Fliess on 8 March 1895: 'The next moment came a flood of blood, the patient turned white, her eyes bulged, and she had no pulse.' Emma Eckstein almost died as a result of Fliess's surgical incompetence. Freud was so affected by the sight of the 'poor creature' and his simultaneous understanding of what, or rather who, had made her that way that he felt sick and had to flee into the next room, where he was given 'a small glass of cognac'.[36] He explained to Fliess why he needed to be revived:

> I do not believe it was the blood that overwhelmed me — at that moment affects were welling up in me. So we had done her an injustice; she was not at all abnormal, rather a piece of iodoform gauze had gotten torn off as you were removing it and stayed in for fourteen days, preventing healing; at the end it tore off and provoked the bleeding.[37]

Thus the 'affects welling up' in him concerned the injustice done to Emma. Freud realised that Fliess's actions had caused Emma's suffering. It was Fliess's surgical incompetence, not Emma's underlying emotional abnormality, that caused her bleeding. Yet over time Freud's attitude undergoes an emotionally charged shift that closely parallels the one which occurred in the retraction of his original theory of hysteria. He is progressively able to persuade himself that the assault, a medical one in this case, is of little psychological importance in Emma's overall condition. He soon surmounts the uncomfortable feeling that an injustice has been done to Emma.

When Emma continues to fare poorly, with symptoms of pain, swelling and bleeding, the weight of Freud's emotional concern shifts from her to Fliess in a way that does not augur well for any conflict between patient welfare and his own emotional needs. By 20 March he tells Fliess: 'In my thoughts, I have given up hope for the poor girl, and am inconsolable that I involved you and created such a distressing affair for you. I also feel very sorry for her, I had become very fond of her.'[38] In using the past tense, 'had become very fond of her', it is almost as if Emma is dead and Freud is detaching himself from what are now felt to be inappropriate and inconvenient sentiments.

By 26 April, in a wonderful reversal of the true state of affairs, the victim becomes the perpetrator and Freud is writing to Fliess of Emma as 'my tormentor and yours'.[39] Freud's ability to transform tangible injuries so that they not only disappear as injuries but also metamorphose into something entirely praiseworthy is also shown in the same letter when he fulsomely compliments Fliess on his medical competence — a bizarre tribute in the circumstances.

Freud's emotional response to anti-Semitic accusations about atavistic, incestuous Jewish sexuality might have both played some role in the theoretical revision of his first theory of hysteria and helped to elucidate aspects of its replacement, namely the emphasis on childhood sexual fantasies in the Oedipus complex. By moving from a consideration of actual incest, so closely and specifically linked at the time to Jewish degeneration, and focusing instead on universal fantasies of incest shared by non-Jews and Jews alike, Freud was able to transform and dispel a pressing racist and religious calumny. Far from Jews committing incest, Freud might be saying in this revision, no one actually commits incest, including Jews. Further, it is not the sexual acts of adults and fathers that should concern us but the sexual wishes of infants and children.

Freud's treatment of the legend of Oedipus strengthens this possibility. In speaking of the legend of King Oedipus Freud wrote:

> It is the fate of all of us, perhaps, to direct our first sexual impulse towards our mother and our first murderous wish against our father. Our dreams convince us that this is so. King Oedipus, who slew his father Laius and married his mother Jocasta, merely shows us the fulfilment of our own childhood wishes.[40]

The concentration on the repressed wishes or fantasies of the child towards its parents allows the part played by the sexual impulses and acts of the parents, especially the father, to elude scrutiny.

More than forty years ago, George Devereux, an American anthropologist, published a paper in the *International Journal of Psychoanalysis* entitled 'Why Oedipus killed Laius'. He discusses parts of the legend Freud left out and therefore the corresponding issues raised, which psychoanalysis had hitherto neglected.

> Numerous Greek sources and fragments reveal that Laius was deemed to have been the inventor of pederasty. In his early manhood, long before he married Jocasta and fathered Oedipus, Laius fell violently in love with Chrysippus, son of King Pelops ... He chose to kidnap him ... The enraged Pelops ... laid upon Laius the curse that his own son should slay him and then marry his own mother. According to a later version it is ... Zeus' decision that Laius' son would kill him in retribution for the rape of Chrysippus. This curse seems to suggest that the Greek mind linked Oedipus with Chrysippus — an inference which is further substantiated by still another version of this myth, according to which Hera was so greatly angered by the rape of Chrysippus that she sent the Sphinx to ravage Thebes in order to punish the Thebans for having tolerated Laius' homosexual escapade. The Oedipodeia is even more specific in conjoining the fates of Chrysippus and of Oedipus.[41]

It is highly probable that Freud knew this part of the myth, not only because of his own education and his selective use of the various Greek myths to illustrate various aspects of his theories but also because it was specifically reported by his disciple and colleague, Otto Rank.

Although very well educated in the Greek myths, Freud nevertheless omitted certain telling details of the legend. Significantly, their omission served what might have been the implicit purpose of his theory: to shift attention from the forcible sexual acts of the father, Laius, who raped the son of another ruler, by focusing on the sexual fantasies of the child.

Freud's earliest published work on hysteria demonstrates incontrovertibly that he believed what his patients said to him about their childhood sexual experiences. Consequently, his letter to Fliess on 15 October 1897, in which he gives his version of the Oedipus complex, is especially significant because it signals the end of Freud's early approach of believing his patients' stories and makes the emotional universality of the myth contingent on its concordance with Freud's own experience as revealed through self-analysis: 'I have found in my own case too, falling in love with the mother and jealousy of the father and I now regard it as a universal law of early childhood.'[42]

But in rejecting the veracity of patients' narratives, Freud moved on to no less perilous epistemological ground in choosing his own experience as the norm against which his patients' experiences were evaluated. This reliance on self-analysis and what he judged to be intuitively credible potentiated a kind of theoretical solipsism. By this I mean that everything that was supposed to be observed and to function as evidence inevitably looped back to and confirmed Freud's interpretive framework and its premises. In principle, the only thing that could be known was fundamentally self-referential. In this way, the realm of the observable became overdetermined by what the theory expected according to its self-regarding conceptual categories. Observation and proof cannot be disentangled, as the theory has created the criteria that dictate the terms of proof, and these saturate and overwhelm the observations. Of course, if only those observations and interpretations that potentially confirm Freud's theories are selected, then the theories are literally proofed against refutation.

As chief discoverer of the laws of human behaviour, Freud became the arbiter who decided on the credibility, reliability and validity of his patients' experiences. If there was concurrence between his patients' and his own experience of the world, a law could be posited. But if concurrence constitutes evidence of the 'truth' of universal laws of behaviour, then what of non-concurrence? Might this be taken to indicate 'lies', 'resistance', 'denial' or 'fantasy'? The non-concurrence of patients' experiences with Freud's own necessarily gendered, partial ones is a highly significant issue with far-reaching implications for his ability to hear and believe what his female patients said to him.

In the following chapter I will use the case history of Dora to illustrate how Freud's theoretical tenets and overriding desire to prove them effectively precluded him from listening to Dora objectively.

6

ALMOST BESIDE HERSELF: THE CASE OF DORA

D ora's treatment illuminates the pitfalls inherent in the process of attribution Freud employed when he instructed patients in the truly significant but unconscious meanings of their behaviour and actions.

Freud was seeking to provide an understanding of human beings from within so that their symptoms and responses became understandable and believable. In attempting to understand human psychology, his abiding interest was in unconscious phenomena, and this meant that the age-old philosophical problem of other minds was rendered even more formidable than if his attention had been confined to examining the conscious thoughts of others. He was well aware of the perceived difficulty of his undertaking:

> The decidedness of my attitude on the subject of the unconscious is perhaps specially likely to cause offence, for I handle unconscious ideas, unconscious trains of thought, and unconscious impulses as though they were no less valid and unimpeachable psychological data than conscious ones. But of this I am certain — that anyone who sets out to investigate the same region of phenomena and employs the same method will find himself compelled to take up the same position, however much philosophers may expostulate.[1]

Freud was certain the psychoanalytic method ensured that his attribution of beliefs and desires lying outside his patients' consciousness would be convincing and intuitively credible to 'anyone who sets out to investigate the same region of phenomena', in other words, to anyone like him, working within the boundaries he has defined. There is a tautological quality in this position, which Freud extends to his readers. He assumes that they are of like mind and all too often like gender to himself and, on this basis, will agree with him. Likewise, if a patient's behaviour is incomprehensible to Freud, he is sure that it will be incomprehensible to his readers too; they are assigned the role of impartial but ever-supportive endorsers of his insights.

Unless this congruence between Freud and a wider audience is assumed, that is, unless they are an extension of him, it can be objected that when he finds a patient's behaviour incomprehensible his perception is no more than an individual and idiosyncratic failure of insight. For example, in referring to Dora's behaviour he writes in the imperative form: 'Her behaviour must have seemed as incomprehensible to the man after she had left him as to us.'[2] But if Freud's attributions fail to convince on this level of intuitive credibility, if we do not find her behaviour puzzling, let alone incomprehensible, then why should we not dismiss his interpretations as saying more about him than they do about Dora? And Freud possessed just the kind of closed-minded conviction about his theoretical correctness that was conducive to projection and the misattribution of motives to patients.

In his letters to Fliess, he comments more than once on his determination to prove his theories. As early as February 1894, in discussing the link between obsessional neurosis and sexuality he tells Fliess: 'If it had been sought for by anyone less obstinately wedded to the idea, it would have been overlooked.' And in May of the same year, in another letter about his work on the neuroses, Freud admits: 'They regard me rather as a monomaniac, while I have the distinct feeling that I have touched on one of the great secrets of nature.'[4] When the friendship with Fliess was almost over, Freud took umbrage at Fliess' accusation that he was a 'thought reader' in a letter written on 7 August 1901: 'In this you came to the limit of your penetration, you take sides against me and tell me that "the thought-reader merely reads his own thoughts into other people", which deprives my work of all its value.'[5]

The case history of Dora richly illustrates how these various difficulties were played out in therapeutic practice. Dora, as Freud called her, after a maid in his sister's family, was born in 1882. Her real name was Ida Bauer. She was the Eastern European Jewish daughter of Philip Bauer. But as Sander Gilman points out, 'There is no sign in the case study of the "racial" identity of Ida Bauer.'[6] In nineteenth-century racist science there was an indelible link between disease, specifically syphilis, hysteria and being Jewish, all of which, Gilman argues, Freud wished to avoid discussing in Dora's case. To justify publication, Freud tried to convince himself and his readers that no one would ever find out Dora's true identity. She first came to see him as a 16-year-old in 1898 but did not begin psychoanalytic treatment until 1900.

Freud's determination to prove his theory of hysteria dominated his therapeutic encounter with Dora. Claire Kahane, one of the editors of the collection *In Dora's Case: Freud–Hysteria–Feminism*, characterises him as 'an unreliable narrator relentlessly pursuing his own demon of interpretation'.[7] Dora's case demonstrates the cultural and ideological assumptions that allowed Freud to find his theory intuitively credible despite, or rather because of, Dora's disagreement with his interpretations of her desires and wishes. It shows him to be relentless in insisting that Dora accept his interpretations; evidences Freud's hostility when she would not concur with his interpretations; describes how he proceeded to attribute feelings, motives and most especially 'fantasies' to her and constantly and at times brutally imposed his sexual interpretations on her, with the therapeutic rationale that her denial and resistance had to be overcome because a genuine 'no' cannot exist in the unconscious.

Freud describes Dora as a girl in the first bloom of youth, intelligent and with engaging looks but a 'heavy trial' to her parents. More significantly, he tells us that she is a 'mature young woman of very independent judgement, who had grown accustomed to laugh at the efforts of doctors and in the end to renounce their help entirely'.[8] Dora walked out of therapy after three months, a gesture Freud interpreted as an 'unmistakable act of vengeance on her part'. He was inclined to categorise all autonomous decisions and actions on Dora's part as evidence of revenge or vengeance. In 1902, fifteen months after she has left, Dora goes back and asks about resuming treatment. Freud justifies his refusal to take her back on the ground that 'one glance at her face was enough to tell she was not in earnest'.

Contemporary commentators do not accept Freud's estimation of his own prescience about Dora's motives and lack of sincerity. The French psychoanalyst Jacques Lacan, like many others, asserts that Freud's refusal was related to the powerful counter-transference affecting him. As we have seen, Freud identified very strongly with the positivistic model of late nineteenth-century science. He was convinced that facts could be observed and measured in an objective fashion. In the case history of Dora he assures the reader: 'He that has eyes to see and ears to hear may convince himself that no mortal can keep a secret.'[9] The positivistic view that everything besides the variable of interest can be controlled, thereby enabling the clearest observation, description and testing of the phenomenon in question, influenced Freud's early conception of his role in therapy. The patient was positioned as the only variable of interest in the therapeutic relationship. Freud, on the other hand, saw himself as an impartial observer, a neutral man of science, not a significant actor in a joint psychotherapeutic drama. As a consequence of this model, he was able to discern the operation of transference — the feelings of the patient for the analyst — late in Dora's case, but he did not recognise the countertransference — the analyst's feelings for the patient — until 1910. By this time, Freud realised that the analogy with the natural scientist did not hold up and that the feelings of the analyst for the patient, relating to the analyst's own complexes and inner resistances, determined the entire course of therapy.

Freud was unable to recognise the strength of his hostility to Dora. He was outraged at her for sabotaging his therapeutic quest and, in calling her after his sister's maid, expressed anger at her for having dismissed him as if he were one. Most of all, he was angry at her for interfering with the satisfactory completion of his analytic work, as if she had engineered a psychotherapeutic form of *coitus interruptis*: 'Her breaking off so unexpectedly, just when my hopes of a successful termination of the treatment were at their highest, and her thus bringing these hopes to nothing, this was an unmistakable act of vengeance on her part.'[10]

Clearly Freud hadn't finished with Dora, even though she had finished with him. He was obsessed by the notion of completion, of having complete knowledge and a complete case history, instead of what he called the study, 'A fragment of an analysis of a case of hysteria'. The case seems to have niggled at Freud for a long time, and he put off publishing it until 1905. On three occasions he got the date of the treatment wrong.

The first thing one notices about the case is the intricate relations between Dora's family and the K family, which Philip Reiff called a 'group illness'. He writes:

> The sick daughter has a sick father, who has a sick mistress, who has a sick husband, who proposes himself to the sick daughter as her lover. Dora does not mean to hold hands in this charmless circle — although Freud does, at one point, indicate that she should.[11]

Illness was such a feature of this family that it is almost like an additional character in the story, one that plays a crucial role for everyone. The sicknesses of Dora's father include tuberculosis, syphilis, a detached retina, a confusional attack, a nervous cough, which became one of Dora's symptoms, and partial paralysis. He has been a patient of Freud's at the recommendation of his friend, Herr K, the husband of the woman with whom he is having an affair. Herr K tries over a number of years to draw Dora into a similar arrangement with himself.

Frau K, the lover, has also been ill and spent months in a sanatorium for 'nervous disorders' because she couldn't walk — presumably a hysterical paralysis, but since her affair has been 'a healthy and lively woman'. Both Dora and Frau K have acted as nurse to her father when he was ill, and Dora has been a nurse–companion to the Ks children. Dora is very fond of Frau K and has stayed with the Ks on occasion.

Dora's symptoms and her neurosis were dated by Freud from the time she was eight years old, when they included bed-wetting and dyspnoea. In 1899, the year before she commenced treatment with Freud, she had an attack of appendicitis, and just before seeing him she had written a letter threatening to kill herself. Dora also suffers from migraine, a nervous cough, a limp, depression, loss of voice, hysterical unsociability and *taedium vitae* (weariness of life). She also has a vaginal discharge, which Freud assumes, conveniently for his revised theory, is not an infection but a somatic sign of her hysteria.

Dora's mother also has a vaginal discharge due to the venereal disease she has contracted from her syphilitic husband. Freud is contemptuous of her, accepts her husband's story that she no longer has sex with him and dismisses her as an insignificant figure, suffering a 'Housewife's Psychosis', who is disliked by both her husband and her daughter. In the course of the history, however, we learn that it is to her mother, the psychotic housewife, that Dora confides the unwelcome sexual attentions she has received from Herr K.

Dora also has one brother, eighteen months older, who like her mother plays little role in Freud's story, an aunt who is dying from a wasting disease and an uncle described as a hypochondriacal bachelor.

Dora's father is the dominating figure in the family circle and for good reason, according to Freud, who cites his intelligence, his character and his wealthy circumstances. Dora is said to be most tenderly attached to him, and this affection has been heightened by his illnesses. But she was also critical of him or, as Freud says, 'took all the more offence at many of his actions and peculiarities'.[12] The peculiarities that loom large in Dora's case concern his untrustworthiness, his relationship with Frau K, about which he lies, and his readiness, from Dora's point of view, that she should be willing to hand herself over to Herr K in exchange for Frau K.

The case history of Dora articulates the power relationships in a turn-of-the-century patriarchal family. It illuminates that when a whole family is ill psychologically, and possibly everyone could do with treatment, one person can be singled out as the 'sick' one and then assume the mantle of symptom bearer for the entire family. Dora did not seek treatment herself, she was sent by her father: 'It was only her father's authority which induced her to come at all.' Behind the authority Dora's father brings to bear on her, there is an even higher authority. Philip Bauer intended to enlist nineteenth-century medical science in his cause.

> No doubt owing to this fortunate intervention [for syphilis] that four years later he brought his daughter, who had meanwhile grown unmistakably neurotic, and introduced her to me, and that after another two years he handed her over to me for psychotherapeutic treatment.[13]

And why did Dora's father hand over his daughter in this way? What did he want Freud to achieve? Her father's plea to Freud was: 'Please try and bring her to reason'. Now, reason can be thought of as an impartial, neutral matter clear to and agreed upon by everyone, or it can be seen as something partial, a matter of self-interest that expresses relative positions of power and authority. It makes sense to ask whose 'reason' was Dora meant to be brought to see.

As the case unfolds, the relationship between power, authority and knowledge becomes increasingly clear. We learn, for example, the sort of reason Dora's father wants her to be brought to see:

> But it must be confessed that Dora's father was never entirely straightforward. He had given his support to the treatment so long as he could hope that I should 'talk' Dora out of her belief that there was something more than a friendship between him and Frau K.[14]

Following the initial handing over of Dora by her father, Freud's reason, his knowledge and his sense of reality are constantly privileged and Dora's are subjugated.

The history of Dora's dealings with Herr K as recounted by Freud involve a concerted campaign over four years, from the time she is 14, to get her to submit to him sexually. The first incident, when he forces a kiss on her, is carefully orchestrated by Herr K to take place in his office when no one else is about. Two years later, in 1898, Herr K approaches Dora again. She told her mother that he had had 'the audacity to make her a proposal while they were on a walk after a trip upon the lake'.[15] Shortly after this, Herr K goes into Dora's room when she is asleep, and she wakes to find him standing over her. Dora tells her mother what has happened, and she informs her husband. But when Dora's father confronts Herr K, he flatly denies Dora's account and adds for good measure that she has 'fancied it'. Much to Dora's distress, her father prefers to accept this claim over her own. Herr K also adds that his wife, the woman with whom Dora's father is having an affair, has told him that Dora thinks of nothing but sex and has read Paolo Mantegazza's *Physiology of Love*. Herr K then tells Dora's father that she is morally worthless: '… no girl who read such books and was interested in such things could have any title to a man's respect. Frau K, therefore, had betrayed and had calumniated her'.[16]

But Frau K's betrayal is not the only one with which Dora has to contend. Dora, in all her emotional connections, lives within a finely tuned conspiracy that functions to use and, if it cannot use, to denigrate her. Dora makes a suicide threat after having an argument with her father over his continued relationship with Frau K. He refuses to give her up, and he repeats this refusal to Freud in their interview even though he lies to him about the nature of his involvement. Freud supports him in his refusal, saying that giving up Frau K because Dora wanted it would show her 'what a powerful weapon she had'. After her suicide threat Dora spends three months in psychoanalysis.

Since its publication the case has been much commented on by psychoanalytic as well as feminist commentators, so I will confine my discussion to the epistemological conflict between Dora and Freud over reason and reality. Dora's case can be read as a contest over whose version of reality will be given credence and about who decides what shall count as a reason. Dora's father wants her to be made to see reason, his reason; Freud, the archaeologist, wants to restore what he reasons is missing and vindicate his theory; Herr K says there is no reason for Dora's distress and complaints against him, only fantasies; and Dora is 'beside herself', portrayed and betrayed by everyone as a fantasist devoid of reason. Throughout the analysis, Freud and Dora struggle over what has caused Dora's hysteria, what actually happened and what it really meant. Dora won't accept Freud's interpretations, and he does not support hers.

The case is now generally regarded as a therapeutic failure that missed vital material relating to transference and countertransference. In a recent review of the case in the *American Journal of Psychiatry*, Peter Buckley says Dora represents 'a classic case of the symptom carrier for the whole family'. He goes on:

> ... the sexual intrigue involving her father and the K family, the disavowal by everyone around her of the sexual subterfuge to which she was subjected, and the disruption of her adolescence by her immersion in this intrigue give the case, by today's standards, indications for concurrent family therapy. Such a therapy would address the secrets and dissimulation in which Dora's father participated and help to validate her reality, something Dora spontaneously did herself when she confronted her father and Herr K after she broke off her treatment with Freud.[17]

Far from helping to validate her reality, Freud's treatment of Dora systematically undermined and invalidated it.

WHAT FREUD WANTED FROM DORA

Freud was eager to cure Dora of hysteria — the daughter's disease — but was even more eager to prove his theory. He wanted to establish that psychoanalysis, alone among psychiatric treatments, could solve the age-old psychological problem of hysteria and prove its sexual aetiology. His secondary aim was to use the case to forge a connection with his work on the interpretation of dreams. The work's original title was 'Dreams and hysteria'.

In Freud's theory of hysteria three necessary conditions had to be met. They were a psychical trauma, a conflict or reversal of affect, and a disturbance in the sphere of sexuality.

A PSYCHICAL TRAUMA

Although Freud first saw Dora in 1898, only two years after he gave his lecture on 'The aetiology of hysteria', the case history contains no trace of his earlier theory's emphasis on the aetiological significance of actual childhood sexual abuse. Instead, Freud fulfils his theoretical need for a psychical trauma by appealing to two different kinds of experience. One concerns Dora's various encounters with Herr K, but the other relates to her childhood, or a reconstituted psychoanalytic facsimile of her childhood.

Freud's new theory of hysteria, incorporating the Oedipus complex and the role of childhood sexual fantasy, means that he has to look back to Dora's childhood and find evidence of a 'genetic reality' there: fantasies from childhood that have led to the current neurosis. The other reason her childhood needs to be included is to make sense of symptoms that predated her experience with Herr K.

Freud determines that certain of her symptoms, like bed-wetting, began when she gave up masturbating at the age of eight. Other current symptoms, like her shortness of breath, are linked, using the mechanism of somatic compliance, to overhearing her father's heavy breathing during sex with her mother. The revised theory of hysteria cannot contemplate for a moment that it might have been sex with Dora that caused her symptoms.

Yet there are many clues that actual abuse by her father was worth considering as no doubt it would have been a few years earlier. In a letter to Fliess, written on 28 April 1897, Freud discusses a new case, a young woman, rather like Dora in many ways, including the wetness in her bed. Freud says to this patient: '"Then let us speak plainly. In my analyses I find it's the closest relatives, fathers or brothers, who are the guilty men." "It has nothing to do with my brother." "So it was your father, then."' Then it came out that when she was between the ages of eight and 12 her allegedly otherwise admirable and high-principled father regularly used to take her into his bed and practise external ejaculation (making wet) with her. Even at the time she felt anxiety. A six-year-old sister to whom she talked about it later admitted that she had had the same experiences with her father.[18] It seems almost inevitable that if Freud had seen Dora at this time he would have interpreted her bed-wetting in quite a different way. From what Freud tells us, Dora's father was a self-interested liar who wants to use Freud to use Dora in order to achieve his own ends. His exploitative attitude towards Dora is so seasoned that he has no compunction in pursuing his own desires even when he knows they harm will her.

Dora knew her father well. Her criticisms of him were that 'he was insincere, he had a strain of falseness in his character, he only thought of his own enjoyment, and he had a gift for seeing things in the light which suited him best'. Freud grudgingly accepts this estimation: 'I could not in general dispute Dora's characterisation of her father.'[19]

Dora seems to exist only in relation to her father's emotional, physical and sexual comfort. When he is ill, which is often, he uses her as a nurse: '… he would allow no one but her to discharge the lighter duties of nursing'.[20] What these duties consisted of we do not know, although Dora, who began these duties as a child, is carrying out a role that would more usually be performed by an adult, most often a wife. We do not know why Dora's mother did not nurse her husband when he was ill. Perhaps her mother detested nursing duties as much as she detested conjugal ones; perhaps they amounted to the same thing.

At this distance in time and on the evidence Freud presents it is impossible to know whether her father sexually abused Dora, but that he sexualised her seems certain: '… he had made her his confidante while she was still a child'.[21] Thus, Dora as a child was placed in two wifely roles by her father, that of nurse and that of emotional confidante. Then there is the explanation Dora's father gives Freud about his relationship with Frau K, which is the standard rationalisation given by men who sexually abuse their daughters: 'You know already that I get nothing out of my wife.'[22]

Freud does not bother to consider that Dora's discharge might be an infection like her mother's and transmitted in the same way, or that her somatic symptoms and depression might issue from the same cause. We learn from the case history that he does not even ask Dora about the discharge but convinces himself the question is unnecessary:

> The persistence with which she held to this identification with her mother almost forced me to ask her whether she too was suffering from a venereal disease; and I then learnt that she was afflicted with a catarrh (leucorrhoea) whose beginning, she said, she could not remember.
>
> I then understood that behind the train of thought in which she brought these open accusations against her father there lay concealed as usual a self-accusation.[23]

Interestingly, when Dora, the patient, makes accusations about her father or asserts the veracity of her beliefs about what has taken place, we are instructed that these accusations have no status as knowledge claims. What seems to apply to the external world — open accusations — is asserted to have greater relevance to the internal world of Dora's psyche. Her accusations, then, reflect more on her intrapsychic pathology and are ultimately self-accusatory.

By contrast, when Freud, the physician, makes assertions, his subjective experience functions as the final arbiter of the existence of universal laws of behaviour. Dora's experience and perceptions only produce a 'sick', particularistic unconscious solipsism, while Freud's creates a healthy, universalisable conscious knowledge. Moreover, it is interesting how often Freud refers to Dora's assertions as if they emanate from her eyes rather than her brain; she is described as 'pitilessly sharp' and the 'sharp-sighted Dora' on numerous occasions, but is precluded from knowing anything.

Freud is equally unperturbed about the age at which her symptoms started. Bed-wetting does not usually begin for the first time at eight years of age. Secondary enuresis, or enuresis that occurs after a child has achieved voluntary bladder control, as Dora had, is rare and is likely to have a psychogenic cause. Fewer than 10 per cent of children, with a preponderance of boys, are enuretic after the age of seven.[24] A change in a child's behaviour with the sudden onset of symptoms like secondary enuresis is now accepted as indicating sexual abuse.[25] Yet the onset of Dora's bed-wetting at the age of eight does not make Freud reconsider the possibility of actual sexual abuse; his explanation is that she began wetting her bed because she had given up masturbating. There is now conclusive evidence that the ages of greatest reported risk for sexual abuse in children are from eight to twelve years.[26]

Finally, there is Dora's first dream about a fire. Two dreams were reported in the course of the case, but the first dream was a recurrent one and amenable to a fuller and more satisfying analysis from Freud's viewpoint. He admitted that the second dream could not be 'made as completely intelligible as the first'.[27] The successful analysis of the dreams in the case history was crucial to Freud's bid to establish the similarity between the formation of dreams and symptoms. Dora's first dream could just as easily be interpreted, using Freud's own criterion — 'every dream is a wish which is represented as fulfilled' — as expressing Dora's wish that her father would save her from the fire rather than forcing her into the one he had lit.

REVERSAL OF AFFECT

Freud's writing up of the case reveals that Dora's cure was contingent on her accepting his interpretations, and his attempts to persuade her to do so are distinctly coercive. Freud's manner of proving both Dora's supposed disturbance in the sphere of sexuality and her reversal of affect demonstrates his approach. For almost the entire case history, despite endless refusals by Dora, Freud is adamant that she loves Herr K. Coincidentally this 'love' fulfils all the conditions for hysteria, accommodating the need for a psychical trauma, then reversal of affect and a disturbance in the sphere of sexuality.

In Dora's case her conscious 'repulsion' of Herr K's physical advances is said to conflict with her repressed love and desire for him. This is really a central part of Freud's argument, and its acceptance depends on us agreeing with his view of female sexuality and on finding his attribution intuitively credible. Freud writes of the kiss Herr K gives Dora as follows:

> This was surely just the situation to call up a distinct feeling of sexual excitement in a girl of fourteen who had never before been approached. But Dora had at that moment a violent feeling of disgust, tore herself free from the man, and hurried past him to the staircase and from there to the street door.[28]

Freud takes as certain what could be viewed as highly problematic, namely that any girl of 14 would be overwhelmed by desire when a middle-aged man suddenly clasped her to him in a lonely spot. Freud comments that her response was conclusive evidence of her hysteria: 'I should without question consider a person hysterical in whom an occasion for sexual excitement elicited feelings that were preponderantly or exclusively unpleasurable.'[29] An 'occasion for sexual excitement' is synonymous in this explanation with any occasion whatsoever and leaves no room for a woman's wishes, no choice of sexual partner. In this account of sexual 'normality', on which the whole of Freud's theory of hysteria rests, there is no difference between love-making and rape.

Freud argues that Dora's response to Herr K caused the reversal of affect and the somatic effect of an upward displacement of sensation from the genital area to pressure on the upper body, a sensation that Dora still said she experienced. In countertransferential mode, the middle-aged Freud avers that Herr K is 'still quite young and of prepossessing appearance'. He sees the scene by the lake so much through Herr K's eyes that he thoughtfully provides him with an erection. He then uses this imagined 'fact' in his explanation of Dora's hysteria, deftly replacing the repressed, guilty memory she is meant to feel about it with the current innocent symptom of pressure on the thorax. The hypothesised connection between the two demonstrates the existence of 'somatic compliance', another vital element in Freud's theory.

DISTURBED SEXUALITY

Freud assumes that Dora is frigid because she refuses to 'yield' to Herr K's advances and accept herself as an object of his desire. This same argument does duty on several occasions and has an intellectual correlate in psychotherapy in the necessity Freud imposes on Dora to yield to his interpretations. This intellectual and emotional yielding also operates as a requirement for her recovery. In Freud's mind, not yielding was what made Dora sick in the past and what stops her from getting well in the present.

Perhaps the most memorable example of Freud's insistence of the role of yielding in hysteria is offered by his interpretation of the much commented on first dream. Freud reports the dreams as follows:

> A house was on fire. My father was standing beside my bed and woke me up, I dressed quickly, mother wanted to stop and save her jewel case; but father said: 'I refuse to let myself and my two children be burnt for the sake of your jewel case'. We hurried downstairs and as soon as I was outside I woke up.[30]

Freud, in a particularly overbearing and didactic frame of mind, tells Dora:

> The dream confirms once more what I had already told you before you dreamt it — that you are summoning up your old love for Herr K. But what do all these efforts show? Not only that you are afraid of Herr K, but that you are still more afraid of yourself, and of the temptation you feel to yield to him. In short, these efforts prove once more how deeply you loved him.[31]

Freud is so sure that his theory will be confirmed he knows in advance what Dora's dream will signify before she has it. This indicates either his extreme prescience or an extreme expectancy bias.

His confidence allows him to accept yet another refusal by Dora in a sanguine fashion — 'naturally Dora would not follow me in this part of the interpretation'.[32] What Dora said or thought was almost irrelevant to Freud's project, as his next comment shows:

> I myself, however, had been able to arrive at a further step in the interpretation, which seemed to me indispensable both for the anamnesis

[recollection] of the case and for the theory of dreams. I promised to communicate this to Dora at the next session.[33]

But the point is that she continued to refuse to follow him and yield to his interpretations, preferring to leave treatment. Her announcement to this effect made Freud feel like a governess or servant being given notice.

Freud does not question the cultural and ideological assumptions that inform his view of female desire and cause him to interpret her refusal to 'yield' to Herr K as repressed desire. This line of thought preserves the status quo of heterosexuality and its pattern of dominant, active male and ever-submissive, passive female. For Freud the desirability of women yielding is tantamount to a moral injunction. And in marriage, yielding is a duty: 'Dora realised that the presence of the husband had the effect of making his wife ill, and that she was glad to be ill so as to escape the *conjugal duties* which she so much detested.'[34]

Reversal of affect, or the implicit desire to yield despite explicit refusal, also accords with the conventional, sexist rationale that when a woman says no, she means yes. Feminist commentators have argued that when Dora said 'no' she might actually have meant 'no'. And if 'no' means 'no', the ground for accepting the importance of reversal of affect effectively disappears.

WHAT DORA WANTED FROM FREUD

What Dora wanted from Freud was to have her reality validated — to be listened to and believed when she spoke about her father and Herr K. At one level, Freud could grant that Dora's reproaches were justified, that her judgement was sound, that she did know:

> and there was one particular respect in which it was easy to see that her reproaches were justified. When she was feeling embittered she used to be overcome by the idea that she had been handed over to Herr K as the price of his tolerating the relations between her father and his wife; and her rage at her father's making such a use of her was visible behind her affection for him.[35]

At the same time, Dora's ability to know is continually displaced and diminished by Freud's higher knowledge of her. For instance, Freud knows that her reproaches against her father had a 'lining' or 'backing' of self reproaches. So while Dora thinks she is talking about her father, she is really talking about herself. Dora literally doesn't know what she is saying, she is deluded, and this delusion undermines any of her claims to know and reinforces Freud's superior epistemological position in relation to her.

Moreover, when Dora goes back to confront the Ks in order to validate her own reality after terminating the treatment that had failed to assist her in this task, Freud can only conceive of her behaviour, as he saw her decision to terminate therapy, as an act of 'revenge'.

> She made it up with them, she took her revenge on them, and she brought her own business to a satisfactory conclusion. To the wife she said: 'I know you have an affair with my father'; and the other did not deny it. From the husband she drew an admission of the scene by the lake which he had disputed, and brought the news of her vindication home to her father.[36]

Although Dora's behaviour and her words must figure in Freud's interpretations at some level, and do appear at several junctures, they only illustrate aspects of his preferred narrative. At other times what she wants to say seems to register with Freud as so much impedimenta obstructing his privileged position as narrator: 'My powers of interpretation were at a low ebb that day; I let her go on talking ...'.[37] Only after the metamorphosis demanded by his interpretation do Dora's words and actions assume a form that interests and satisfies Freud. What her words signify for Dora is of little or no interest to Freud. He cannot envisage her occupying the same position towards them that he does; that is, she literally cannot be the neutral 'man of science' whose claims to know will ever be taken seriously.

Gilman argues that this split between doctor and patient was psychologically necessary for Freud as a Jewish doctor treating Jewish patients:

We find Jewish biological and medical scientists of the late nineteenth century forced to deal with what is for them the unstated central epistemological problem of late nineteenth-century biological science: how one could be the potential subject of a scientific study at the same time that one had the role of the observer; how one could be the potential patient at the same moment one was supposed to be the physician. This was especially a problem in Vienna, where the domination of the 'second Viennese' school stressed the central role of the physician–scientist as diagnostician.[38]

It is imperative for Freud to occupy clearly the role of scientific authority, and he cannot do this if Dora's judgements and self-insight are on an equivalent plane to his. As the doctor, Freud must know and must know that he knows better: 'I informed her of this conclusion';[39] 'I could then go on to say that in that case she must be thinking ...';[40] 'I will explain to you presently'.[41] And even when he experiments, the results are just what he expects: 'I opened the discussion of the subject with a little experiment, which was, as usual, successful.'[42]

In one sense, Dora has typical adolescent concerns over fidelity, trust and betrayal, but Freud was apparently not interested in the development of the adolescent identity. He treated Dora as if she were an experienced, sexually mature woman and assailed her with one sexual interpretation after another. Most especially he was oblivious to Dora's need to have her assessment of circumstances verified and that a positive sense of her own identity depended on this verification. The psychologist Erik Erikson, in one of the collection of essays *In Dora's Case*, argues that in adolescence the 'pursuit of factual-historical truth may be of acute relevance to the ego's adaptive strength'. This was precisely the quest that consumed Dora but failed to engage or interest Freud. Instead, he was intent on pursuing what he called a 'genetic reality'. The pursuit of genetic reality saw Freud in his favourite role of intrepid archaeologist, restoring what was buried in Dora's unconscious psychosexual history: 'I had no choice but to follow the example of those discoverers whose good fortune it is to bring the light of day after their long burial the priceless though mutilated relics of antiquity.'[43]

In *Against Therapy* Masson views Freud's determination to pursue and privilege his version of Dora's genetic reality while ignoring Dora's concern for 'material reality' as psychologically injurious to Dora. 'It is as if he (F) is saying, Look, Dora was suffering from internal fantasies, not external injuries. The source of her illness was internal, not external. Fantasy, not reality; libido, not "rape".'[44] What Dora had experienced was pallid by comparison to the excitements of Freud's psychosexual dig into genetic reality. Dora's intensely significant material left Freud curiously, even callously, unmoved.

The psychological distress Dora experienced when faced with her father's disbelief of her account of what happened with Herr K, which Freud shares, is a poignant example of frustrated communication. It exemplifies how the failure to have her reality validated maddened and muted Dora and caused her to become 'beside herself'.

> None of her father's actions seemed to have embittered her so much as his readiness to consider the scene by the lake as a product of her imagination. She was almost beside herself at the idea of its being supposed that she had merely fancied something on that occasion. For a long time I was in perplexity as to what the self-reproach could be which lay behind her passionate repudiation of this explanation of the episode.[45]

Freud noted her distress just as he registered but did not see the significance in transference terms of Dora consistently and anxiously checking 'to make sure whether I was being quite straightforward with her'.

Freud's countertransference and inability to empathise with Dora indicates that he remained unaware of what it was in him that reminded Dora of Herr K. He says:

> In this way the transference took me unawares, and because of the unknown quantity in me which reminded Dora of Herr K, she took her revenge on me as she wanted to take her revenge on him and deserted me as she believed herself to have been deceived and deserted by him.[46]

His complete lack of insight into his similarities with Herr K and with Dora's father, 'the unknown quantity in me', do not augur well for Freud's ability to hear, let alone help, Dora. Ironically, because Freud kept putting himself in the place of Herr K, he was unable to see what it was Dora thought they had in common. At one point he was even taken with the idea that Dora and Herr K might marry and thoroughly approved of this solution to the problem of Dora, calling it a 'triumph of love' — in a viper's nest.

Lacan, in *Dora's Case*, writes that this countertransference keeps on making Freud revert to the love that Herr K might have inspired in Dora and 'it is odd to see how he always interprets as confessions what are in fact the very varied responses that Dora argues against him'.[47]

A number of feminist critics have also commented on Freud's identification with Herr K and how it causes him to misread the nature of Dora's desires and be blind to any evidence that conflicts with his preferred explanation. For example, Toril Moi comments that Freud untiringly tries to 'ascribe to her desires she does not have and ignores those she does' — that is, for Frau K.[48]

Immediately before referring to the unknown quantity in him that reminded Dora of Herr K, Freud writes:

> At the beginning it was clear that I was replacing her father in her imagination, which was not unlikely, in view of the difference between our ages. She was even constantly comparing me with him consciously, and kept anxiously trying to make sure whether I was being quite straightforward with her, for her father 'always preferred secrecy and roundabout ways'.[49]

Despite having such an unequivocal admission from Dora about her concern with issues relating to honesty, trust and openness, his countertransference maintains Freud's ignorance of what it is in him that reminds Dora of Herr K and her father.

Even though he acknowledges the importance of transference, Freud adheres to his belief that Dora really desired and loved Herr K right to the end of the case history. Only in a footnote does he bring up another possibility that throws all his previous interpretations into disarray. This is, that the real object of Dora's desire was Frau K — and her 'adorable white body'. Indeed Freud generally ignores all Dora's relationships with women and only concentrates on those with men. Thus his final surprising footnote, about Dora's homosexual love for Frau K, is a sizeable omission: 'I failed to discover in time and to inform the patient that her homosexual (gynaecophilic) love for Frau K was the strongest unconscious current in her mental life'. He concludes this footnote with the sentence: 'Before I had learnt the importance of the homosexual current of feeling in psychoneurotics, I was often brought to a standstill in the treatment of my cases or found myself in complete perplexity.'[50]

It must be said that this complete perplexity is nowhere in evidence in his previous confident assertions, which dominate his writing up of Dora's case study to the effect that 'he that has eyes to see and ears to hear, may convince himself that no mortal can keep a secret'.

Freud seems distinctly uncomfortable with Dora's complaint about her father that she is being used as an object of erotic barter, both accepting her proposition but wanting to occlude and trivialise her judgement.

Dora's reproach against her father is that she had been handed over to Herr K so he would tolerate the affair between her father and Frau K. Behind this is a further reproach that she has also been handed over to Freud for her father's ulterior motives and in turn was used by Freud to supply the raw material for his theories. Perhaps it is his own usage of Dora that unconsciously prompts Freud to refer to her act of revenge. The use of the word *revenge* immediately draws our attention to the likely grievance Freud believed Dora harboured against him. It is not something he pursues, preferring to concentrate on Dora's criticisms of her father, especially the way her father 'handed [her] over to Herr K as the price of his toleration the relations between her father and his wife'. Freud immediately backs away from accepting this proposition and effectively denies it. However, he does not acknowledge his denial but rather transfers it to Dora and makes her the one who cannot believe her own characterisation: 'At other times she was quite well aware that she had been guilty of exaggeration in talking like this.'

He then goes on to make a rather gratuitous comment, as if to reassure himself: 'The two men had of course never made a formal agreement in which she was treated as an object for barter.'[51] Apparently Freud wants to convince himself that nothing less than the existence of a formal contract should count as evidence of an agreement. To refute Dora's claim, Freud switches from his usual role of genetic archaeologist to become the most mundane materialist, wanting signatures on the dotted line.

Jane Gallop comments: 'Dora and Freud have discovered a fragment of the general structure which thirty years later Claude Levi-Strauss will call elementary kinship structures, that is the exchange of women between men.'[52] It would seem that, of the two, Dora was more conscious of the rates and cost of this exchange, and more reliable as a narrator concerning her feelings towards Herr K, than Freud.

When Freud does recognise Dora's desires for Frau K, he exhibits no corresponding sense that his constant demands on Dora to accept that she wanted to yield to Herr K might have inflicted psychological damage on her. Moreover, the nature of this damage, coercion to form an unwanted sexual liaison, is exactly the same as she has already experienced from her father and Herr K. Similarly Freud's recognition that he has been mistaken all along about Dora's feelings do not affect in the slightest his regard for his own powers of observation and interpretation. In the very last paragraph of the case history he writes:

> Years have again gone by since her visit. In the meantime the girl has married, and indeed — unless all the signs mislead me — she has married the young man who came into her associations at the beginning of the analysis of the second dream.[53]

The young man in question was an engineer. Dora had not married him. All the signs had again misled Freud. The assumed prescience underlying his claims to know the unconscious minds of others, and to attribute to them feelings and motives of which they were unaware, was seriously flawed. And while Freud was confident he knew other minds, he could not permit Dora, permanently positioned as 'other' because of her gender, to know even her own mind.

How should the fragments from this analysis of a case of hysteria be regarded? Freud believed it was up to him to construct a 'coherent narrative' and fill in the gaps of memory, self-knowledge and understanding in the patient's memory:

> It is only towards the end of the treatment that we have before us an intelligible, consistent and unbroken case history. Whereas, the practical aim of the treatment is to remove all possible symptoms and to replace them by conscious thoughts, we may regard it as a second and theoretical aim to repair all the damage to the patient's memory.[54]

Can the fragments only form one fixed shape, in the same way as the pieces of a child's puzzle can only form a rabbit or a car, or are they more like the fragments in a kaleidoscope where a shift of angle, a turn or rotation will produce an entirely new configuration? Freud's own view seems much closer to the first suggestion — truth is fixed and attainable by he who has 'eyes to see and ears to hear'. In fact, he used the image of the child's puzzle in describing how he put together a case history in 'The aetiology of hysteria': 'It is exactly like putting together a child's picture puzzle: after many attempts, we become absolutely certain in the end which piece belongs in the empty gap.'[55]

Postmodern and feminist readings are more suggestive of the second possibility — there is no fixed truth, and what is perceived is always perceived and interpreted by someone. Rereading and rewriting Dora is pertinent because, as Chris Weedon puts it, 'In rewriting the meaning of the feminine ... feminists make language the site of a struggle over meaning which is a prerequisite for political change.'[56]

Dora's case demonstrates how Freud's theory of hysteria and the therapeutic practice it informed actively worked against Dora's mental and emotional well-being. Her experience in psychoanalysis can be seen to exemplify the effect of a dominant ideology on a young woman who refuses to submit to its demands for passivity and compliance. Dora is accused by Herr K, her father and Freud of having fantasies. All these accusations work to protect the interests of the person who makes them: Herr K protects his behaviour from scrutiny and avoids censure, Dora's father protects his affair and Freud protects his theory. Could it be that when the truths of the powerless — in this case, Dora's truths — threaten the authority and self-interest of the powerful, they will be called fantasies?

Dora's unsuccessful attempts to be heard during her three months of treatment are a classic case of frustrated communication. She speaks but she cannot be heard on her own terms, only on Freud's. It is his theory whose truth status needs to be proved and protected. Her account is reduced to the status of 'raw data' that will be fitted into the configuration demanded by his theory. Freud accords her story almost no independent authenticity or meaning.

Dora's case raises the spectre of psychogenic science and therapy — when the terms of getting better are liable to make the patient ill; when acts of self-validation are perceived as acts of revenge and where 'yielding' to the analyst's view is mandatory. Dora's recovery was made contingent on her accepting Freud's account of her intrapsychic, 'genetic reality', no matter how little it meshed with her own view nor how much she had to reorder her consciousness and values to accommodate it. Within this model of psychological health for women, the emotional costs of therapeutic cure involve disowning the significance of one's own material reality, accepting that what feels like revulsion is really desire, that accusations against others convict the self and that what seems like an external injury, an injustice that can and should be righted, is probably a fantasy and a sign of one's intrapsychic pathology. From a psychoanalytic perspective, then, the greatest reversal of affect necessary in becoming well is in accepting that one should change oneself rather than wanting, as Dora did, to change the world around her.

The shift from 'material' to 'psychical reality' in the aetiology of hysteria and neurosis was to have far-reaching effects on women, inside and outside psychiatric treatment, for the next eighty years.

7
THE FREUDIAN LEGACY

Apart from the discovery of the Oedipus complex, with its emphasis on the universality of childhood sexual fantasy, Freud's retraction of his original theory of hysteria derived from his scepticism about the prevalence of sexual abuse in childhood. If what all his patients were saying was true, then, Freud reasoned, sexual abuse would have to be rampant in society; almost every female child would have experienced it and almost every father, including his own, would have perpetrated it. Freud baulked at this possibility — surely not everyone, his own father particularly, could be guilty of sexually abusing children.

It hardly needs to be pointed out that the logic Freud used was faulty. He failed to consider that the sexual experiences of his patients might not be representative of the rest of the population and could not serve as a basis for making generalisations about them. Failure to consider the likelihood of selection bias set in train an increasingly spurious line of argument. Freud began by making an unsupported generalisation — if all my patients have been abused, then everyone has been abused — and ended by using his rejection of that generalisation to draw a false inference. He used his conclusion about the general — not everyone can have been abused — to return to and reject the veracity of the particular — my patients can't have been abused.

The beauty of Freud's theoretical revision was that it accommodated and overcame the difficulty posed by the invariant presence of abuse in the histories of his patients. The revision allowed him to reformulate their reports of abuse as expressions of the universal fantasy he identified as the Oedipus complex. In this way, their stories did not overstrain his sense of credibility. While the fact of universal childhood sexual abuse had to be denied, hearing his patients express the universal fantasy demanded by his new theory was another matter entirely.

In the 1920s, as we have seen, Freud attributed his earlier acceptance of his patients' stories to the technical procedure he used at the time, his own credulity and his lack of theoretical sophistication regarding the importance of wishful fantasies in hysteria. Although he reserved a small, 'humbler' role for early traumatic sexual experiences in the development of hysteria, the fact of abuse lost theoretical interest for Freud because he became convinced that 'as far as neurosis was concerned psychical reality was of more importance than material reality'. In an important sense, the distinction between material and psychical reality fell away, and what had happened or not happened to the child became ablated in this therapeutic revision. Only what went on within the woman's own psyche, as determined by Freud's theories of the unconscious, became a suitable object of therapeutic endeavour. Nothing external to her could or should be changed; real trauma was relatively unimportant. Freud further justified this stance on the ground that childhood sexual abuse occurred so infrequently that it could only make a small contribution to the vast majority of cases of neurosis and hysteria in adult women.

The damaging impact on subsequent psychiatric thinking and practice of Freud's privileging of fantasy over fact, and on the wishful fantasies of the 'seductive' child rather than the tangible acts of the abusive adult, cannot be overestimated. Elaine Showalter has argued that throughout the history of psychiatry men such as Pinel, Conolly, Charcot, Freud and Laing have claimed that they would free women from the 'chains of their confinement to obtuse and misogynistic medical practice'. However, until women

speak for themselves, Showalter argues, these 'dramas of libera-
tion become only the opening scenes of the next drama of confinement'.[1] In what follows, I will argue that Freudian theories on
women and hysteria are a driving force in this continuing drama
of mental and emotional confinement and are antagonistic to the
very possibility of women being able to speak for themselves.

One of the givens of feminist critiques of knowledge in the
social sciences is that previous theories have never been constructed by women or based on their experiences.[2] Psychoanalytic
thinking, with its emphasis on internal rather than external reality, suggests that the simple exclusion of women's voices from the
theories of social science is not the sole difficulty. Alongside exclusion, there is a problem of distortion when women are spoken for
and heard through a theoretical model they have had no part in
devising. Culturally significant theory, whether it consists of nineteenth-century beliefs regarding a conflict between the uterus and
the brain for a fixed amount of energy, or twentieth-century
Freudian orthodoxy, has imposed strange filters and strictured
categories of explanation through which women have had to
attempt to see and understand themselves and have been seen and
understood by their professional 'helpers'.

Whether an individual woman identifies positively or negatively with the image of her difference created by Freudian theory,
the ubiquity of the theory in its multiple representations within
Western culture makes some reaction unavoidable and, in so
doing, necessarily configures self-perception and identity. Juliet
Mitchell has defended Freud's theorising about women and femininity on the grounds that it was descriptive rather than prescriptive.[3] My own view is more that his theory functions as a
description of what woman's nature, determined by its biology,
her biology, must be.

Regardless of his intentions, the prescriptive force of his ideas
in psychiatric research papers and in the textbooks used to train
several generations of psychiatrists is unmistakable. Until the
1980s, both research papers and textbooks were replete with
notions of women's passivity, narcissism and masochism, and

both uncritically accepted Freud's view that childhood sexual abuse was so rare as to be theoretically insignificant in understanding or treating the psychological ills disproportionately experienced by women. As a result of this malignant blind spot, the sexual abuse of children has for most of this century either been ignored, dismissed as a fantasy, considered a rare 'sexual deviation' for which 'seductive' children were largely responsible or otherwise disregarded as a possible cause of psychological distress among women seeking psychiatric help.

Women, whether in formal therapy or simply seeking to understand their emotional responses to abusive experiences, have been equally benighted. Not only has the dominant Freudian model of explanation been unable to accommodate what they might be attempting to say but also the explanations it does offer are honed to exacerbate feelings of frustration and distress. Where Freudian premises inform therapy, a curious situation obtains. Women are rendered most incomprehensible and muted by precisely those people whose professional credentials promise to provide them with their best chance of being well understood.

Indeed, the female patient and her analyst are in a remarkable relationship to one another. The analyst listens to what the patient is saying but 'knows', psychoanalytically speaking, that what she says happened did not happen and that what she says she does not want is, in fact, what she deeply desires. A double crossover is effected in the psychoanalytic translation of the patient's narrative, and this translation is something that the patient can never do on her own behalf. Not only does she want what she says she does not want but also what she says happened never occurred. Consequently, the true state of her desire is the opposite of what she thinks: unconsciously, she is deeply desirous of something that did not take place, and consciously, she is deeply distressed by something that did not occur. How many women, labelled as hysterics as Dora was, felt as she did and were beside themselves at not being believed, at their doctors supposing they had merely fancied something that had made them ill? And how many doubted their sanity as a result?

The term *gaslighting* has been coined by English psychologists Gertrude Gass and William Nichols to describe the emotional effect of the lies told by one partner to another during an extramarital affair.[4] It has, however, a much broader application in understanding the way Freud's revised theory of hysteria acted as a psychogenic, 'gaslighting' force in women's lives by repudiating, reinterpreting and explaining away their accounts of abuse so that nothing remained but their own neurotic fantasies.

The idea comes from the 1944 classic film *Gaslight* with Charles Boyer and Ingrid Bergman, in which the husband attempts to drive his wife insane in order to prevent her from discovering his guilty secret. Thus it refers to a systematic attempt to drive someone mad by telling her that she has imagined something that never happened. Gaslighting proceeds by utilising deceit and concealment and by falsifying and denigrating the victim's perceptions, judgements and experiences. The person being gaslighted is ultimately forced to question her sanity. At its most successful, gaslighting is a form of soul murder. The self is destroyed through the agency of a more powerful person or, in the case of psychiatric theories, an extremely powerful and authoritative way of thinking that undermines and destabilises one's experienced reality, causing the person to deny her insight into and knowledge of events.

If the 'truth' of the gaslighter is accepted over one's own, the internalisation of it will bring about a more insidious but complete repudiation of self than could ever be attained if the threat to self were perceived as external and separate. Gaslighting would seem to be most easily achieved when there is an imbalance of power, such as that which still characterises the social position of women. This imbalance overdetermines the outcome of any disagreement over what is real or true or significant. What is first transmitted sociologically, for example, through Freudian theory, becomes internalised or laid down intrapsychically. Thus, the person being gaslighted is already primed, through her weaker position in the social hierarchy, to doubt herself and her opinions and to defer to those who are confident they know better. There is ample evidence that this takes place. Exactly the damage predicted to occur as a result of gaslighting — weakened self-belief, chronic lowering of confidence in one's ideas and knowledge, poor self-esteem and the depression and anxiety that can flow from not being valued or believed — are the forms of emotional distress that have been documented in women over and over again.[5]

Reiker and Carmen have theorised that making accommodations to the judgements of others about child sexual abuse can result in a fragmented sense of identity. They also maintain that the defenses which need to be used in dealing with abusive and traumatic events subsequently form the core of survivors' psychopathology.[6] Within this theoretical context, it seems highly likely that the incomprehension, distortion or repudiation of women's accounts of child sexual abuse by the 'helping' professions in the not so distant past were highly salient characteristics of this process of accommodation. In so far as this psychiatrically endorsed accommodation fragmented rather than supported attempts to fuse an integrated identity, it was a process of self-alienation that jeopardised rather than fostered psychic survival.

The 'gaslighting' to which women were subjected when they sought help is painfully obvious in psychiatric textbooks until quite recently. Even in 1990, Susan Ogata and her co-workers writing in the mainstream psychiatric journal, the *American Journal of Psychiatry*, felt impelled to advise psychodynamic clinicians not to dismiss their patients' recollections of sexual abuse as 'merely oedipal wishes or fantasy'.[7]

Only the year before, Morrison published a paper entitled 'Childhood sexual histories of women with somatization disorder', which demonstrated that such advice was still timely and revealed a profession seemingly united in an emperor's new clothes attitude to childhood victimisation.[8] All papers published between 1950 and the late 1980s were scrutinised for Morrison's comprehensive review of the research. Of the seventy-five papers that appeared over this period, Morrison found only two that provided any data at all on patients' childhood sexual histories.

One of the papers, by Coryell and Norten, published in 1981, reported an 18 per cent incidence of childhood sexual abuse in patients with somatisation disorder. This compared with no incidence in patients with primary affective disorders. Interestingly, the authors managed to discount their own findings in a way that delineates how resistant Freudian theory can be to disproof and how theory is privileged over evidence. The reported incidence of childhood sexual abuse, which, on the face of it, posed an uncomfortable threat to the theory, was able to be invalidated by, and at the same time 'save', the same theory by appealing to its unfalsifiable premises. The authors, in retreating from their own data, advised that 'questions concerning the validity of [early sexual molestation] are classic'.[9] The 'classic' nature of questions over the validity of child abuse comes directly from 'classic' Freudian theory, which positioned women as unreliable informants, whose reports should be discounted as fantasies.

Morrison, whose own research found a 35 per cent incidence of sexual molestation among women with somatisation disorder, concluded: 'The paucity of research into the sexual backgrounds of women with somatization disorder may stem from the traditional belief that women with hysteria have only imagined early sexual molestation.'[10]

THE SEDUCTIVE CHILD AND HER FANTASIES

The same Freudian perspective that caused psychiatric researchers to ignore the possibility of childhood sexual abuse also permeates the psychiatric textbooks that moulded clinical practice. Psychiatric textbooks writtten between the 1940s and the 1970s continued to represent the mental world of female children and adults through the same Freudian prism that vivified Gregory Zilboorg's fantasies of malignant psychoses related to childbirth in the 1920s.[11]

Freudian orthodoxies also left an indelible mark on obstetrics and gynaecology textbooks written during the same period. As critical attention has already been directed to these texts, only brief mention of them will be made here.

Probably the best known critique of gynaecology textbooks, and one of the earliest salvos of second wave feminism, came from sociologists Diana Scully and Pauline Bart. Their seminal 1973 paper, 'A funny thing happened on the way to the orifice: Women in gynecology textbooks', found that women were routinely portrayed in these textbooks in terms of their reproductive functioning.[12] A content analysis of twenty-seven gynaecological textbooks published in the USA between 1943 and 1972 revealed that Freudian views on women and their sexuality, such as the presumption that the psychosexually mature woman should experience vaginal orgasm, kept on being expressed long after contrary evidence was amassed by Kinsey and Masters & Johnson. Gynaecology textbooks consistently upheld Freud's 'biology is destiny' arguments and described women as 'anatomically destined to reproduce, nurture and keep their husbands happy'.[13] Women were positioned as passive, submissive and somewhat feeble-minded creatures.

More than sixteen years after the publication of Scully and Bart's paper in the *American Journal of Sociology*, the same topic was re-examined by an Australian researcher, Glenda Koutroulis, with the aim of finding out how much these textbooks had changed in the meantime. She found some improvement in the newer textbooks used in Australian medical schools in that they communicated more up-to-date knowledge about female sexual response, but overall the same Freudian-inspired notions of rigid sex roles prevailed.[14]

In some psychiatric textbooks published between the 1940s and 1970s, the dominance of Freud's views is obvious because his theories are simply summarised and presented as objective truths. Importantly, his theories on femininity and female sexuality inform and sustain those on hysteria and, as such, virtually determine the way child sexual abuse is conceptualised. The Oedipus complex, the various stages in psychosexual development, the passive, masochistic and narcissistic nature of women, the 'seductive' child and her sexual fantasies and an almost total silence about the existence or effects of childhood sexual abuse, let alone sexual and physical violence in adult women's lives, are standard elements in the psychiatric textbooks of the 1940s, 1950s and 1960s. While an exhaustive analysis of all textbooks is impossible in the context of this chapter, the texts mentioned are a representative selection.

Beginning in the early 1940s with Ross's textbook, *The Common Neuroses*, we find a discussion of hysteria that contains no reference to sexual abuse in childhood nor the possibility that it might be linked to hysteria.[15] Freud's theoretical revision effectively severed the connection between the two ideas in psychiatric thinking. Ross barely touches on the notion that symptomatic fears might have a basis in reality when he describes a hysterical patient, whose reactions and fears are very similar to Dora's:

> A girl of nineteen, the subject of emotional attacks, always locked her bedroom door for fear that a man might come in at night; this would happen even at home. One cannot, of course, be sure that this was not a necessary precaution, but it is an unusual one to take. She dreaded to go to sleep, for the man might come through the window; she believed that she might be assaulted in her sleep and not waken, and therefore not know whether she were deflowered or not.[16]

After noting that it might not be possible to reassure the girl that such an event could not place without her knowing, Ross observes that 'hysterical patients are apt to distrust the reassurances which doctors give'. The girl's distrust thus comes to be seen as another symptom of her hysteria, not a marker of her perception of the inadequacy of her doctor's understanding of what ailed her.

The focus on the intrapsychic characteristics of 'neurotic' patients in many textbooks bordered on the tautological. Attention was so firmly directed by the belief that distress was a product of a disordered psyche that nothing besides intrapsychic conflict could be recognised as playing a part in symptom development. For psychiatrists of this persuasion, other possible sources of patient distrust and disquiet, including their own unbreachable complacency and incomprehension, were literally unthinkable. Empathy was impossible; how can you be empathic with someone whose stated experiences you deny in prinicple?

Instead of the therapeutic alliance meant to exist between patient and doctor, the theory pertaining to hysteria almost ensured that there had to be a therapeutic mismatch. It comes as no surprise, then, that in a recent study by Elizabeth Pribor and Stephen Dinwiddie of women who had been victims of incest during childhood, nearly 80 per cent had seen at least one mental health professional before the present therapist, but the overwhelming majority (82.9 per cent) had not found the prior therapist helpful.[17]

What psychiatrists found in their patients' psyches neatly coincided with what Freudian theory predicted would be there. Helene Deutsch, one of Freud's most loyal disciples, endlessly reiterated the holy trinity of Freudian femininity — narcissism, masochism and passivity — in her influential two-volume work, *The Psychology of Women*, published in 1945. From her acceptance of the biological basis of women's penis envy and its parlous consequences, everything else followed. For example, Deutsch asserted that because women were naturally masochistic they had a deeply feminine need to be sexually overpowered by men: 'A painful bodily injury — the breaking of the hymen and the forcible stretching and enlargement of the vagina by the penis — are the prelude to woman's first complete sexual enjoyment.'[18]

Otto Fenichel's *Psychoanalytic Theory of Neurosis*, published in 1946, amounts to another facsimile of Freud's theory of psychosexual development. It is replete with references to the 'ideal Oedipus complex' and how the 'specifically feminine disappointment' of not having a penis prepares the ground for subsequent femininity in which the 'idea "penis" is replaced by the idea "child," and the clitoris as a leading zone may again be regressively replaced by anal and especially oral — that is receptive — demands'.[19] Fenichel does briefly mention traumatic experiences and 'seduction', but stalwartly upholds the primacy of the Oedipus complex over traumatic reality. Trauma only becomes a problem if the 'Oedipus complex has not been surmounted in a normal way'.[20] If the Oedipus complex has been resolved, albeit with difficulty for most women, then apparently they can have sexual experiences after this time with little or no ill effect on their psychological development.

While a strict adherence to Freud's tenets is only to be expected in a psychoanalytical text like Deutsch's or Fenichel's, it also features in *Modern Clinical Psychology*, published in the same year by Dr T.W. Richards, Professor of Psychology at Northwestern University. Richards reproduces the same Freudian stereotypes of masculinity and femininity and the same outline of psychosexual development, which ordains that 'masculinity is identified with aggression and femininity with passivity'. Furthermore, this identification is enjoined because 'in courtship and in social customs these roles are necessary and typical of adjustment'.[21] Childhood sexual abuse is not mentioned, but Richards warms to the theme, fully developed by Deutsch, of women's 'natural' masochistic pleasure in being overpowered. Women, as natural masochists, want and enjoy sexual aggression from men: 'It is true, however, that in the normal sex act the woman is highly stimulated by aggression of increasing intensity and even violence.'[22]

To what extent psychiatric opinions both reflected and shaped ideas in the broader culture and its institutions is debatable. What cannot be doubted is that these opinions could be called upon scientifically to legitimate attitudes and beliefs about the nature of women, which were and still are used to discriminate against them. In Australia, in August 1992, Mr Justice Bollen of the South Australian Supreme Court caused a furore over his comments in a rape-in-marriage trial. Justice Bollen warned the jury that it was very easy for women to make false allegations of rape, and instructed them that there was nothing wrong with a husband, faced with his wife's initial refusal to engage in intercourse, to use 'a measure of rougher than usual handling' to persuade her to agree.

The subject of childhood sexual abuse is not addressed directly in Rees's *Modern Practice in Psychological Medicine*. It contains a mere two paragraphs on 'early sex relations with adults'. Rees acknowledges that these relations are damaging, but isn't quite sure why, saying the reasons are 'still incompletely worked out'. Despite this perplexity, he opts for the likely 'fundamental importance' of the guilt feelings experienced by the adult.[23] The gender neutrality of 'the child', the even-handed 'he or she' and then the use of the masculine pronoun — '*his* parents' — all help to conceal the fact that little girls were and still are the ones most likely to be sexually assaulted. All community studies conducted since the 1970s have reported that female children are twice as likely to be sexually abused as their male counterparts.[24]

Skottowe's *Clinical Psychiatry for Practitioners and Students*, with its section on social factors in mental illness, promises to provide a more accurate examination of the social conditions that cause mental distress. This promise is not fulfilled as the discussion turns out to be little more than a recitation of the psychological dangers that attend the flouting of the rigid sex roles of the 1950s. Domestic incompetence is identified as a cause of psychoneurotic illness. The androcentrism of Skottowe's perspective is apparent:

> The most ardent affection is liable to wilt under the continued strain of bad cooking, slovenly housework and ill-managed shopping; but not all those who fail in this way do so by reason of constitutional incapability; some of them do so because they have the wrong attitude about their obligations and some because they have never been instructed in the technicalities of simple domestic arts.[25]

The text speaks from an entirely male viewpoint, male gender being implied in the person whose affection is liable to 'wilt' and in the likely victim of the domestic incompetence. Skottowe acknowledges the psychological significance of 'a sense of being exploited or frustrated' when talking about the male-identified workplace but ignores the same feelings in discussing psychological problems arising in the female-identified domestic sphere.

Skottowe's judgements on domestic incompetence and his stress on social and sex role obligations essentially reproduce nineteenth-century notions of moral insanity. If a woman showed the wrong attitude towards her domestic duties she was threatened with loss of love and was morally culpable of causing neurosis in the unhappy victim of her bad cooking, slovenly housework and ill-managed shopping.

It would be mistaken, however, to think that this equation of sanity with a compliance to conventional sex role stereotypes was confined to the 1950s. Psychiatric drug advertisements continue to convey potent messages about appropriate social and sex roles for women, as Kleinman and Cohen illustrated in their analysis of advertisements, targetted at psychiatrists and their management of female patients, which appeared in the *American Journal of Psychiatry* between 1980 and 1988.[26]

Advertisements portraying women stressed that the taking of medication would achieve 'maintainability' and 'manageability' of the traditional domestic division of labour. While reinforcing the view that women should perform all domestic work, the advertisements failed to recognise how inadequate social support, a more equitable division of domestic labour and the absence of social recognition or alternative job opportunities could cause psychiatric symptoms. Instead, their implicit message was that 'the problem lies within individual women themselves'.[27] The decontextualisation of mental illness evident in the advertisements and their corresponding focus on intrapsychic pathology is, of course, congruent with their aim of selling large quantities of psychotropic drugs.

Although the 1950s saw little change in the type or amount of attention paid to childhood sexual abuse, explanations for the initiation of sex in childhood increasingly began to implicate the child.

Leo Kanner, in the third edition of *Child Psychiatry*, like his predecessors, relies on Freud's theory of personality development with its basis in infantile sexuality. Like so many other psychiatric texts of the 1940s and 1950s, curt notice is paid to child sexual abuse and incest. In his one-paragraph treatment of the topic, Kanner upholds Freud's opinion that such behaviour is extremely rare: 'It takes considerable abandon of all inhibition to pierce one of the strongest taboos of the culture.'[28] He repeats this opinion in the revised 1972 edition of *Child Psychiatry* and reiterates the conviction that when incest does take place it is because the 'home setting' is 'utterly disorganized and disastrous' and characterised by 'feeble-mindedness, alcoholism and absence of all restraint'.[29] In

1957 and again in 1972, Kanner refers to the 'several dozen instances' of 'incest' that have come to his attention. Through the use of the identical phrase in both editions he creates the impression that no additional cases have appeared in the interim. Naturally, this lends added weight to his claim about the rarity of incest.

Kanner gives far more attention to the problem of 'sex misconduct' by girls. Compared with incest, which happens so rarely thanks to the great strength of inhibition in fathers, the sexual misconduct of girls is presented as being almost ludicrously easy to trigger. According to Kanner, it could be set off by a girl being on 'hostile' terms with her family (without further elaboration) or being 'infatuated with some man'; it could happen when the girl 'craves excitement', a 'gay life' including 'booze parties' or goes about 'picking up a fellow who has a car' or is working in 'music shows' or 'taxi dancing academies'.[30]

A rare example of the piercing of one of the strongest taboos is cited in the section on 'juvenile delinquents'. Here the 'seduction' of feeble-minded children by adults is put forward as a cause of juvenile delinquency along with 'loose sex standards in the home' and 'parental cruelty, persuasion by companions, desire for adventure and the expectation of pay'.[31]

The sexual precocity of the child is singled out as a 'prominent etiologic feature' in delinquency. The emphasis on the child's sexuality is continued in Kanner's discussion of what were thought of at the time as 'promiscuous children'. He devotes considerably more space to this subject than the one paragraph on incest. The concentration on promiscuous children reinforces the idea that the sexual behaviour of children towards adults is the critical issue; that of adults towards children is almost a hypothetical problem by comparison. Kanner gives the following brief but florid account of 'Alice O':

> Alice O., daughter of an alcoholic loafer and skirt-chaser and a nagging deaf mother, had been promiscuous since the age of 8 years, preferably with sailors and married men. Her mother shielded her and blamed the men 'for everything.' Alice said in court: 'I run away from home because I get devilishness in my head.' Neither she nor her older

sister, who was in reform school because of sex delinquency, had any guilt or anxiety with regard to their sex behavior.[32]

Child sexual abuse is not something that Dr D. Russell Davis, author of *An Introduction to Psychopathology*, considers a problem either.[33] Like his peers, Russell Davis writes of the Oedipus complex and gives credit to Freud for recognising young children's sexual behaviour. That adults might be involved in this sexual behaviour is not contemplated. What is more, Russell Davis says that 'patriarchal' Western cultures, which encourage strong oedipal complexes, safeguard against sexual expression. In a restatement of the evolutionary arguments that placed Western man on the pinnacle of the phyletic scale, he asserts that while sexual activities might be elaborate and frequent in 'permissive' cultures resulting in a 'less intense' Oedipus complex, they are restrained in 'range and frequency' in 'restrictive cultures, e.g. Western cultures' where there is 'a strong dominance of the father in the family'.[34]

THE SIXTIES

In the 1960s, the fiction that child sexual abuse hardly ever occurred continued. It coexisted with a form of denial that held that such abuse was of meagre psychological import, even in the few cases where its existence was acknowledged. Avoidance of the subject was buttressed by the tactic of stigmatising certain groups of materially or intellectually disadvantaged people and, increasingly, by blaming the child victim. The preoccupation with these out-groups in the psychiatric literature ensured that those closest in social position to the authors — intelligent, middle-class, professional men occupying positions of power and high social regard — were, almost by definition, placed outside the ranks of possible offenders. Some texts, like Howells' 1968 *Theory and Practice of Family Psychiatry*, contain no discussion of either incest or the sexual assault of children, referring only to the importance of the Oedipus complex on several occasions, including a report on its role in an experiment on sibling rivalry.[35]

Those texts that do mention intrafamilial abuse favour Kanner's view that incest was caused by feeble-mindedness, alcoholism and poverty. The few lines Hale Shirley spends on childhood sexual experiences in *Pediatric Psychiatry* (published in 1963) contain no direct reference to incest. Instead, Shirley speaks more euphemistically about how: 'Occasionally, one finds parents who, driven by their own sexual conflicts and frustrations, more or less unwittingly overstimulate their children's sexual feelings, even obtaining vicarious pleasure from their children's behavior.' The children likely to be affected come from 'poverty stricken neighborhoods or from intellectually underprivileged homes' where they are 'sometimes exposed to sexual life which is not far removed from the ordinary barnyard variety'. Not only is the prevalence of such behaviour extremely low, only happening 'occasionally', but also it is concentrated among those who, once again, are far removed from the author, occurring among the 'poverty stricken' and/or 'intellectually retarded' or the small aberrant group of 'sexually abnormal adults or adolescents [who] may seduce children with gifts or bribes'.[36]

The explanations provided by Shirley, like those by Kanner and Russell Davis before him, help to deny that the sexual abuse of children is a pressing social problem. Taken together, all use rationalisations that employ minimisation, containment and social distancing to maintain this comforting illusion. In fact, child sexual abuse occurs in all social classes. One of the first studies of childhood sexual abuse by David Finkelhor in the late 1970s was of 795 college students of whom 20 per cent of women and almost 10 per cent of men reported being sexually abused as children.[37] Thus even among university students, the most educationally and materially privileged group of young adults, sexual abuse in childhood was by no means the unknown phenomenon these authors preferred to believe.

Even when the topic began to receive more attention towards the end of the 1960s, the same premises remain and victim-blaming reaches new heights. For instance, Ian Gregory spends about a page discussing incest in his 1968 text, *Fundamentals of Psychiatry*. It appears under the heading of 'Sexual deviation', again stressing its rarity.

Gregory quotes Sloane and Karpinski's view that more emotional damage was done when incest occurred during adolescence than when it took place before puberty. The only emotional aspect of the experience affecting the child in which writers of this time seemed to be interested was whether children expressed anxiety about what had happened. If there was no overt anxiety then apparently no harm had been done. Gregory uncritically accepted Barry and Johnson's assertion that 'incestuous daughters experienced little anxiety when they were young, and when the mother accepted the fact of incest'.[38] It is disconcerting to attempt to assimilate this 'finding'. Do the authors believe it is psychologically better for daughters if mothers accept incest, so as to reduce anxiety in their daughters?

In keeping with the mentality that sees incest somehow inhering in those who are abused, that is, in the incestuous daughters, Gregory devotes a section of his work to 'The role of the victim and other precipitating factors'. Here, he repeats Freud's theories on female sexuality and endorses his belief, so forcefully expressed in Dora's treatment, that it is woman's nature to want to 'yield' even, or especially, when she is refusing to do so.

Gregory asserts that: 'Often the role of the female is to stimulate the male by tantalizing him, to invite pursuit by running away, and to resist mildly before finally submitting.' And in another reiteration of nineteenth-century writings on woman's position on the phyletic scale, Gregory assures us that:

> Many women, particularly in primitive societies or among the lower socioeconomic levels of our own society, may expect men to establish their worth as a sexual partner through a display of dominance that may involve physical force and even some bodily pain.[39]

Even 'civilised' women, according to Gregory, can experience a desire to be violated, and 'willing submission to pain may result from a desire to intensify sexual excitement'.[40]

For Gregory, 'primitive' women, or their modern counterparts — women 'among the lower socioeconomic levels of our own society' as well as 'civilised' women — in other words, all women — share a desire to 'yield' as prescribed by Freud. To ensure that no woman is left out, Gregory cites two psychopathological types of women who make 'deliberate or unintentional' invitations to be sexually assaulted. One is the 'sadistic' woman who knowingly arouses a man sexually with the 'conscious intention of frustrating him, only to find that he will not be denied what she had in effect promised him'. The other is the 'hysterical or otherwise neurotic woman' who unwittingly provides the 'temptation' and hence provokes the sexual assault.[41]

Although references to sexual assault appear more commonly in psychiatric textbooks by the late 1960s, they are accompanied by what sometimes amounts to a vilification of the child victim and the unfounded conviction that sexual abuse has no deleterious effect on long-term psychological functioning. Both these attitudes are apparent in Myre Sim's 1968 *Guide to Psychiatry*. Somewhat unusually for the time, Sim devotes three pages to 'Sexual assaults on children'. After warning readers against accepting the pre-Freudian view that the child victims of such assaults are 'innocent', he proceeds to instruct readers according to the scientific wisdom of the time.

Close scrutiny, Sim opines, 'may reveal the most unexpected situations'. Using the 1946 publication of Brill, another psychoanalytically inclined psychiatrist, Sim informs us that 'a nine year old girl may be capable of seduction'. This nine-year-old was a patient of Brill, who was referred to him because of her unfortunate habit of 'importuning lorry drivers' and had recently been the chief witness against her father in an incest case. Sim's explanation of the situation makes it clear that he sees the child as responsible for bringing about the incestuous relationship:

> An older sister had in fact been having an incestuous relationship with the father and the patient was *envious* and reported the father for having relations with her too. Physical examination revealed the effects of her *importuning* and medical evidence was conclusive.[42]

The psychological motives attributed to the child by Sim encompass envy, vindictiveness for reporting her father and importuning, that is, soliciting for an immoral purpose. All are hostile emotions, and all are seen as actively directed by the girl towards her father. By comparison the father, in a curious way, appears not to have acted at all. It is as if he had no choice but to comply with his nine-year-old daughter's importuning.

The imbalance in power inherent when sex occurs between a child and an adult is present in Sim's description but in a completely inverted form. The child is invested with all the power, and the father is a shadowy, motiveless, powerless victim — the one who has things done to him. Rape is not mentioned, yet this was a man convicted by conclusive medical evidence of committing incest with both his daughters. Sim's focus is so firmly on what the girl has done to her father through her envy, reporting and importuning that he cannot grasp the likely emotional effects of what has been done to her: the violation of her physical and emotional integrity, her sexual exploitation, the breaking of bonds of trust, the absence of proper paternal care, affection and protection. Nothing is mentioned about the complete disruption of her childhood, first through the incest itself, then through its legal re-enactment in which she is called upon to be the chief witness and finally through her psychiatric treatment by someone who seems to see her as a vindictive, under-age prostitute.

Sim goes on to quote one of the few studies of child victims of sexual assault carried out during the 1960s, that of Gibbens and Prince, published in 1963. This study is also mentioned uncritically in the 1968 edition of Henderson and Gillespie's *Textbook of Psychiatry*. Once again the 'findings' of a study purporting to be scientific, seamlessly meld into Freudian premises about the troublesome 'seductive' child. We are informed that two-thirds of the child victims of sexual assault are 'sufficiently willing participants to co-operate in assaults more than once or by more than one assailant'.[43] This 'willingness' is not considered to be psychologically problematic; rather it seems to be thoughtlessly equated with the absence of any emotional distress on the child's part. Some understanding of what cooperation might signify emotionally only became possible many years later, when investigators began to ask relevant and empathic questions about abuse from the child's perspective.

Lest the budding psychiatrist be alarmed that sexual assaults on children could cause them some psychological harm, Sim is ready with this reassurance:

> The surprising thing is, how little *promiscuous children* are affected by the experiences, and how most settle down to become *demure housewives*. It is of interest that Henriques lists two categories — the unaffected and the guilty — and that seems to put the matter in a nutshell.[44]

This assurance had no empirical basis whatsoever. At the time Sim gave his guarantee about abused children turning into demure housewives, no studies of the long-term effect of child sexual abuse had been carried out.

Freud's influence is even discernible in the economical two-category explanation of Henriques that Sim cites so approvingly. It recalls Freud's rationalisation that he can be doing no harm to Dora when he presses her with one explicitly sexual interpretation after another: 'There is never any danger of corrupting an inexperienced girl ... and where hysteria is found there can no longer be any question of "innocence of mind".'[45]

In the Oedipus complex, Freud put forward a theory that highlighted the sexual fantasies of the child towards its parents but, as the psychiatric textbooks show, professional preoccupation with these fantasies increasingly took precedence over the facts themselves. It is almost as if professional belief in the importance of fantasies caused them to become realised. Children did not just have sexual fantasies about their parents, they also acted on them. Acceptance of this 'fact' created a need, amply fulfilled in the textbooks, to ponder the problems caused by the seductive child, the sexually precocious child, the incestuous child and the promiscuous child. If there was a problem with sexual misconduct at all, by the end of the 1960s, it was easy to believe that it derived from the sexual misconduct of female children.

SOMATISATION DISORDER

In the remaining part of this chapter, I will appraise Freud's repudiation of the significance of childhood sexual abuse in psychological distress and disorder in adult life in the light of contemporary evidence on somatisation disorder.

Among the various patient groups to have been studied the one of most interest, because of its relevance to Freud's arguments, are patients who appproximate to his diagnosis of hysteria. His doubts about the authenticity of these patients' reports led him to revise his beliefs about the prevalence and psychological significance of childhood sexual trauma and to minimise its role in the aetiology of hysteria.

The term *hysteria* is no longer used in psychiatry. It was eliminated from the *Mental Disorders Diagnostic Manual* of the American Psychiatric Association in 1952 and replaced by the term *conversion symptom*. The name change recognised the conversion of mental states or disorders into physical symptoms as a crucial feature of the disorder.

In the latest *Diagnostic and Statistical Manual of Mental Disorders* (DSM IV)[46] what Freud called hysteria is now included in a category known as somatoform disorders. This group includes somatisation disorder, which historically has been referred to as hysteria or Briquet's syndrome, undifferentiated somatoform disorder, conversion disorder, pain disorder, hypochondriasis, body dysmorphic disorder and somatoform disorder not otherwise specified. Somatisation disorder is probably the closest modern diagnostic category to the disorder Freud treated. The manual reports that its essential feature is a pattern of recurring, multiple, clinically significant somatic complaints that cannot be fully explained by any known general medical condition. Diagnostic criteria demand four pain symptoms, two gastrointestinal symptoms, one sexual symptom and one pseudoneurological symptom for positive diagnosis. It is also necessary that the symptoms start before the age of 30.

Although many of the symptoms mentioned in the manual are familiar from Dora's case history, there is not, nor would it be expected for there to be, a complete congruence between Dora's symptoms and those enumerated for somatisation disorder in the manual. The lack of congruence is partly a function of changing definitions and partly to do with the way symptoms are culturally constructed idioms of distress. These are historically specific and change over time. It has been argued that there is a 'sociosomatic' as well as a psychosomatic formulation of illness, with the social course of illness being determined by a dialectic between between body and society.[47] Dora's hysteria, for example, expressed the characteristic symptoms of the time, namely a preponderance of pseudoneurological or 'conversion' symptoms. They included impaired coordination and balance — her gait was affected and she dragged one foot, localised weakness, difficulty in breathing and swallowing, a nervous cough, loss of voice (aphonia) and dissociative symptoms. However, she did meet some of the other modern criteria for somatisation disorder. Dora had two and possibly three pain symptoms: severe headaches from the age of 12, 'piercing gastric pains' and an unconfirmed attack of appendicitis. She also complained of a vaginal discharge, which might count as a sexual symptom.

It is diagnostically significant, too, that Dora suffered from low spirits, chronic fatigue and depression, as the most common psychological accompaniments to somatisation disorder noted in the manual are depression and anxiety. Likely additional diagnoses are panic disorder, substance-related disorders and personality disorders such as histrionic, borderline and antisocial personality disorders. In women, reported prevalence rates of somatisation disorder range from 0.2 per cent to 2 per cent, whereas in men they are reported as being less than 0.2 per cent, which echoes the imbalance in the ratio of childhood sexual abuse (CSA) between men and women.

In the light of what has been documented about somatisation disorder, any studies that investigate the relationship between childhood sexual abuse and this disorder are of absorbing interest for their relevance to Freud's arguments.

An interesting study by Elizabeth Pribor and her colleagues examined the relationship between childhood abuse, Briquet's syndrome (somatisation disorder) and dissociative symptoms in ninety-nine female psychiatric patients attending outpatient clinics.[48] About half the patients in the study met the criteria for Briquet's syndrome while the other half had somatic complaints but did not meet the criteria for Briquet's syndrome. High rates of childhood abuse, including sexual, physical and emotional abuse, were found among both groups of patients, but those with Briquet's syndrome or somatisation disorder had significantly higher rates than the other group. Child sexual abuse was reported by nearly 60 per cent of the women with Briquet's syndrome, just over 43 per cent reported physical abuse and 72 per cent reported emotional abuse. When all forms of abuse, both in childhood and adult life, were included, a staggering 92.2 per cent of patients with Briquet's syndrome were affected.

Dissociative experiences were related to a history of abuse independent of Briquet's syndrome. In other words, patients with the same disorder — somatisation disorder — as those seen by Freud exhibited particularly high levels of dissociation and abuse. Furthermore, women with high dissociation scores and many somatic complaints were more likely to report CSA than women with low dissociation scores or few somatic complaints. This relationship between CSA, dissociation and somatisation has also been reported by Briere and Runtz.[49]

High rates of CSA in patients with somatisation disorder have been found in numerous other studies,[50] suggesting that multiple, somatic symptoms unexplained by any demonstrable organic pathology should arouse a high degree of suspicion about early abuse. CSA has also been connected to hysterical seizures.[51] Linking with the findings on somatisation disorder, an association between pelvic pain and other gynaecological complaints and sexual abuse has been documented.[52] Harrop-Griffiths and co-workers, for example, found that 63 per cent of women undergoing laparoscopy for chronic pelvic pain had been sexually abused as children compared with 23 per cent of women undergoing laparoscopy for other reasons.

Somatic complaints are not confined to gynaecology; some women with a history of abuse have extensive histories of medical and surgical intervention. Arnold and his colleagues illuminate the kind of medical presentation that somatic idioms of distress can assume.[53] The seven psychiatric patients in their study had an average of eight operations each, despite normal pathology findings. The women had been investigated by the following specialities: obstetrics, gynaecology, gastroenterology, urology, rheumatology, haematology, orthopaedics, neuropsychiatry and neurology, which raises the distinct possibility that large numbers of costly and futile surgical procedures are one important consequence of a failure to recognise and deal directly with a history of CSA.

Despite the small sample size of Arnold's study, the disproportionate number of investigations and treatments per patient was striking. Even so, it probably underestimates the actual number of encounters these patients have with the medical profession as only their hospital notes were examined. Investigations by general practitioners and those done in other medical facilities were not included.

As far as Dora is concerned, there is no way of knowing with absolute certainty that she or any other of Freud's 'hysterical' patients were sexually abused as children. What contemporary evidence does suggest, with some force, is that her symptoms were more consistent with this interpretation than any other.

What we know from Felix Deutsch, who treated Ida Bauer when she was 42, is that symptoms in adult life reinforce this supposition.[54] Everything described by Freud — her limp, attacks of migraine, difficulties in breathing, dizziness, coughing spells and vaginal discharge — persisted into adult life, and additional symptoms of tinnitus and severe constipation had been added. Most tellingly in the context of contemporary understanding of somatisation disorder, Deutsch found out that later on she underwent several minor gynaecological operations in the hope of curing the same worrying vaginal discharge she had as an adolescent.

It has also been established by recent reseach that women who have been sexually abused as children are significantly more likely than non-abused women to seek and receive psychiatric treatment.[55]

That is, the very women Freud saw in his clinical practice were the ones most likely to have high rates of childhood sexual abuse.

Freud's theoretical revision deflected professional attention from CSA for more than seventy years. Along with this lack of attention and absence of scientific investigation went a massive 'gaslighting' of women's experiences. Women's realities were infused with male subjectivities; malignant fantasies of the other were thus transubstantiated into women's own neurotic desires. The artificial illumination of women's neurotic fantasies took precedence in psychiatric discourse over confronting the cruelty, sexual exploitation and misery of the abused child, and was incompatible with the delivery of sensitive, humane, effective psychiatric services.

When there was no research on CSA and the standard psychiatric stance towards it was one of disbelief and even hostility towards the 'incestuous' child, what women encountered when they sought psychiatric help came perilously close to mirroring the initial abusive experience. The professional response bore out what the perpetrator probably told the abused child: no one will believe you and, if they do, you will be the one to be blamed or punished.

Recent research demonstrates that women continue to be affected by these beliefs and that mental health services, although changing, are still unlikely to provide therapeutic assistance to women who have experienced CSA. In one study of the long-term psychiatric consequences of incest published in 1992, the researchers reported that:

> The incest victims in our group were unlikely to perceive benefit from mental health services in general. Half reported that they had never seen a psychiatrist; of those who had, almost none indicated that they found the experience beneficial. Many of the women volunteered that they had never told their psychiatrist about the abuse, nor were they ever asked. This outcome is made more disturbing by the fact that, excluding tobacco dependence, all subjects had at least one psychiatric disorder and on average met criteria for seven on a lifetime basis.

Given the high rates of anxiety disorders and depression, potentially treatable by pharmacotherapy or a combination of psychotherapy and pharmacotherapy, psychiatric intervention might be of unique benefit in this population.[56]

In the next chapter, the prevalence and psychological impact of childhood sexual abuse in the general community and among women seeking psychiatric help will be discussed more fully. Particular attention will be paid to the factors that influence the attainment of accurate estimates of prevalence and studies that illuminate the relationship between the frequency, severity and duration of abuse and the corresponding nature and severity of psychiatric disorder in adult life.

8
INCREASED ATTENTION, INCREASED EVIDENCE

The 'battered child syndrome' was described by the paediatrician Charles Kempe and his co-workers in 1962.[1] That health professionals recognised child physical abuse long before child sexual abuse was hardly surprising. Freud's theoretical influence on several generations of psychiatrists efficiently proscribed awareness of the subject. The first research studies on child sexual abuse (CSA) did not appear until the 1970s. Again, Kempe was one of the first doctors to draw the attention of his professional colleagues to what had until then been so comprehensively excised and censored from their professional gaze.[2] The American journal, *Child Abuse and Neglect*, first appeared in 1977, and substantial professional engagement can probably be dated from the early 1980s when the first national conference on child abuse took place in the USA and research on CSA began to burgeon. However, it was not until 1992 that the *Journal of Child Sexual Abuse*, indicating the existence of enduring professional interest and sufficient research to maintain the journal, came into being.

The huge amount of research now being published on childhood sexual abuse belatedly substantiates Freud's opinion, expressed in his 1896 lecture on hysteria: '... it is to be expected that increased attention to the subject will very soon confirm the great frequency of sexual experiences and sexual activity in childhood.'[3] Only his prediction about the timing was wrong, and he was the prime mover behind the delay. Now that increased attention has come and the relevant questions have begun to be asked, evidence is not lacking.

PREVALENCE: THE SIZE OF THE PROBLEM

The magnitude of child sexual abuse (CSA) is still being reliably established. Nevertheless, there is incontrovertible evidence that the problem of CSA is serious and widespread, a social pattern of major significance that affects close to one in three girls. Boys are also affected at a lower rate, probably around one in ten, and need to be studied in their own right.[4,5]

The most reliable findings on prevalence come from well-designed studies, which have high rates of participation (that is, most of those who are eligible to participate do so), cover a wide range of ages so that various cohorts of women born at different times can be compared, and use large, random representative samples so that unbiased generalisations can be made. However, even in large community studies, underestimation of prevalence can occur because of low rates of disclosure and the non-inclusion of certain high-risk groups, such as homeless girls, who are difficult to contact.

Leventhal, in a comprehensive 1990 review of community studies of the prevalence of CSA carried out mainly during the 1980s, found a wide variation in reported rates.[6] For women, prevalence rates from different studies ranged from 6 to 62 per cent, and for men they ranged from 3 to 31 per cent.[7-14,5]

One of the most reliable recent studies on prevalence was reported in the *Journal of the American Academy of Child and Adolescent Psychiatry* in September 1993. Jessie Anderson and her colleagues in Dunedin, drawing on a randomly selected community sample of 3000 women, of whom 73 per cent responded, found that nearly one woman in three reported having one or more unwanted sexual experiences before the age of 16.[15] This finding falls midway in the range of prevalence rates reported in the earlier studies and is likely to provide a stable estimate of community prevalence. The majority of unwanted sexual experiences were serious assaults involving genital contact, intercourse or attempted intercourse. Nearly two-thirds of the abuse reported took place before menarche, with the ages of greatest reported risk being between 8 and 12 years. Seventy per cent of episodes lasted less than a year, but intrafamilial abuse lasted significantly longer than extrafamilial abuse. The majority of abusers were known to the child, with 38.3 per cent of episodes occurring with family members and only 15 per cent occurring with strangers. Other studies support the finding that stranger abuse accounts for the smallest number of cases of abuse.[7,5,16,17]

Most community studies include both intrafamilial and extrafamilial abuse,[11,13,14,18] but at least one, conducted by Diana Russell, has concentrated on intrafamilial abuse. Russell, in probably the best designed study of intrafamilial abuse, utilised a random sample of more than 900 women living in San Francisco.[19] She found that 16 per cent of the total sample of women had been victims of exploitative incest, and 38 per cent of the sample reported CSA before the age of 18. Finkelhor in his study of college students found that 28 per cent reported incest, defined as a 'sexual experience with a family member', but half of it was incestuous contact between siblings.[20]

Although intrafamilial abuse makes the largest contribution to overall rates of CSA, and reported rates for intrafamilial abuse range between 12 per cent and 38 per cent,[9,15,19,20] estimates of father–daughter incest are harder to establish as they are rarely reported separately from other forms of intrafamilial abuse. One study of 286 working-class mothers in the United Kingdom, by Bifulco and co-workers, did distinguish between different perpetrators. It found that 16 per cent of all CSA was by the natural father.[21] However, this study found a relatively low overall rate of CSA (9 per cent) and cannot therefore be directly compared with Russell's study.

Psychiatric patients

While the prevalence of CSA in the general community based on the best available evidence appears to be at least 30 per cent, rates of CSA reported among psychiatric patients are often much higher. In general, studies of patient groups that are heterogenous with regard to psychiatric diagnosis report lower rates of abuse than those that concentrate on a specific psychiatric diagnosis, such as posttraumatic stress disorder. Sometimes the rates among patient groups are lower than those reported in the general community. For example, Brown and Anderson, in a large study of 947 patients (41 per cent women) admitted to psychiatric wards of Wilford Hall Medical Centre, the largest tertiary care medical centre of the US Air Force, found that nearly 25 per cent of women reported either child sexual abuse or combined sexual and physical abuse during childhood.[4] Other researchers have reported much higher rates of CSA in psychiatric patients. Carmen, Rieker and Mills in a review of charts found that 43 per cent of 188 psychiatric inpatients reported abuse,[16] Jacobson and Richardson reported a rate of 57 per cent CSA among 100 psychiatric inpatients,[22] and Chu and Dill found that 35.7 per cent of female psychiatric inpatients reported CSA.[23]

Twenty-one per cent of perpetrators in Brown and Anderson's study were the natural fathers,[4] a higher figure than that reported in studies of the general community and male family members (that is, fathers, stepfathers, brothers, uncles, grandfathers, stepbrothers and stepuncles) constituted two-thirds of all perpetrators. In another study of sexually abused children referred by a child protection agency, 83 per cent of perpetrators were family members or lived with the children.[24]

Psychiatric outcomes

For some specific disorders, extremely high rates of CSA have been documented. The disorder for which the highest rates have been reported is multiple personality disorder. Putnam and co-workers, in a study of 100 patients, found that 97 per cent had histories of abuse during childhood.[25] In another large study, Ross and co-workers discovered that 74.4 per cent of 207 female patients with multiple personality disorder had histories of childhood sexual abuse.[26]

For borderline personality disorder, one of the likely additional diagnoses mentioned in DSM IV in relation to somatisation disorder, CSA has been put forward as having an etiologic role.[27] Of all the DSM III R diagnoses made in Brown and Anderson's study, borderline personality disorder accounted for 48 per cent. Certainly very high rates of CSA have been reported in this group of patients. For example, Susan Ogata and her colleagues, in a small mixed gender study (most patients were women), found that 71 per cent reported CSA.[28] Other studies confirm this relationship.[27,29,30,31]

High rates of CSA have been documented in women with somatisation disorder (as discussed in the previous chapter), including unsubstantiated polysomatic complaints attributed to sensitivity to environmental chemicals,[32] alcohol and other substance abuse disorders,[4,8,33] eating disorders[31,34,35,36] and posttraumatic stress disorder.[24,37,38,39]

In addition, CSA has been found in relation to self-harm, including repeated self-harm and suicidality,[4,40,41,42,43,44] difficulties in sexual and interpersonal relationships[20,41,45,46] and a heightened vulnerability to revictimisation, prostitution and early unplanned pregancy, a pattern common in homeless girls.[19,47,48,49]

But perhaps the best documented psychological outcome of CSA in adult life relates to depression and anxiety. Markedly increased rates of depression and anxiety among women who have a history of CSA have been identified in community samples,[11,13,14,15,21,33,50] student samples[40] and psychiatric samples.[4,50,51] Like the variation in overall rates of CSA, studies of depression as an outcome of CSA have reported rates that vary from 13 per cent in a large community study[53] to 64 per cent in a group of working-class British mothers.[21]

CSA: A METHODOLOGICAL QUAGMIRE

The wide range of reported rates of CSA in the general community and in different groups of psychiatric patients calls for some explanation. Two issues emerge: first, why is there such variation in reported rates, and second, are currently available rates more likely to be an over- or underestimate of the true size of the problem? A significant amount of the reported variation in prevalence appears to be a function of both methodological differences and methodological inadequacies in the various studies rather than a reflection of true variation in prevalence. Methodological complications are so numerous that some researchers have dubbed research in this area a 'methodological quagmire'.[53]

Few studies have used standardised data collection and outcome measures or a control group, or have addressed the question of whether early sexual abuse is causally related to the outcomes measured.[41,54,55]

Another obstacle that prevents comparison of findings from different studies has to do with the duration in time between when abuse occurred and when the study was conducted. Similarly, there is variation between studies over the age definition of a child, with some using a cut-off in age of 12 years and some using 16. Obviously, studies using the higher age will obtain higher estimates of child abuse as more years during which abuse can occur are counted.

Another source of possible inaccuracy in estimating prevalence derives from the variation among studies in how child sexual abuse is operationalised. Depending on the study, it might cover acts from fondling to intercourse, single incidents or chronic abuse, and include both sexual intercourse between adolescents of similar age and violent attacks by adults on small children.

An overwhelming number of studies are retrospective. On the other hand, prospective, cohort studies, which from a methodological point of view are better suited to establishing whether there is a cause and effect relationship between childhood abuse and adverse emotional consequences, are constrained by ethical considerations. It would, for example, be unethical for psychiatrists not to intervene in the 'natural history' of abuse that they were attempting to research, and it is questionable whether children are able to give informed consent to participate in research. Further, if parents were to provide consent for their children to be included in such studies, there is an issue regarding the type of bias likely to occur. What kind of parents would be willing to participate in such a study, and how would this willingness relate to the likelihood or unlikelihood of abuse taking place and being disclosed over the course of the study?

The best method of eliciting accurate information has also been debated. Wyatt and Peters have argued that in-depth interviews with multiple questions about abuse are superior to short interviews in determining the actual prevalence of abuse in any population.[56] However, Anderson and her co-workers found that shifts in the numbers of women disclosing abuse occurred between a postal survey and an interview.[15] Further, the shifts did not necessarily occur in the direction predicted by Wyatt and Peters because, while some women found that the interview clarified the definition of abuse, others found the interview too threatening a situation in which to disclose abuse.

The number of screening questions to establish the diagnosis of child sexual abuse can also vary from study to study, as can the definition of abuse and whether it is defined by the researcher or comes from the victim's own definition. For example, Bifulco, Brown and Adler asked women in their study two general questions at different points in an interview.[21] One was: 'Have you at any time in your life been sexually abused?' and the second, relating to childhood, 'Were you ever interfered with sexually?' By contrast, Anderson and her co-workers in the survey part of their study asked the following series of questions to determine the occurrence of CSA:

> Has an adult or older person ever involved you in any unwanted incidents of the following types before you reached the age of 16? a) touched or fondled your private parts, b) made you touch them in a

sexual way, c) attempted or completed sexual intercourse, d) other unwanted sexual activities (specify if you feel able).[15]

In the interview that followed the survey, additional questions were posed, all interviews were conducted by female researchers and the interviews lasted between one and five hours.

Finkelhor found that the more questions asked and the more specific those questions were about the type of abuse experienced, the higher the rates obtained.[57]

UNDERREPORTING

Despite the methodological problems described that contribute to variation in rates between studies, evidence to date strongly suggests that underestimation of the true magnitude of CSA is more of a problem than overestimation. If we look at the most serious sexual assault — rape — and only consider cases reported to officials, the disproportionate brutalisation and victimisation of female children becomes apparent.

In the USA, the first major law enforcement effort to document the problem of child sexual abuse was carried out in 1992 by the Justice Department. A study of eleven states and the District of Columbia found that 10 000 women, about half the total number of reported rapes, were under 18 at the time of the rape, and at least 3800 were children under the age of 12. Although females under 18 made up only 25 per cent of the nation's total female population in 1992, in the twelve reporting jurisdictions they made up 51 per cent of rape victims. In three of the states surveyed, 20 per cent of the girls under 12 were raped by their fathers, 46 per cent were attacked by relatives and 50 per cent by 'friends' and acquaintances. Only 4 per cent of children under 12 were attacked by strangers.[58]

It is known that the incidence of reported abuse cases and of rape is increasing and that girls are more commonly abused than boys. One estimate is that one in six women will be raped in her lifetime.[59] The Justice Department study reveals that, for an alarmingly high number of women, these rapes will occur while they are children. Yet there is substantial evidence that CSA is seriously underreported, especially to official agencies.[53] Estimates based on officially reported cases of CSA, such as those from the Justice Department study, cannot provide a sound basis from which to infer prevalence in the general community.

On the basis of her research, Diana Russell concluded that up to 98 per cent of incest cases go unreported.[19] A slightly lower but consistent figure, using a random, representative community sample, comes from the work of Jessie Anderson and her colleagues.[15] They, too, found that disclosure of abuse was infrequent, especially to official agencies. Only 7.5 per cent of all abuse reported in their study had been officially notified either to social workers or to police investigators. Figures from both studies indicate that more than 90 per cent of cases of CSA are not reported to official bodies, and thus actual rates of abuse are at least ten times higher than official rates.

Another consequence of underreporting is that the small, selected number of cases that are notified to officials are likely to differ in significant, systematic ways from the vast bulk of unreported cases. In other words, officially reported cases will provide biased information on associated social and demographic features of the victims and the perpetrators. With the introduction of mandatory reporting of child abuse in various countries, this situation will presumably change and, with better ascertainment of cases, official rates will become a more reliable indicator of rates in the wider community.

The issue of underreporting and the possible psychological motives behind it have critical implications for understanding and theorising about the emotional impact of abuse and the methodological assumptions that typically guide scientific research.

THE PSYCHOLOGY OF DISCLOSURE

Accurate estimates of prevalence depend on all those factors that affect the ascertainment of cases. Especially pertinent is how scientific theories and evidence on CSA inform clinical practice and, in turn, how these factors interrelate with women's perceptions of abuse and their willingness to disclose it. There is a continuous, fluid interchange or dynamic between the inner and the outer; between how women construct and interpret their experience of CSA, privately and intrapsychically, and how it is represented in the public, outer world of scientific and psychiatric discourse. Meaning is, to some extent, intersubjective and shared, and consequently the meanings the individual can bring to her understanding of CSA, whether or not she accepts, contests or repudiates the discourse, are saturated by its presence. At any time there is only a limited array of available explanations, even though, as we have seen, they can and do shift quite dramatically over time.

One way in which culture and science impinges on how women perceive and construct their experience of CSA is evident in the motives they give for not disclosing or reporting abuse. In a recent study by Jessie Anderson and her co-workers, women advanced a number of reasons for not disclosing abuse.[15] Nearly a third expected to be blamed, and a quarter were either embarrassed, did not want to upset anyone or expected disbelief. Eighteen per cent said they were not bothered by abuse, 14 per cent wished to protect the abuser, 11 per cent feared the abuser and 3 per cent wanted to obey adults. These attitudes towards the perpetrator — fear, protectiveness and the tragically misplaced wish to be 'good' and obey the person who has violated and betrayed them — are a far cry from the incestuous, seductive, envious, importuning, punitive child of Brill and Sim's imagination. And for women who have been sexually abused as children, engaging with these still-extant virulent caricatures of themselves undoubtedly exacerbates emotional distress.

Another indication of how expected reactions to abuse can effectively suppress disclosure is provided by evidence on timing. Only 37 per cent of women in the same study had disclosed abuse within a year of its happening. For 10 per cent disclosure came between one and ten years after the abuse, and for 24 per cent it did not occur for ten or more years. For another 28 per cent of women, disclosure did not come until they participated in the survey and were asked the relevant questions.

Underreporting would seem to be intimately connected to the psychological process of accommodation that women make to deal with CSA. The very efforts, cognitive and emotional, that go towards coping with and containing the abuse can minimise perception of its severity. Koss, in her 1985 study, found that 43 per cent of women who said 'yes' to questions about assaults that met the legal definition of rape answered 'no' to the question 'Have you ever been raped?'[60] Similarly, Martin and her co-investigators discovered a trend during their interviews for women who had been sexually abused as children to downplay the seriousness of the assaults.[61] The women frequently applied such terms as 'it was only' or 'that was all' to these assaults. These comments illustrate quite poignantly how minimisation simultaneously acts as a defence against the abuse and is a symptom of the psychological damage sustained.

Now that research has begun to ask questions of women about the reactions they expected to encounter if they disclosed abuse, their responses make it plain why there have been and continue to be such low rates of disclosure and are another reminder of the noxious emotional consequences of the gaslighting discussed in the previous chapter. The reluctance to disclose runs on dual tracks between the personal and the public. On a personal level, women minimise abuse to themselves and, on a public level, they are inhibited from disclosing out of fear of being disbelieved, punished or blamed.

To begin to understand the magnitude and psychological significance of CSA it is vital that researchers and clinicians legitimate disclosure by asking the relevant questions. Indeed, the basic failure to inquire about the existence of CSA, let alone its role in psychiatric disorder, obstructed the link between the two for a very long time:

> It may be wondered why the connection between psychiatric disorder and abuse had not been noted earlier. In large part this reflects the failure to ask the relevant questions. This clinical shortcoming was

compounded by a tendency to discount histories of sexual abuse when they were volunteered spontaneously by the patient.[62]

Researchers on CSA have been recommending systematic inquiry to clinicians for some time now. For example, Mullen and his co-workers gave this advice in the *New Zealand Medical Journal* in 1989: 'What is clear is that clinicians dealing with psychiatrically disturbed patients need to inquire carefully into past experiences of sexual and physical abuse.'[62] The following year, Susan Ogata made almost the identical recommendation: 'Inquiry and assessment of sexual abuse experiences should become standard in evaluating borderline patients.'[28]

Routine enquiry has also been recommended to family physicians considering the use of psychotropic drugs with female patients,[63] clinicians dealing with general psychiatric patients,[4,64] psychiatrists treating patients with dissociative symptoms[65] and those dealing with drug and alcohol problems[66] among others.

Yet this basic first step of inquiry remains largely untaken at the level of routine medical history taking. For example, Yeo and Yeo, in a 1993 study of women who deliberately and repeatedly harmed themselves and presented in an emergency department, undertook a review of medical records to elicit information on any history of CSA. What they found, given the already oft-documented relationship between the two conditions, was disturbing.

> Reading through individual case records, it was found that no one, not even psychiatrists, elicited a past history of physical, let alone sexual, abuse in a systematic fashion. No written record of any patient gave an indication that the question 'were you abused' was ever asked. Considering its relevance to psychiatric practice this was unexpected and unfortunately limits the results of this study.[44]

So far, the abundance of empirical evidence on the psychological consequences of CSA appears to have brought about little corresponding change in clinical practice, or in the policies made in hospitals and other treatment facilites, that would direct resources and facilities to women with CSA. Swett and his co-workers, commenting on the coexistence of CSA and alcohol problems among women attending a psychiatric outpatients clinic, lamented the lack of facilities: 'However, there is no walk-in service, no crisis management program, and no special service for abused patients.'[66]

LEGITIMATING DISCLOSURE

One of the beneficial consequences of contemporary research, in contrast to that of the 1960s, is that it signals to the women involved that the issue of CSA is being taken seriously by medical and social scientists. The asking of the relevant questions in itself assures women that it is safe to disclose and that their accounts will be accepted as true and meaningful.

Nevertheless, reliance on women's self-reports is regarded as scientifically suspect. As Mark Yama and his colleagues put it: 'The use of self-reports about a history of sexual abuse is similarly open to criticism; here the subject is presumed to be both honest and capable of recalling childhood sexual experiences.'[67] Yet when CSA was not regarded as a significant problem, and women were not perceived as being honest and capable of recalling childhood sexual experiences, accurate estimates of the prevalence of CSA were out of the question. Underreporting continues to be a problem today precisely because these derogatory attitudes are still apparent. Indeed it could be argued that, as far as CSA is concerned, scientific acceptance of women as both honest and reliable witnesses is a necessary precondition for disclosure and the ascertainment of good-quality evidence on this subject.

Reasons given by women for not wishing to disclose abuse and the delayed timing of their disclosures also illustrate that the scientific adequacy of studies on CSA is inextricably bound up with the salience of the questions researchers ask. The matter of salience directs attention to the cognitive and emotional context from which questions arise in the first place and how they are informed by experience, especially, in this case, a gendered experience of the world. This experience relates to the problem of intuitive credibility already discussed in relation to Freud's theorising and enters into clinical practice and the therapeutic relationship as a function of the clinician's ability to empathise or imaginatively occupy the same emotional plane as the patient. Psychotherapeutically, it is difficult to conceive how it would be possible to be empathic with someone whose stated experience you repudiated and denied as a matter of theoretical principle.

It is probably no coincidence that most researchers publishing on CSA are women. Diana Russell, Jessie Anderson, Judy Martin, Sarah Romans-Clarkson, Geri Anderson, Elizabeth Pribor, Susan Ogata, Lenore Terr, Judith Herman, Elaine Carmen, Patricia Rieker and Carol Sheldrick are just some of the researchers involved in improving knowledge of CSA. Books by survivors of abuse like Katherine Brady's *Father's Days: A True Story of Incest*,[68] Ellen Bass and Louise Thornton's *I Never Told Anyone*[69] and Ellen Bass and Laura Davis's *The Courage to Heal*[70] have been instrumental in drawing scientific attention to this widespread social problem, by breaking the long-standing silence and contesting previous psychiatric theories.

By asking questions that proceed from the premise that women are reliable informants whose experiences, understanding and concerns about CSA need to be incorporated into research, theories that purport to represent women will, for once, be grounded in their realities.

As the psychiatry textbooks of an earlier era attest, no study was able to ask the questions posed by Anderson and her colleagues.[15] Why would anyone enquire about a lack of disclosure of abuse when such abuse was not meant to happen in the first place? In fact, the theoretical assumptions that guided earlier perceptions of CSA were incompatible with the establishment of accurate prevalence rates. The inability to find out about prevalence had nothing to do with the availability of evidence and everything to do with theory about what was permissible. Anderson and her co-workers found no variation in rates of reported CSA in any of the age cohorts compared between the period from the late 1930s until the time of the study in the 1990s.[15] In other words, the same evidence was there all along; only the science changed over time.

CSA AND PSYCHOLOGICAL OUTCOMES

Despite differences in the definition of child abuse and the type of sample employed, childhood sexual abuse has now been established as a significant predictor of long-term mental health impairment.

Studies of adults suggest that from one-fifth to three-fifths exhibit serious psychopathology.[14,55] And in the short term one-fifth to two-fifths of abused children who are seen by clinicians show pathological disturbance.[71] Initial effects of rape and sexual abuse include fear of injury and death, anxiety, depression, anger and hostility.[40,41,42,46,72] Guilt and shame are universal responses.[73] Nevertheless the exact nature of the relationship between CSA and adverse psychological outcomes is still being elucidated. CSA is firmly established as a potent risk factor for a great number of negative psychological outcomes, but there remains a need to clarify whether its role is causal. The chief difficulty is that CSA typically coexists with other factors that independently predict mental disorder in adult life, such as coming from a disrupted, unstable home characterised by conflict or mental disorder or experiencing physical or emotional abuse or all these factors at once.

So while there is now a large quantity of evidence on the long-term psychological effects of CSA the quality of the available evidence is somewhat patchy. A unique syndrome, if there is one, that takes into account both the nature and severity of the abuse experienced and precisely delineates the kind of emotional consequences that follow has yet to be described.

In order to develop a more integrated theory, it is critical for research to identify factors that predict differential outcomes of sexual abuse. There is no longer any need for researchers to establish that there is an association between CSA and psychological distress or disorder in adult life — that much is now proven beyond doubt. What is needed and what researchers have been pursuing with more precision most recently is good-quality information on the interrelationship between the frequency, severity and duration of abuse and different patterns of psychological outcome, and in designing studies able to distinguish the effects of CSA from the effects that stem more generally from an upbringing in a broadly pathogenic home environment.

So far, factors definitely implicated in adverse psychological outcomes include the use of force and threats of force, penetrative sex, chronic abuse and abuse by fathers and stepfathers. Evidence regarding the age at which abuse takes place remains equivocal. These factors may occur separately or act in concert with one another, for example, more than one perpetrator may be involved,[67] and intrafamilial abuse generally takes place over a longer period than extrafamilial abuse.[74] Browne and Finkelhor, in their 1986 review of research, concluded that abuse by fathers and stepfathers had a more negative impact than abuse by other perpetrators.[41]

A LINEAR RELATIONSHIP?

Only conceptually and methodologically sophisticated research is able to disentangle the interrelationships between a variety of risk factors and to quantify the independent contribution of CSA to outcome.

One study of women in the community, by Mullen and his co-workers, does provide strong evidence of a linear relationship between severity of abuse and the severity of subsequent psychiatric disorder. More severely abused women reported more psychiatric admissions. Women who had experienced abuse involving intercourse were sixteen times more likely to report psychiatric admissions than those subjected to lesser forms of abuse and, of all the women who gave a history of abuse, 85 per cent had been admitted to a psychiatric unit or hospital at some time in their lives. Mullen et al. comment:

> This finding goes some way to explaining the high rates of childhood sexual abuse reported in samples from in-patient psychiatric units. Such abuse would appear, from this study, not only to be associated with increased vulnerability to psychiatric disorder, but also to make it more likely that admission will be required when disordered.[52]

These researchers were able to distinguish between various degrees of sexual abuse and their associated psychological outcomes and at the same time statistically control for the presence and contribution of other risk factors. They found that women who reported intercourse had the highest psychiatric intervention rate of all and that CSA remained a significant predictor of psychiatric disorder in adult life even after other factors that might account for such disorder were statistically controlled for in the analysis. Such factors included having come from a disrupted, unstable home where one or both parents were absent or had mental health problems or an unsatisfactory or conflict-ridden relationship. In other words, the results of this study suggest very strongly that CSA is in its own right a highly significant factor that presages the development of psychological problems independently of and in addition to any other family and social disadvantages. The same relationship between severity of abuse, such as forced penetrative sex, and an increased likelihood of serious adverse psychological outcomes has also been documented by Finkelhor[8] and Russell.[19]

As well as being more than twice as likely as their non-abused counterparts to have depressive and anxiety disorders, women who reported CSA in Mullen et al.'s study also had higher rates of eating disorders, both anorexic and bulimic types, substance abuse and suicidal behaviour.

Another large-scale community study with a design rigorous enough to examine the aetiological and causative role of CSA in adverse psychological outcomes in adult life was conducted by Stein and his co-workers.[14] The resulting Los Angeles Epidemiologic Catchment Area (ECA) report used a probability sample of more than 3000 men and women. Compared with controls, women who had been sexually abused as children experienced greater severity and frequency of depression and anxiety. Nearly 60 per cent of the women who reported CSA had at least one psychiatric diagnosis, and many had more than one, including major depressive disorder, drug abuse and dependence, and phobias.

This study is particularly important as the data collected enabled rates of psychiatric disorder before and after the assault to be estimated. In this way, the causal sequence between the two was able to be established. The results demonstrated that increased pathology was a consequence of abuse, not an antecedent of it. Both this study and the two New Zealand studies by Mullen et al. quantified the increased risk of depression in women who reported CSA compared with controls.

In Mullen et al.'s first study of 2000 randomly selected women, 20 per cent of the women reporting CSA compared with 6.3 per cent of the non-abused population were identified as having psychiatric disorders on the two measures of psychiatric morbidity employed in the study.[13] Confirming the findings of other studies, 75 per cent of the disorders were predominantly of the depressive type, and the remainder were phobic and anxiety conditions. In the second study, with a different cohort of nearly 1400 Dunedin women, 13 per cent of abused cases were found to be depressed compared with 5 per cent of non-abused women.[52] Similarly, Stein and co-workers found that 17 per cent of women who reported CSA were currently depressed compared with only 3 per cent of the controls.[14] The lifetime prevalence of major depression showed that it affected 22 per cent of CSA women compared with 6 per cent of controls. Taken together, these studies suggest that women are three or more times at risk of developing depression in adult life if they have been sexually abused as children.

While studies of the general community are an excellent way of reliably establishing prevalence and comparing rates of psychiatric disorder between women who report CSA and those who do not, another method, which allows for greater focus on both severe forms of abuse and rare but serious psychiatric disorders, is the study of psychiatric patients. Such studies select women on the basis of their having a diagnosed psychiatric disorder and then proceed to find out the incidence of CSA in their history. If it exceeds base rates of CSA established by community studies, aetiological links are suggested between CSA and the development of the particular psychological disorder or disorders under investigation.

An allied method is to focus on clinical samples of women who all share a history of CSA and then determine whether they also share certain psychiatric disorders. For example, in putting forward the hypothesis that posttraumatic stress disorder is the most likely consequence of CSA and the one that best accommodates and explains the most commonly reported psychological outcomes, Rowan and co-workers only selected women with a history of CSA. They ascertained that 69 per cent met full DSM III R criteria for this disorder.[39]

The best studies of psychiatric patients include a control or comparison group where possible to aid in the interpretation of results. One methodologically strong study of this kind was conducted by Elizabeth Pribor and Stephen Dinwiddie.[51] They compared women who had been victims of incest, defined as 'unwanted sexual contact' with a relative 'too close to marry', matched them for age and race with women who had no history of either physical or sexual abuse and then compared findings for both groups with lifetime prevalence rates for a comparable group of women aged 18–55 reported in the St Louis ECA study.

It is now well established that several of the factors known to result in long-term damage have been found to act in concert with one another, such as chronic abuse and intrafamilial abuse or physical abuse and sexual abuse. It might also be considered axiomatic that, if women have experienced physical and sexual abuse as children, they have suffered severe emotional abuse. Similarly, women who have been sexually abused as children are more likely to be diagnosed with more than one adverse psychological outcome, or receive more than one psychiatric diagnosis, and are all too likely to have experienced more than one form of sexual abuse.

Many subjects in Pribor and Dinwiddie's study reported several forms of abuse.[51] Almost all, for example, reported fondling, but more than a third reported all of the following: cunnilingus, fellatio and sexual intercourse. Attempted sexual intercourse was reported by 5.8 per cent, while 11.5 per cent reported anal intercourse, 13.5 per cent reported group sex, 5.8 per cent had either been forced to watch pornography or had had pornographic pictures or movies taken of them, and 7.7 per cent had undergone some other sexual activity.

The likelihood of having any psychiatric diagnosis was significantly higher for incest victims than for comparison subjects. For most major psychiatric disorders, incest victims had significantly higher lifetime prevalence rates for seven disorders, as defined in DSM III, including agoraphobia, alcohol abuse or dependence, depression, panic disorder, posttraumatic stress disorder, simple phobia and social phobia.

Among incest victims subjected to vaginal intercourse, higher rates were found for agoraphobia, simple phobia, panic disorder and somatisation disorder. When physical force was also a feature of the abuse, the psychiatric outcomes were slightly different again, with significantly higher prevalence rates for four disorders: obsessive-compulsive disorder, simple phobia, somatisation disorder and posttraumatic stress disorder. These slightly differing outcomes suggest that both the nature and severity of abuse encountered is predictive of somewhat different patterns of psychiatric disorder.

Lifetime prevalence rates for a whole range of psychiatric illness were significantly higher than community base rates. For example, 88.5 per cent of the women met DSM III criteria for depression, 69.2 per cent for generalised anxiety disorder and 69.2 per cent for psychosexual dysfunction. These women also had significantly higher rates of agoraphobia, alcohol abuse and substance abuse or dependence, antisocial personality disorder, atypical bipolar disorder, dysthymic disorder (chronic mood disturbance), egodystonic homosexuality (distress about one's sexual orientation), obsessive compulsive disorder, posttraumatic stress disorder, simple and social phobia, somatisation disorder and transsexualism.

Studies of psychiatric patients help to provide further insight into the relationship between severe abuse and increased psychological disorder identified in the large community study by Mullen and his colleagues. Not only is the rate of CSA higher in psychiatric patients than in the general population, but also the severity of abuse they have suffered appears to be reproduced in the severity of the psychiatric symptoms and disorder that follow the abuse. The degree of difference in severity can be gauged by the fact that in the large community study by Anderson and co-workers 70 per cent of abusive episodes lasted less than a year and generally took place between the ages of 8 and 12.[15] By contrast, in one clinical study the average period of abuse was twelve years, almost five different types of abuse occurred and more than two perpetrators were involved,[75] and in another, the average duration of abuse was six years and began when the child was five years old.[76]

In particular, an aetiological relationship has been suggested between the traumatic experience of severe CSA and the development of dissociative symptoms of the kind found in multiple personality disorder and posttraumatic stress disorder.[25,77,78,79,80,81] Further evidence of this relationship is the finding that while dissociative symptoms are highly prevalent in female psychiatric inpatients, they are even more common in patients with a history of childhood abuse, both physical and sexual. Chu and Dill reported that women with both types of abuse manifested significantly greater dissociation than those reporting only one form of abuse.[23] Similarly, Anderson and co-workers found, in their study of dissociative symptoms in a group of women with histories of CSA, that 78 per cent had also experienced physical abuse as children.[15]

Probably the most detailed analysis of the relationship between different aspects of the abuse experience and dissociative symptomatology in female psychiatric patients was carried out by Janet Kirby and her co-workers.[65] Abusive experiences were graded in severity from least severe to most severe (this category included attempted intercourse and completed vaginal, oral or anal intercourse). Nearly all women (95 per cent) had at some time been pressured against their will into sexual contact, and for four-fifths this was abuse of the most severe kind. Eighty-three per cent had experienced physical force, such as being 'hit really hard, kicked, punched, burned, stabbed or thrown down', and 78 per cent had experienced both physical and sexual abuse.

For 59 per cent of women in this study, abuse had begun at or before the age of five, while only 5 per cent were first abused between the ages of 16 and 21. The age at which abuse began was inversely correlated with the severity of dissociative symptomatology; that is, the younger the child when the abuse begins, the higher the level of dissociative symptoms in adult life. As to the question of frequency of abuse, four-fifths were categorised as having experienced chronic abuse, but the women found it difficult to report a finite number, instead writing in comments like 'countless', 'all my life' or 'every day'.

The results of this study confirm Diana Russell's earlier finding that more invasive abuse is associated with a higher level of perceived trauma,[7] and it expands our understanding of what this is likely to imply in terms of symptomatology. The interrelationship of greater dissociation, younger age at onset of abuse and more traumatic and invasive abuse is particularly significant.

On a theoretical level, the findings are congruent with other research that shows an inverse relationship between age and dissociative capacity. Interestingly, a relationship has also been documented between age and hypnotisability, in that younger children tend to be more hypnotisable.[82,83] One study of multiple personality disorder and dissociative symptoms, in which abuse began before the age of five years and lasted for nearly twelve years, 81.4 per cent of the women reported amnesia for large parts of their childhood.[84]

These findings support Lenore Terr's view, based on clinical work with children who have experienced psychic trauma, that dissociation is a learned response that begins as a conscious effort at self-hypnosis.[85] Dissociation can thus be interpreted as the psychological defense that symbolises the victim's attempt to escape overwhelming experience. With repeated use this defence becomes an automatic response to abuse and to any stimulus associated with abuse. The finding of such high levels of dissociative symptoms in women who have experienced the most severe and chronic forms of abuse equally supports Rieker and Carmen's theory that the initial defences used to deal with severe trauma subsequently form the core of survivors' psychopathology and result in a fragmented sense of identity.[16] The evidence supporting a relationship between dissociative symptoms and multiple personality disorder is especially significant in this regard.

While the coexistence of higher rates of CSA, worse abuse and an increase in frequency as well as severity of psychiatric disorder is highly suggestive of aetiological links between them, it is perhaps still too early to claim that direct causal relationships obtain. On the other hand, the wealth of evidence accumulated so far is entirely consistent with the central assertion of Freud's initial theory of hysteria, that childhood trauma in the form of sexual abuse is a potent source of long-term psychiatric morbidity. Contemporary research has confirmed Freud's hypothesis that childhood sexual traumas lead to hysterical reaction, dissociation, depression and somatisation.

Research has implicated CSA in a plethora of psychological disorders, most particularly in markedly increased rates of depression and anxiety, but also in various personality disorders, drug and alcohol abuse, suicidality and self-harm, eating disorders and difficulties in sexual and interpersonal relationships. Previously it had not been considered that CSA might play a role in causing most of these disorders. A massive conceptual remapping of the theoretical domain is warranted to address this inadequacy for disorders in which women predominate.

Depression, which a range of studies show is diagnosed in women twice as often as in men, is a leading candidate for such revision. Until very recently, an individual, intrapsychic and pathologising approach to women's mental health, largely attributable to Freud's theoretical influence, dominated explanations of why women experienced higher rates of depression and other forms of mental illnesses. Interestingly, even in research on depression ostensibly guided by a social model of health, CSA has only been included as a factor in the explanatory model of depression in women very recently.

For instance, the classic 1978 study of Brown and Harris, *Social Origins of Depression: A Study of Psychiatric Disorder in Women*, as its name implies, concentrated on exploring the role of social factors in the development of depression in working-class English mothers.[86] At the time, their work represented a departure from theorising about depression in women that dwelt on intrinsic biological, hormonal and reproductive factors in its model of mental health. Their study was seminal in underscoring the importance of social factors and stressful life events in bringing about depression. Four vulnerability factors that increased the chances of a woman developing depression in the presence of a stressful life event or difficulty were enumerated. The factors were parental loss before the age of 17, particularly the loss of one's mother before the age of 11, the presence at home of three or more children younger than 14, a poor, non-confiding marriage and the lack of full- or part-time employment.

For all the reasons already discussed, childhood sexual abuse was not enquired about at this time. However, once established, the vulnerability factors identified by Brown and Harris continued to receive attention in later research, becoming almost standard elements in other researchers' domains of concern. And most of these factors, especially the quality of a woman's relationship with her husband, have been confirmed in other studies.[87,88,89,90,91,92] None of these studies have conceptualised CSA or concurrent sexual or physical violence as a 'vulnerability factor', a significant negative element in 'self-esteem' or 'social support' or even as a 'stressful life event' in their social model of depression. This theoretical oversight is reminiscent of nineteenth-century views that placed women outside culture. Here, scientific research has placed the specific risks to which their gender exposes them outside its social model of health.

None of the studies sought nor received any information on abuse, nor would it be expected that women would spontaneously disclose childhood sexual or physical abuse in the absence of any reassurance that it was of interest to the researchers or that they would be likely to believe it. The implications of this omission for understanding depression in women only becomes clear once the relevant questions are asked.

Fourteen years after *Social Origins of Depression* was published, George Brown's name is found again as a co-investigator on another study of 286 working-class British mothers living in Islington.[21] The focus of research continued to be on vulnerability factors in the onset of depression among working-class mothers. Women were interviewed three times a year apart. Questions about child sexual abuse were only administered at the third interview. Nine per cent of the mothers reported CSA before the age of 17, but a staggering 64 per cent of them were categorised as being depressed over a three-year period preceding the study. Several childhood factors significantly predicted depression in adult life, including lack of care from a parent, parental violence and having stayed in an institution before the age of 17. While CSA was correlated with these stresses, analysis revealed that CSA was responsible in its own right for an increased risk of depression over and above these other factors, and that women who reported CSA were significantly more likely to have experienced chronic episodes of depression.

It is also worth pointing out that, although this study employed a sample of working-class mothers, the available evidence has not found a relationship between lower social class status and CSA,[7,8] contrary to the beliefs expressed in the psychiatric textbooks canvassed in the previous chapter.

In the past when questions on CSA were not asked, the effect of abuse would have remained hidden in the large amount of unexplained variance in the statistical model. It is impossible not to feel concerned about how many aetiological explanations of psychiatric disorders in women might be marred by this same failure to obtain relevant histories of abuse.

As the British study shows, some researchers are beginning to incorporate the increasingly large literature on the psychological effects of abuse into their main research focus. But at present it seems as if two non-communicating lines of research exist, a bit like parallel play in children. One has CSA as the primary focus of research and proceeds to find associations with depression, anxiety and a whole host of other psychological outcomes. The other has these psychological outcomes as their primary focus and as a result seems far less likely to include CSA in its aetiological model, especially if there is an already established tradition of research on the topic.

Postnatal depression (PND) is a good example of this phenomenon. Around 10–15 per cent of women experience depression after becoming mothers,[93],[94],[95] and there is a large research literature on this condition. Many studies, predictably enough, have concentrated on finding a biological explanation. To date, biologically based research has considered thyroid dysfunction, changes in the levels of oestrogen and progesterone, hypersensitivity of central D2 receptors (i.e. receptors of the central nervous system) and alterations in plasma cortisol, beta endorphin and corticotrophin releasing hormones.

Despite seeing 'exciting times ahead' in which a 'multitude of pathogenetic hypotheses' could be tested, Wieck, writing in 1989, had to admit that 'few encouraging data have yet emerged' in the history of biological research into postnatal mental illness.[96] In particular, there is no proven association between breastfeeding and PND.[97] The absence of encouraging data has, however, done little if anything to blunt enthusiasm for research that looks for the cause of women's depression in their biology.

Another focus in postnatal research has been on 'within-woman' pathology. Evidence exists for previous psychiatric illness,[96] higher levels of neurotic symptoms when well,[93] higher levels of depressive symptoms during pregnancy and a higher incidence of mood disorder, such as premenstrual depression.[98] There is also evidence that supports the importance of events or experiences in the social context to which postnatal depression may be viewed as an understandable reaction, including an increased number of adverse life events in the previous twelve months,[96] marital disharmony,[94] financial worries, poor housing and physical illness or disability.[99] In addition, research that seeks to understand PND by relying on women's own views and experiences has begun to appear.[97] But even in this research (as far as I know) there has never been a systematic investigation of the role of CSA as a vulnerability factor in, or predictor of, postnatal depression.

Yet the known psychological effects of CSA suggest that it should be. For one thing, CSA might be useful in explaining the link between past psychiatric illness and an increased likelihood of experiencing depression after becoming a mother. For another, the research on the emotional consequences of CSA appears highly relevant to the concerns voiced by mothers who are depressed. That is, research has revealed that psychological effects of childhood abuse — fear, hostility, a sense of betrayal and lack of basic trust in others — can compromise the possibility of forming close and satisfying intimate relationships. What, then, could be more emotionally stressful and likely to trigger depression than the task of becoming a mother and feeling responsible for establishing an intimate relationship with a small, dependent and often anxiety-provoking infant?

Perhaps somewhat sentimental notions of motherhood, even when depression is being investigated, have militated against researchers enquiring into the grim reality of past or present sexual violence. But if the evidence from Bifulco, Brown and Adler study[21] are used as a guide, up to two-thirds of mothers who report CSA are depressed, and in their study only 9 per cent of the sample made this admission; thus around 6 per cent of their total sample had a history of CSA and was depressed. Currently, there is no direct evidence of how many of the 15 per cent of women in the community with postnatal depression would also report a history of CSA but, extrapolating from Bifulco et al.'s work, CSA might be significantly related with PND in more than 50 per cent of cases. If this turns out to be the case, it would be the most significant risk factor for PND identified so far.

Moreover, it is essential that the violence women experience in adult life is incorporated into any aetiological model of PND or other forms of emotional distress in which women predominate. Not only is there a proven connection between CSA and revictimisation in adult life, but also violence against women is highly prevalent, and its contribution to emotional distress and disorder should be evaluated independently of any previous history of CSA. Like CSA, research on the prevalence of violence against women only began in the mid 1970s. Before that time social concern about violence was focused on violence that occurred outside the home. The majority of studies were concerned with investigating violence that occurred between men and boys as both perpetrators and victims, and effort was put into improving the safety of streets and neighbourhoods against attacks by unknown assailants.

Intimate violence, that is, violent attacks by those known to the victim, and violence occurring within the home, were largely ignored within a model that owed a lot to the nineteenth-century ideology of separate spheres and preferred to believe, like Auguste Comte, that women and children were 'free in the sacred retirement' of their own homes. Yet research from the 1970s has conclusively established that the family, which ideally provides the structure for nurturance, security and mental health, is often in reality 'the most frequent single locus for violence of all types including homicide'.[100] And while violence outside the family is publicly condemned, violence inside the family has been and still is condoned by many as private, normal and legitimate.

An Australia-wide survey in 1987 found that nearly half the population knew personally either a perpetrator or a victim of domestic violence.[101] Similarly Hilberman, reviewing studies carried out in the USA, reported that violence occurs in at least 50 per cent of American families.[100] It has been estimated that up to two million American wives are battered each year.[73] Like CSA, however, the actual rates remain unknown. The most recent findings from the USA, based on a probability sample of women, revealed that at least 13 per cent — more than 12 million women — had experienced sexual violence, defined as forcible rape.[102]

The public response to family violence is inconsistent. Both disbelief and denial that such violence occurs at all,[103] and a view accepting and condoning violent behaviour to women, have been reported.[101] Violence in the family is disproportionately directed towards women and children, and the assailants are typically men with whom these women have intimate relationships, rather than strangers.[60,99] Ninety per cent of physical and sexual assaults reported by psychiatric patients were committed by family members.[16]

Koss, in a review of research on the mental health impact of violence, notes a set of common core responses.[103] They include a postvictimisation distress response, which if not resolved develops into longer-term, chronic symptom patterns consistent with the criteria for posttraumatic stress disorder. Further, what is interpreted by clinicians as depressed mood might in fact be long-term posttraumatic responses to intimate violence. Carmen and her co-workers have argued that victimisation histories in psychiatric patients tend to be ignored or misunderstood.[16] Similarly, Rosewater, in analysing the diagnoses given to women who had experienced violence from their partners, found that abused women were frequently misdiagnosed becuase their reactions to the violence approximated to and were therefore explained in terms of borderline and other personality disorders.[104]

Yet as Bassuk and co-workers have observed: 'Personality disorder is a diagnosis of social dysfunction and does not take into account the influence of environmental factors extrinsic to the organization of the personality such as poverty, racism, and gender bias.'[105] And, as Dutton has determined, what are seen to be characteristics of personality can in fact be the consequences of marital violence and a result of severe and frequent battering, which did not exist before the violence occurred.[106]

The need to take into account the presence of real danger in women's lives and the likely emotional reactions to it is now beginning to be incorporated into the measures used in assessment of their psychological state. For example, the Minnesota Multiphasic Personality Inventory has been adapted so that it can be used with battered women.

Victims of violence are also at increased risk for repeated victimisation and of using violence against their own children.[107] However, Finkelhor has shown that, while both female and male children may be violently abused, many more men than women go on to become abusers as adults.[8]

MENTAL HEALTH EFFECTS

As pointed out in the Australian National Women's Health Policy, '... women who suffer sexual and physical violence are at greater risk of psychological problems'.[108] Medical attention is sought in fewer than half of known cases.[109] Adult female victims of sexual violence, like children who have been sexually abused, exhibit more psychiatric symptoms, especially depression, anxiety, somatisation, obsessive compulsive disorder and paranoid ideation, than non-victims.[110,111,112] A community-based study in 1990 found that recent rape victims were significantly more likely to meet DSM III criteria for current major depression and drug abuse diagnoses than for other disorders.[113]

Various attempts have been made to develop a theoretical model to explain the psychological effects of living with a violent partner and why it is so difficult for women to extricate themselves from such a situation. This theoretical direction based on evidence and clinical work with women contrasts with the earlier, Freudian-influenced view of which several examples were cited in the previous chapter, that women tolerated if not enjoyed violence because they were 'naturally' masochistic.

Walker has outlined a three-phase violence cycle based on a tension-reduction hypothesis.[116] The three phases are first, a period of tension-building, in which the woman has some minimal control over the abusive incidents; second, a period of inevitability when the acute battering incident occurs; and third, a period of loving contrition and/or no tension.

Psychological responses accompanying each stage are shock and denial, terror and then attempts at ingratiation and appeasement followed by depression, characterised by withdrawn and self-accusatory behaviour.[114] The battered woman in this situation develops learned helplessness,[115] a concept utilised to explain the loss of the ability to predict outcomes after exposure to repeated random and variable aversive stimuli (i.e. psychologically harmful stimuli that cannot be avoided).

Cognitive distortions, including minimisation, denial and dissociation, and a loss of faith in the ability to predict whether one can stop the violence, are common. Victims fear confrontation and learn methods of hiding their pain to protect themselves and of covering up the abuse. Such women might appear to be coping well and to be emotionally stable, and therapists unaware of the psychological effects of family violence might terminate treatment prematurely.[116]

CONCLUSION

The inadequacy of existing scientific knowledge relating to gender differences in mental disorder and its treatment has been increasingly recognised since the mid 1980s. A significant change of perspective on women's mental health was signalled by the priority areas outlined in both the National Institute of Mental Health's document in the USA[117] and the National Women's Health Policy in Australia.[108] Both documents highlighted the way women's subordinate position in society and their gendered life experiences contributed to their mental health. This sociocultural perspective is relatively new in women's mental health, and research on the relationship between women's social position and health is in its infancy. There is an urgent need for the social model of health to be expanded to incorporate the specifically gendered conditions of women's lives that affect their health and to obtain data on most aspects of women's health outside the narrow confines of their reproductive health.[118]

It is not disputed that the frequencies and patterns of mental disorder do differ for men and women, as found by the National Institute of Mental Health's Epidemiological Catchment Area (ECA) Program.[119] Women predominate in diagnoses of depression, agoraphobia, simple phobia, dysthmia, obsessive compulsive disorders, somatisation disorder, panic disorder and histrionic personality disorder. There is evidence to implicate CSA in all of these disorders. What has been questioned throughout this book is the notion that these differences in psychological morbidity are reducible to intrinsic, biologically based differences, rather than very real differences in the traumatic experiences, stressful roles and social position of women, and that the contribution of these factors needs to be accounted for before any alternative, biologically based aetiological formulation is advanced.

In my discussion of neurotic science I have concentrated on one of these significant influences on women's mental health, that of childhood sexual abuse. It is arguably the most blatant but by no means the only example of the way supposedly impartial scientific theories have been intensely partial and have, because of this partiality, been able to ignore those events and experiences extrinsic to women's biology that so significantly, and often so negatively, affect their physical and emotional realities. If the idea of 'proneness' to emotional distress is to be retained at all, then research increasingly needs to turn to these events and experiences in looking for explanations.

Other gendered conditions of women's social lives that demand and are increasingly receiving attention include physical and sexual violence in adult life, the increased likelihood of living in poverty with or without dependent children to care for, the effect of having multiple roles and multiple workloads, of working in lower-paid, lower-status occupations and in experiencing gender-based discrimination and harassment. How these conditions, separately and together, configure women's emotional well-being requires separate treatment beyond the scope of this book.

In examining the relationship between the adequacy of theory and the adequacy of subsequent evidence relating to women's mental health, I have suggested that science for most of this century has been 'neurotic'. It has generated its problematic from what have often been odious fantasies of the other and created evidence in line with these fantasies. Moreover, by reifying these preconceptions into immutable facts of woman's nature, the same theories have actively fomented frustration, distress and neurosis in women, especially in those most likely to seek psychiatric help.

It is ironical that psychoanalysis, whose theories have played such a pivotal role in silencing and misrepresenting women to themselves, was called the 'talking cure' by one of its earliest female patients. Analysis of Freud's revised theory of hysteria and its legacy on more than sixty years of psychiatric thinking about childhood sexual abuse strongly suggests that talking about CSA in therapy was designed to be an exercise in futility. The revised theory might be regarded as a self-sustaining theoretical system sealed against disproof. As far as CSA was concerned, those who didn't do it, psychiatrists like Freud, couldn't believe that it happened; those who did do it, like Herr K, wouldn't admit it and called it a fantasy; and those who experienced it, all the hysterical patients like Dora, could not 'penetrate' this phallocentric discourse of denial and were 'beside themselves'.

For much of this century, then, what has presented itself as impartial science has involved the production of partial and perverse understanding of women's psyches based on biologically reductionistic premises. This is only to be expected when one gender presumes to speak about the nature of the other from a standpoint of unexamined androcentrism. Moreover, I have argued that while these distorted messages are imparted sociologically, through the agency and authority of science, they become lodged intrapsychically and are actively psychogenic.

There is no compelling reason to believe that the discourse that effected this lodgement can be the means of its enlightenment. Until science generates its problematic from those it claims to represent in its theory and research, and women actively contribute to the cultural construction of knowledge, theories of their psychiatric disorder will continue to inscribe the other neurotically. Only when categories of explanation are produced that freely accommodate women's experiences, instead of muting and binding them in the distorting strictures of science's own yellow wallpaper, will theories on women and the causes of their madness have any claim to the strong objectivism Sandra Harding believes possible.[120]

In the meantime, what science needs is a 'listening cure'.

NOTES

1 INTRODUCTION: PRONENESS AND DISORDER

1 Dennerstein, L.D., Astbury, J., Morse, C. (1993) *Psychosocial and Mental Health Aspects of Women's Health*. World Health Organisation, Geneva.

2 Mill, J.S. (1869; 1965) *The Subjection of Women*, Dent, Everyman's Library, London, p. 242.

3 Tan, A. (1989) *The Joy Luck Club*, William Heinemann, London, p. 103.

4 Showalter, E. (1989) 'A historical overview: Opening up the woman's case'. In E. Van Hall and W. Everard (eds), *The Free Woman: Women's Health in the 1990s*, Parthenon, Carnforth, UK, and New Jersey.

5 Wilkerson, I. (1989) 'Charges against doctor bring ire and questions'. *New York Times*, 11 December.

6 Austen, J. (1818; 1975) *Persuasion*, Folio Society, London, p. 219.

7 Benjamin, M. (1992) *Science and Sensibility: Gender and Scientific Enquiry 1780–1945*, Basil Blackwell, Oxford.

8 Harding, S. (1991) *Whose Science? Whose Knowledge?* Open University Press, Buckingham.

9 Ratcliffe, J.W. (1976) 'Analyst biases in KAP surveys: A cross-cultural comparison'. *Studies in Family Planning*, 7:322–330.

10 Gould, S.J. (1989) *Wonderful Life: The Burgess Shale and the Nature of History*, Penguin Books, London, p. 28.

11 Showalter, E. (1987) *The Female Malady: Women, Madness and English Culture, 1830–1980*, Virago, London, p. 150.

12 Showalter, *The Female Malady*, p. 151.

2 THE RAZOR'S EDGE: IDEOLOGY AND SELF-LIMITATION

1 Showalter, E. (1987) *The Female Malady: Women, Madness and English Culture 1830–1980*, Virago, London.

2 Mead, M. (1928; 1971) *Coming of Age in Samoa*, Penguin Books, London.

3 Weedon, C. (1987) *Feminist Practice and Poststructuralist Theory*, Basil Blackwell, Oxford.

4 Simmel, G. (1926) *Philosophische Kultur*, quoted in K. Horney (1967) *The Flight from Womanhood*, in Horney, K., *Feminine Psychology* (ed. Harold Kelman), W.W. Norton & Company, New York, p. 56. Originally published in the *International Journal of Psychoanalysis*, 7, 324–339.

5 Broverman, I.K., Vogel, S.R., Broverman, D.M., Clarkson, F.E., Rosencratz, P.S. (1972) 'Sex role stereotypes: A current appraisal'. *Journal of Social Issues* 28, 58–78.

6 Broverman et al., 'Sex role stereotype', p. 76.

7 Fabrikant, B. (1974) 'The psychotherapist and the female patient: Perceptions, misperceptions and change'. In Franks, V., Burtle, V. (eds), *Women in Therapy*. Brunner/Mazel, New York, pp. 83–112.

8 Fabrikant, 'The psychotherapist and the female patient', p. 91.

9 Watkins, S.C. (1993) 'If all we knew about women was what we read in *Demography*, what would we know?' *Demography* 30, 551–577.

10 Brown, S., Lumley, J., Small, R., Astbury, J. (1994) *Missing Voices: The Experience of Motherhood*, Oxford University Press, Melbourne.

11 Crammond, W.A. (1954) 'Psychological aspects of uterine dysfunction'. *Lancet*, 2, 1241–1245.

12 Ringrose, C.A.D. (1961) 'Psychosomatic influences in the genesis of toxaemia of pregnancy'. *Canadian Medical Journal* 84, 647–651.

13 Blau, A., Slaff, B., Easton, K., Welkowitz, J., Springarn, J., Cohen, J. (1963) 'The psychogenic aetiology of premature births'. *Psychosomatic Medicine* 25, 201–211.

14 McDonald, R.L., Gunther, M.D. (1965) 'Relations between self and parental perceptions of unwed mothers and obstetric complications'. *Psychosomatic Medicine* 27, 31–38.

15 Davids, A., DeVault, S., Talmadge, M. (1961) 'Anxiety, pregnancy and childbirth abnormalities'. *Journal of Consulting Psychology* 25, 76–77.

16 Palmer, R.L., Evans, D. (1971) 'Psychoneurotic status, hostility and complications of pregnancy'. In *Proceedings of the Third International Congress of Psychosomatic Medicine in Obstetrics and Gynaecology*. London.

17 Uddenburg, N., Fagerstrom, C.-F. (1976) 'The deliveries of daughters of reproductively maladjusted mothers'. *Journal of Pyschosomatic Research* 20, 223–230.

18 Deutsch, H. (1945; 1973) *Psychology of Women*, vol. 2. Bantam Books, New York, p. 220.

19 Deutsch, H. (1925) 'The psychology of woman in relation to the functions of reproduction'. Eighth International Psycho-Analytic Congress, Salzburg.

20 Horney, K. (1926; 1967) 'The flight from womanhood', p. 60. Originally published in the *International Journal of Psychoanalysis*, 7, 324–339.

21 Zilboorg, G. (1928) 'Malignant psychoses related to childbirth'. *American Journal of Obstetrics and Gynaecology* 8, 145.

22 Zilboorg, G. (1929) 'The dynamics of schizophrenic reactions related to parenthood'. *American Journal of Psychiatry* 8, 733–767.

23 Zilboorg, quoted in Deutsch, *The Psychology of Women*, vol. 2, p. 283.

24 Astbury, J., Brown, S., Lumley, J., Small, R. (1994) 'Birth events, experiences and social differences in postnatal depression'. *Australian Journal of Public Health* 18, 176–184.

25 Gitlin, M.J., Pasnau, R.O. (1989) 'Psychiatric syndromes linked to reproductive function in women: A review of current knowledge'. *American Journal of Psychiatry*, 146, 1413–1422.

26 Gilman, S.L. (1991) *Inscribing the Other*. University of Nebraska Press, Lincoln.

27 Ardener, E. (1975) 'Belief and the problem of women'. In Ardener, E. (ed.) *Perceiving Women*, Dent, London, p. 22.

28 Hardman, C. (1973) 'Can there be an anthropology of children?' *Journal of the Anthropological Society of Oxford* 4, 85–99.

29 Foucault, M. (1992) 'Lecture 1: 7 January 1976'. In Gordon, C. (ed.), *Power/Knowledge: Selected Interviews and Other Writings 1972–1977*. Pantheon Books, New York.

30 Freud, S. (1933; 1964) 'Femininity'. In Strachey, J. (ed.) *New Introductory Lectures on Psychoanalysis*, Hogarth Press, London, p. 174.

31 Morrison, T. (1993), interview with David Streitfeld, *Washington Post*, reproduced in the *Age*, 23 October.

32 Ardener, 'Belief and the problem of women', p. 22.

33 Jack, D.C. (1991) *Silencing the Self: Women and Depression*. Harvard University Press, Cambridge, Mass.

34 Ardener, S. (1976) *Defining Females: The Nature of Women in Society*. Croom Helm, London.

35 Gilman, C. Perkins (1892; 1981) *The Yellow Wallpaper*, Virago, London, pp. 10–13.

36 Gilman, C. Perkins (1935; 1975) *The Living of Charlotte Perkins Gilman: An Autobiography*. Harper Colophon Books, New York, p. 96.

37 Ehrenreich, B., English, D. (1979), *For Her Own Good: 150 Years of the Experts' Advice to Women*, Pluto Press, London, 92.

38 Gilman, *The Living of Charlotte Perkins Gilman*, p. 119.

39 Gilman, *The Yellow Wallpaper*, p. 10.

40 Gilbert, S.M., Gubar, S. (1979) *The Madwoman in the Attic: The Woman Writer and the Nineteenth Century Literary Imagination.* Yale University Press, New Haven, Conn. and London.

41 Gilman, *The Yellow Wallpaper*, p. 12.

42 Gilman, *The Yellow Wallpaper*, p. 12.

43 Gilman, *The Yellow Wallpaper*, p. 19.

44 Gilman, *The Yellow Wallpaper*, p. 30.

45 Vertinsky, P. (1990) *The Eternally Wounded Woman: Women, Doctors and Exercise in the Nineteenth Century.* Manchester University Press, Manchester and New York.

3 WILD WOMEN AND SEX IN SCIENCE

1 Linton, E.L. (1891) 'The wild women: As politicians'. *Nineteenth Century*, 30, p. 86.

2 Fee, E. (1978) 'Science and the "woman question", 1860–1920: A study of English scientific periodicals.' Princeton University, PhD dissertation.

3 Fee, 'Science and the "woman question"', p. 12.

4 Benjamin, M. (1991) (ed.), *Science and Sensibility: Gender and Scientific Enquiry 1780–1945*. Basil Blackwell, Oxford, p. 4.

5 Benjamin, *Science and Sensibility*, p. 4.

6 Russett Eagle, C. (1989) *Sexual Science: The Victorian Construction of Womanhood*. Harvard University Press, Cambridge, Mass.

7 Dijkstra, B. (1986) *Idols of Perversity: Fantasies of Feminine Evil in Fin-de-siècle Culture*, Oxford University Press, New York and London, p. 160.

8 Stephen, L. (1883) 'Remarks on the influence of science'. *Popular Science Monthly*, 24, p. 82.

9 Dijkstra, *Idols of Perversity*, p. 160.

10 Darwin, C., *The Descent of Man and Selection in Relation to Sex*, quoted in Dijkstra, *Idols of Perversity*, p. 172.

11 Darwin, *The Descent of Man*, quoted in Dijkstra, *Idols of Perversity*, p. 172.

12 Quoted in Hall, Stanley G. (1904) *Adolescence: Its Psychology and Its Relations to Physiology, Anthropology, Sociology, Sex, Crime, Religion and Education.* 2 vols. Sidney Appleton, London, D. Appleton & Co., New York, p. 578.

13 Cooke, N. (1870) *Satan in Society*, p. 86, quoted in Dijkstra, *Idols of Perversity*, p. 65.

14 Quoted in Fee, 'Science and the "woman question"', p. 12.

15 Quoted in Hall, *Adolescence*, p. 603.

16 Jordanova, L. (1989) *Sexual Visions: Images of Gender in Science and Medicine Between the Eighteenth and Twentieth Centuries.* Harvester Wheatsheaf, Hemel Hempstead, UK.

17 Jordanova, *Sexual Visions*, p. 45.

18 Ehrenreich, B., English, D. (1978; 1988) *For Her Own Good: 150 Years of the Experts' Advice to Women*, Pluto Press, London, p. 74.
19 Vogt, C., quoted in Dijkstra, *Idols of Perversity*, pp. 166–7.
20 McGrigor Allan, J. (1869) 'On the real differences in the minds of men and women'. *Journal of the Anthropological Society*, 7, p. 212.
21 Broca, P. (1868) 'On anthropology'. *Anthropological Review*, 6, p. 47.
22 Hunt, J. (1864) 'On the Negro's place in nature', *Anthropological Review*, 2.
23 Vogt quoted in Dijkstra, *Idols of Perversity*, pp. 191–2.
24 Gilman, S.L. (1991) *Inscribing the Other*. University of Nebraska Press, Lincoln and London.
25 Darwin, *The Descent of Man*, p. 702.
26 Benjamin, *Science and Sensibility*, p. 4.
27 Schopenhauer, A. (1851) 'Of women', quoted in Dijkstra, *Idols of Perversity*, p. 296.
28 Topinard, P. (1878) *Anthropology*, Chapman & Hall, London, p. 145.
29 Mobius, P. (1898), *On the Physiological Debility of Woman*, quoted in Dijkstra, *Idols of Perversity*, p. 172.
30 Mobius, quoted in Dijkstra, *Idols of Perversity*, p. 172.
31 Hall, *Adolescence*, p. 11.
32 Mobius, quoted in Dijkstra, *Idols of Perversity*, p. 172.
33 Hall, *Adolescence*, p. 639.
34 Hall, *Adolescence*, p. 639.
35 Hall, *Adolescence*, p. 632.
36 Quoted in Ehrenreich and English, *For Her Own Good*, p. 128.
37 Hall, *Adolescence*, p. 602.
38 Hall, *Adolescence*, p. 633.
39 Ruskin, J. (1865), *Sesame and Lilies*, Blackie & Son, London, pp. 77–8.
40 Cleaves, M. quoted in Ehrenreich and English, *For Her Own Good*, p. 130.
41 Geddes, P. and Thomson, J.A. (1889; 1901) *The Evolution of Sex*. Walter Scott, London.
42 Hall, *Adolescence*, p. 561.
43 Hall, *Adolescence*, p. 566.
44 Hall, *Adolescence*, p. 562.
45 Hall, *Adolescence*, p. 562.
46 Hall, *Adolescence*, p. 639.
47 Mill, J.S. (1869; 1965) *The Subjection of Women*, Dent, Everyman's Library, London, p. 238.
48 Hall, *Adolescence*, p. 582.
49 Gilman, *Inscribing the Other*.
50 Crichton Browne, J. (1892) 'Sex in education', *Educational Review*, p. 577.
51 Wilson, J.T. (1885) 'Menstrual disorders in schoolgirls', *Texas Sanitarium*, June, p. 574.
52 Engelmann, quoted in Hall, *Adolescence*, p. 588.

53 Hall, *Adolescence*, p. 634.
54 Finch, H. quoted in Hall, *Adolescence*, p. 582.
55 Clouston, T.S. (1884) 'Female education from a medical point of view'. *Popular Science Monthly*, pp. 214 and 319.
56 Beard, G. (1881) *American Nervousness: Its Causes and Consequences*, G.P. Putnam's Sons, New York.
57 Hall, *Adolescence*, p. 640.
58 Hall, *Adolescence*, p. 574.
59 Vertinsky, P. (1989) *The Eternally Wounded Woman*. Manchester University Press, Manchester, p. 79
60 Turner, Dr E.B. (1896) quoted in Vertinsky, *The Eternally Wounded Woman*, p. 79.
61 Benjamin, *Science and Sensibility*.
62 Faludi, S. (1991) *Backlash: The Undeclared War Against Women*, Chatto & Windus, London.
63 Greenstein, B. (1993) *The Fragile Male*. Boxtree, London.

4 FREUD'S SCIENCE

1 Quoted in Bettelheim, B. (1983; 1991) *Freud and Man's Soul*, Penguin, London, p. 8.
2 Quoted in Gay, P. (1988) *Freud: A Life for Our Time*, J.M. Dent & Sons, London, p. 207.
3 The *Malleus Maleficarum* (or *The Witches' Hammer*) was published in 1487. It was written by two Dominican monks, Heinrich Kramer and James Spengler, who were appointed by Pope Innocent VIII in 1484 to investigate and eliminate witchcraft. A violently misogynistic text, which held that 'All witchcraft comes from carnal lust which in women is insatiable', *The Witches' Hammer* went through thirty editions within two hundred years of its publication.
4 Freud, S. (1895; 1954) 'Project for a scientific psychology'. In *The Origins of Psychoanalysis: Letters to Wilhelm Fliess, Drafts and Notes* (eds Bonaparte, M., Freud, A., Kris, E.) Imago, London.
5 Freud, S. (1933; 1964) 'Femininity'. In *New Introductory Lectures on Psychoanalysis, Standard Edition of the Complete Psychological Works of Sigmund Freud* vol. 22 (trans. and ed. J. Strachey), Hogarth Press, London. (Hereafter abbreviated to SE followed by volume number.)
6 Comte, A. (1851; 1875–77) *System of Positive Polity*, 2 vols, Longman's Green, London, vol. 2, p. 197.
7 Comte, *System of Positive Policy*, vol. 1, p. 208.
8 Freud, Ernst L. (ed.) (1961) *Letters of Sigmund Freud, 1873–1939* (trans. Tania and James Stern), Hogarth Press, London, p. 90.
9 Freud, S. (1925; 1991) 'Some psychical consequences of the anatomical distinction between the sexes'. In vol. 7, *On Sexuality* (trans. and ed. J. Strachey; Penguin edn ed. A. Richards), Penguin, London.
10 Quoted in Gay, *Freud: A Life for Our Time*, p. 513.

11 Freud, S. (1925) 'Autobiographical study', SE 20, p. 72.

12 Ritvo, L.B. (1990) *Darwin's Influence on Freud: A Tale of Two Sciences*. Yale University Press, New Haven, Conn.

13 Freud, S. (1915–16) *Introductory Lectures on Psychoanalysis*, SE 15, p. 199.

14 Freud, S. 'Interpretation of dreams', SE 5, p. 548.

15 Freud, S. *Totem and Taboo*, SE 13, p. 126.

16 Freud, S. (1905; 1962) *Three Essays on the Theory of Sexuality*, SE 7, Hogarth Press and the Institute of Psycho-Analysis, London.

17 Masson, J.M. (trans. and ed.) (1985) *The Complete Letters of Sigmund Freud to Wilhelm Fliess 1887–1904*, Belknap Press of Harvard University Press, Cambridge, Mass. and London, p. 272.

18 Freud, S. (1905; 1977) 'Fragment of an analysis of a case of hysteria', *Case Histories 1* (ed. J. Strachey), vol. 8, Pelican, London, pp. 31–153.

19 Gellner, E. (1985) *The Psychoanalytic Movement*, Palladin, London, p. 6.

20 Ritvo, *Darwin's Influence on Freud*.

21 Freud, S. (1931; 1957) 'Female sexuality'. In *Collected Papers*, vol. 5 (ed. Strachey, J.), Hogarth Press, London.

22 Freud, S. (1933) 'Femininity'. In *New Introductory Lectures on Psychoanalysis* (ed. Strachey, J.) SE 22, Hogarth Press, London, p. 170.

23 Freud, 'Female sexuality', p. 259.

24 Freud, 'Some psychical consequences...', pp. 335–6.

25 Freud, 'Femininity', p. 164.

26 Freud, 'Femininity', p. 160.

27 Freud, 'Some psychical consequences...', p. 340.

28 Freud, 'Femininity', p. 151.

29 Freud, 'Femininity', p. 160.

30 Freud, 'Some psychical consequences...', p. 342.

31 Freud, S. (1905; 1991) 'The transformations of puberty', in SE 7, *On Sexuality*, p. 169.

32 Freud, 'Femininity', p. 28.

33 Freud, 'Femininity', p. 145.

34 Freud, 'Femininity', p. 174.

35 Wilby, L., quoted in Gellner, *The Psychoanalytic Movement*, p. 10.

5 A SCIENTIFIC FAIRY TALE

1 Dijkstra, B. (1986) *Idols of Perversity*, Oxford University Press, Oxford.

2 James, A. (1982) *The Diary of Alice James* (ed. L. Edel), Penguin Books, New York, p. 64.

3 Lewis, R.W.B. (1991) *The Jameses: A Family Narrative*, Farrar, Strauss & Giroux, New York, p. 463.

4 Lewis, *The Jameses*, p. 386.

5 Shorter, E. (1989) 'Women and Jews in a private nervous clinic in late nineteenth century Vienna', *Medical History*, 33, 149–183.

6 Freud, S. (1896) 'The aetiology of hysteria', SE 3, p. 203.

7 Freud, 'The aetiology of hysteria', pp. 206–7.

8 Freud, 'The aetiology of hysteria', p. 207.

9 Freud, 'The aetiology of hysteria', p. 207.

10 Freud, 'The aetiology of hysteria', p. 221.

11 Freud, 'The aetiology of hysteria', p. 209.

12 Freud, 'The aetiology of hysteria', pp. 207–8.

13 Kerr, J. (1994) *A Most Dangerous Method: The Story of Jung, Freud and Sabina Spielrin*, Vintage Books, New York, p. 30.

14 Quoted in Shorter, E. (1992) *From Paralysis to Fatigue: A History of Psychosomatic Illness in the Modern Era*, Free Press, New York, p. 244.

15 Freud, S. (1925) 'Autobiographical study', SE 20, pp. 33–4.

16 Appignanesi, L., Forrester, J. (1993) *Freud's Women*, Virago, London, p. 106.

17 Malcolm, J. (1982) *Psychoanalysis: The Impossible Profession*, Picador, London, p. 21.

18 Schur, M. (1972) *Freud: Living and Dying*, International Universities Press, New York.

19 Masson, J. (1984; 1992) *The Assault on Truth*, Fontana, London.

20 Freud, S. (1895; 1954) *The Origins of Psychoanalysis: Letters to Wilhelm Fleiss, Drafts and Notes* (eds Bonaparte, M., Freud, A., Kris, E.), Imago, London, p. 312.

21 Gilman, S.L. (1989) *Sexuality: An Illustrated History*, John Wiley, New York, p. 265.

22 Gilman, S. (1991) *The Jew's Body*, Routledge, New York.

23 Gilman, *Sexuality*, p. 265

24 Gilman, *Sexuality*, p. 267.

25 Weininger, O. (1904; 1906) *Sex and Character*, William Heinemann, London.

26 Quoted in Monk, R. (1991) *Ludwig Wittgenstein: The Duty of Genius*, Vintage, London, p. 19.

27 Weininger, *Sex and Character*, p. 330.

28 Weininger, *Sex and Character*, p. 303.

29 Weininger, *Sex and Character*, p. 306.

30 Weininger, *Sex and Character*, pp. 307–8, 313–14.

31 Weininger, *Sex and Character*, p. 312.

32 Freud, *The Origins of Psychoanalysis*, p. 171.

33 Gilman, *Sexuality*, p. 268.

34 Letter from Ernest Jones, quoted in Masson, *The Assault on Truth*, p. 73.

35 Quoted in Freud, *The Origins of Psychoanalysis*, p. 6.

36 Masson, J.M. (trans. and ed.) (1985) *The Complete Letters of Sigmund Freud to Wilhelm Fliess 1887–1904*, Belknap Press of Harvard University Press, Cambridge, Mass. and London, p. 117.

37 Masson, *Complete Letters of Sigmund Freud*, p. 117.
38 Quoted in Masson, *The Assault on Truth*, p. 69.
39 Masson, *Complete Letters of Sigmund Freud*, p. 127.
40 Freud, S. (1900), 'The interpretation of dreams', SE 4, pp. 262–3.
41 Devereux, G. (1954) 'Why Oedipus killed Laius: A note on the complementary Oedipus', *International Journal of Psychoanalysis*, 34, 132–141.
42 Freud, *The Origins of Psychoanalysis*, p. 233.

6 ALMOST BESIDE HERSELF: THE CASE OF DORA

1 Freud, S. (1905; 1977)) 'Fragment of an analysis of a case of hysteria', *Case Histories* (ed. J. Strachey), vol. 8, Pelican, London, p. 154.
2 Freud, 'Fragment of an analysis', p. 79.
3 Freud, S. (1895; 1954) *The Origins of Psychoanalysis: Letters to Wilhelm Fleiss, Drafts and Notes* (eds Bonaparte, M., Freud, A., Kris, E.) Imago, London, p. 81.
4 Freud, *The Origins of Psychoanalysis*, p. 83.
5 Freud, *The Origins of Psychoanalysis*, p. 334.
6 Gilman, S. (1991) *The Jew's Body*, p. 81.
7 Bernheimer, C. & Kahane, C. (eds) (1985) *In Dora's Case: Freud–Hysteria–Feminism*, Virago, London, pp. 25–6.
8 Freud, 'Fragment of an analysis', p. 52.
9 Freud, 'Fragment of an analysis', p. 40.
10 Freud, 'Fragment of an analysis', p. 150.
11 Quoted in M. Sprengnether, 'Enforcing Oedipus: Freud and Dora', in Bernheimer and Kahane, *In Dora's Case*, p. 254.
12 Freud, 'Fragment of an analysis', p. 48.
13 Freud, 'Fragment of an analysis', p. 49.
14 Freud, 'Fragment of an analysis', p. 150
15 Freud, 'Fragment of an analysis', p. 56.
16 Freud, 'Fragment of an analysis', p. 97.
17 Buckley, P. (1989) 'Fifty years after Freud: Dora, the Rat Man and the Wolf Man', *American Journal of Psychiatry*, 146, 1394–1403.
18 Freud, *The Origins of Psychoanalysis*, pp. 195–6.
19 Freud, 'Fragment of an analysis', pp. 65–6.
20 Freud, 'Fragment of an analysis', p. 91.
21 Freud, 'Fragment of an analysis', p. 91.
22 Freud, 'Fragment of an analysis', p. 57.
23 Freud, 'Fragment of an analysis', p. 112.
24 Steinhauer, P.D. & Rae-Grant, Q. (eds) (1983) *Psychological Problems of the Child in the Family*, Basic Books, New York.
25 Bloch, S. & Singh, B.S. (1994) *Foundations of Clinical Psychiatry*, Melbourne University Press, Melbourne.
26 Anderson, J., Martin, J., Mullen, P., Romans, S., Herbison, P. (1993) 'Prevalence of childhood sexual abuse experiences in a com-

munity sample of women'. *Journal of the American Academy of Child and Adolescent Psychiatry*, 32, 5: 911–919.

27 Freud, 'Fragment of an analysis', p. 133.
28 Freud, 'Fragment of an analysis', p. 59.
29 Freud, 'Fragment of an analysis', p. 59.
30 Freud, 'Fragment of an analysis', p. 99.
31 Freud, 'Fragment of an analysis', p. 106.
32 Freud, 'Fragment of an analysis', p. 106.
33 Freud, 'Fragment of an analysis', p. 106.
34 Freud, 'Fragment of an analysis', p. 71. My emphasis.
35 Freud, 'Fragment of an analysis', p. 66.
36 Freud, 'Fragment of an analysis', p. 163.
37 Freud, 'Fragment of an analysis', p. 94.
38 Gilman, *The Jew's Body*, p. 43.
39 Freud, 'Fragment of an analysis', p. 69.
40 Freud, 'Fragment of an analysis', p. 81.
41 Freud, 'Fragment of an analysis', p. 105.
42 Freud, 'Fragment of an analysis', p. 107.
43 Freud, 'Fragment of an analysis', p. 47.
44 Masson, J. (1988) *Against Therapy*, Collins, London, p. 105.
45 Freud, 'Fragment of an analysis', p. 79.
46 Freud, 'Fragment of an analysis', p. 161.
47 Lacan, J. (1985) 'Intervention on transference' in (Bernheimer, C. & Kahane, C., eds) *In Dora's Case*.
48 See Bernheimer & Kahane (eds), *In Dora's Case*.
49 Freud, 'Fragment of an analysis', p. 160.
50 Freud, 'Fragment of an analysis', p. 162.
51 Freud, 'Fragment of an analysis', p. 66.
52 Gallop, J. (1982) *The Daughter's Seduction: Feminism and Psychoanalysis*, Cornell University Press, Ithaca, NY, p. 133.
53 Freud, 'Fragment of an analysis', p. 164
54 Freud, 'Fragment of an analysis', p. 18.
55 Freud, S. (1896; 1962) 'The aetiology of hysteria', SE 3, p. 205.
56 Weedon, C. (1987) *Feminist Practice and Poststructuralist Theory*, Basil Blackwell, Oxford, p. 9.

7 THE FREUDIAN LEGACY

1 Showalter, E. (1987) *The Female Malady: Women, Madness and English Culture, 1830–1980*. Virago Press, London, p. 250.
2 Harding, S. (ed.) (1987) *Feminism and Methodology*. Indiana University Press, Bloomington.
3 Mitchell, J. (1975) *Psychoanalysis and Feminism*, Penguin, Harmondsworth.
4 Margo, J. (1994) 'Gaslighting snuffs the flame', *Sydney Morning Herald*, 15 September.

5 Dennerstein, L., Astbury, J., Morse, C. (1993) *Psychosocial and Mental Health Aspects of Women's Health.* World Health Organisation, Geneva.

6 Rieker, P.P., Carmen, E. (H) (1986) 'The victim-to-patient process: The disconfirmation and transformation of abuse'. *American Journal of Orthopsychiatry*, 56: 360–370.

7 Ogata, S.N., Silk, K.R., Goodrich, S., Lohr, N.E., Wessten, D., Hill, E.M. et al. (1990) 'Childhood sexual and physical abuse in adult patients with borderline personality disorder'. *American Journal of Psychiatry*, 147: 1008–1013.

8 Morrison, J. (1989) 'Childhood sexual histories of women with somatization disorder'. *American Journal of Psychiatry*, 146: 239–241.

9 Morrison, 'Childhood sexual histories…', p. 241.

10 Morrison, 'Childhood sexual histories…', p. 240.

11 Zilboorg, G. (1928) 'Malignant psychoses related to childbirth'. *American Journal of Obstetrics and Gynecology*, 15:145.

12 Scully, D., Bart, P. (1973) 'A funny thing happened on the way to the orifice: Women in gynecology textbooks'. *American Journal of Sociology*, 78: 1045–1050.

13 Scully & Bart, 'A funny thing happened', p. 1045.

14 Koutroulis, G. (1990) 'The orifice revisited: Women in gynaecological texts'. *Community Health Studies*, 14:73–84.

15 Ross, T.A. (1941) *The Common Neuroses: Their Treatment by Psychotherapy*, 2nd edn. Edward Arnold & Co, London.

16 Ross, *The Common Neuroses*, p. 179.

17 Pribor, E.F., Dinwiddie, S.H. (1992) 'Psychiatric correlates of incest in childhood'. *American Journal of Psychiatry*, 149:52–56.

18 Deutsch, H. (1945; 1973) *The Psychology of Women: A Psychoanalytic Interpretation.* Bantam books, New York, vol. 2, p. 87.

19 Fenichel, O. (1946) *The Psychoanalytic Theory of Neurosis.* Routledge & Kegan Paul, London, p. 90.

20 Fenichel, *The Psychoanalytic Theory of Neurosis*, p. 91.

21 Richards, T.W. (1946) *Modern Clinical Psychology*, McGraw-Hill, New York, p. 126.

22 Richards, *Modern Clinical Psychology*, p. 127.

23 Rees, J.R. (ed.) (1949) *Modern Practice in Psychological Medicine.* Butterworth & Co., London.

24 Leventhal, J.M. (1990) 'Epidemiology of child sexual abuse'. In R.K. Oates (ed.), *Understanding and Managing Child Sexual Abuse*, Sydney, Harcourt Brace Jovanovich; Finkelhor, D., Hotaling, G., Lewis I.A., Smith, C. (1990) 'Sexual abuse in a national survey of adult men and women: Prevalence, characteristics and risk factors'. *Child Abuse and Neglect*, 14, 19–28.

25 Skottowe, I. (1953) *Clinical Psychiatry for Practitioners and Students*, Eyre & Spottiswoode, London, p. 75.

26 Kleinman, D.l., Cohen, L.J. (1991) 'The decontextualization of mental illness: The portrayal of work in psychiatric drug advertisements'. *Social Science and Medicine*, 32: 867–874.

27 Kleinman and Cohen, 'The decontextualization of mental illness', p. 867.

28 Kanner, L. (1957) *Child Psychiatry*, 3rd edition, Blackwell Scientific Publications, Oxford, p. 575.

29 Kanner, *Child Psychiatry*, p. 575.

30 Kanner, *Child Psychiatry*, p. 571.

31 Kanner, *Child Psychiatry*, p. 570.

32 Kanner, *Child Psychiatry*, p. 572.

33 Russell Davis, D. (1957) *An Introduction to Psychopathology*, Oxford University Press, London.

34 Russell Davis, *An Introduction to Psychopathology*, pp. 174–5.

35 Howells, J.G. (1968) *Theory and Practice of Family Psychiatry*. Oliver & Boyd, Edinburgh.

36 Shirley, H.F. (1963) *Pediatric Psychiatry*, Harvard University Press, Cambridge, Mass., p. 340.

37 Finkelhor, D. (1979) *Sexually Victimized Children*. Free Press, New York.

38 Gregory, I. (1968) *Fundamentals of Psychiatry*. W.B. Saunders Company, Philadelphia, p. 517. Emphasis added.

39 Gregory, *Fundamentals of Psychiatry*, p. 520.

40 Gregory, *Fundamentals of Psychiatry*, p. 520.

41 Gregory, *Fundamentals of Psychiatry*, p. 520.

42 Sim, M. (1968) *Guide to Psychiatry*, 2nd edn, E. & S. Livingstone, Edinburgh, p. 682.

43 Batchelor, I.R.C. (1969) *Henderson and Gillespie's Textbook of Psychiatry*. Oxford University Press, London, p. 683.

44 Sim, *Guide to Psychiatry*, p. 683. Emphasis added.

45 Freud, S. (1905; 1977) 'Fragment of an analysis of a case of hysteria', *Case Histories* (ed. J. Strachey), vol. 8, Pelican, London, p. 83.

46 *Diagnostic and Statistical Manual of Mental Disorders* (DSM-IV). (1994) American Psychiatric Association, Washington.

47 Ware, N.C., Kleinman, A (1992) 'Culture and somatic experience: The social course of illness in neurasthenia and chronic fatigue syndrome', *Psychosomatic Medicine*, 54:546–560.

48 Pribor, E.F., Yutzy, S.H., Dean, J.T., Wetzel, R.D. (1993) 'Briquet's syndrome, dissociation and abuse'. *American Journal of Psychiatry*, 150:1507–1511.

49 Briere, J., Runtz, M. (1986) 'Suicidal thoughts and behaviours in former sexual abuse victims'. *Canadian Journal of Behavioral Science*, 18: 413–423.

50 See, for example, Finkelhor, D., Browne, A. (1985) 'The traumatic impact of child sexual abuse: A conceptualization'. *American Journal of Orthopsychiatry*, 55: 530–541; Bryer, J.B., Nelson, B.A., Miller, J.B., Krol, P.A. (1987) 'Childhood sexual and physical abuse as factors in adult psychiatric illness'. *American Journal of Psychiatry*, 144:1426–1430; Morrison, J. (1989) 'Childhood sexual histories of women with somatization disorder'. *American Journal of Psychiatry*, 146: 239–241; and Arnold, R.P., Rogers, D., Cook,

D.A.G. (1990) 'Medical problems of adults who were sexually abused in childhood', *British Medical Journal*, 300: 705–708.

51 La Barbera, J.D., Dozier, J.E. (1980) 'Hysterical seizures: The role of sexual exploitation'. *Psychosomatics*, 21: 890–897.

52 See Backman, G.A., Moeller, T.P., Bernett, J. (1988) 'Childhood sexual abuse and the consequences in adults'. *Obstetrics and Gynaecology*, 4: 631–642; Harrop-Griffiths, J., Katon, W., Walker, E. (1988) 'The association between chronic pelvic pain, psychiatric diagnosis and childhood sexual abuse'. *Obstetrics and Gynaecology*, 71:589–594; and Draijer, N. (1989) 'Long-term psychosomatic consequences of child sexual abuse'. In E. van Hall, W. Everard (eds), *The Free Woman*, Parthenon Publishing, Lancaster, UK.

53 Arnold, R.P., Rogers, D., Cook, D.A.G. (1990) 'Medical problems of adults who were sexually abused in childhood', *British Medical Journal*, 300:705–708.

54 Deutsch, F. (1957; 1985) 'A footnote to Freud's "Fragment of an analysis of a case of hysteria"' in C. Bernheimer & C. Kahane (eds), *In Dora's Case*, Virago, London, pp. 35–43. First published in *Psychoanalytic Quarterly* 26: 159–167.

55 Mullen, P.E., Martin, J.L., Anderson, J.C., Romans, S.E., Herbison, G.P. (1993) 'Childhood sexual abuse and mental health in adult life'. *British Journal of Psychiatry*, 163:721–732.

56 Pribor, E.F., Dinwiddie, S.H. (1992) 'Psychiatric correlates of incest in childhood'. *American Journal of Psychiatry*, 149, p. 55.

8 INCREASED ATTENTION: INCREASED EVIDENCE

1 Kempe, C.H., Silverman, F.N., Steele, B.F. (1962) 'The battered child syndrome'. *Journal of the American Medical Association*, 181:17–24.

2 Kempe, C.H. (1978) 'Sexual abuse: Another hidden pediatric problem'. *Pediatrics*, 62:382–389.

3 Freud, S. 'The aetiology of hysteria', in *The Standard Edition of the Complete Psychological Works of Sigmund Freud* (ed. and trans. J. Strachey), vol. 3, Hogarth Press and the Institute of Psycho-Analysis, London, pp. 191–221.

4 Brown, G.R., Anderson, B. (1991) 'Psychiatric morbidity in adult inpatients with childhood histories of sexual and physical abuse'. *American Journal of Psychiatry*, 148:55–61.

5 Finkelhor, D., Hotaling, G., Lewis, I.A. & Smith, C. (1990) 'Sexual abuse in a national survey of adult men and women: Prevalence characteristics and risk factors'. *Child Abuse and Neglect*, 14:19–28.

6 Leventhal, J.M. (1990) 'Epidemiology of child sexual abuse'. In *Understanding and Managing Child Sexual Abuse* (ed. R.K. Oates). Harcourt Brace Jovanovich, Sydney.

7 Russell, D.E. (1983) 'The incidence and prevalence of intrafamilial and extrafamilial sexual abuse of female children'. *Child Abuse and Neglect*, 7:133–146.

8 Finkelhor, D. (1984) *Child Sexual Abuse: New Theory and Research*. Free Press, New York.

9 Wyatt, G.E. (1985) 'The sexual abuse of Afro-American and white American women in childhood'. *Child Abuse and Neglect*, 9:507–519.

10 Baker, A.W., Duncan S.P. (1985) 'Child sexual abuse: A study of prevalence in Great Britain'. *Child Abuse and Neglect*, 9: 457-467.

11 Bagley, C., Ramsay, R. (1986) 'Sexual abuse in childhood: Psychosocial outcomes and implications for social work practice'. *Journal of Social Work and Human Sexuality*, 4:33–47.

12 Kilpatrick, A. (1986) 'Some correlates of women's childhood sexual experiences: A retrospective study'. *Journal of Sex Research*, 22:221–242.

13 Mullen, P.E., Romans-Clarkson, S.E., Walton, V.A. & Herbison, P. (1988) 'Impact of sexual and physical abuse on women's mental health'. *Lancet*, 16:841–845.

14 Stein, J.A, Golding, J.M., Siegel, J.M., Burnam, M.A. & Sorenson, S.B. (1988) 'Long-term psychological sequelae of child sexual abuse: The Los Angeles Epidemiologic Catchment Area Study'. In G.E. Wyatt and G.J. Powell (eds), *Lasting Effects of Child Sexual Abuse*, Sage, Newbury Park, Cal., pp. 135–54.

15 Anderson, J., Martin, J., Mullen, P., Romans, S., Herbison, P. (1993) 'Prevalence of childhood sexual abuse experiences in a community sample of women'. *Journal of the American Academy of Child and Adolescent Psychiatry*, 32:911–919.

16 Carmen, E.(H)., Rieker, P.P. & Mills, T. (1984) 'Victims of violence and psychiatric illness'. *American Journal of Psychiatry*, 141:378–383.

17 Margolin, L. (1992) 'Sexual abuse by grandparents'. *Child Abuse and Neglect*, 16:735–742.

18 Murphy, S.M., Kilpatrick, D.G., Amick-McMullan, A., Veronen, L.J., Paduhovich, J., Best, C.L., Villeponteaux, L.A. and Saunders, B.E. (1988) 'Current psychological functioning of child sexual assault survivors'. *Journal of Interpersonal Violence*, 3:55–79.

19 Russell, D.E. (1986) *The Secret Trauma: Incest in the Lives of Girls and Women*, Basic Books, New York.

20 Finkelhor, D. (1979) *Sexually Victimized Children*. Free Press, New York.

21 Bifulco, A., Brown, G.W., Adler, Z. (1991) 'Early sexual abuse and clinical depression in adult life', *British Journal of Psychiatry*, 159:115–122.

22 Jacobson, A., Richardson, B. (1987) 'Assault experiences of 100 psychiatric inpatients: Evidence of the need for routine inquiry'. *American Journal of Psychiatry*, 144:908–913.

23 Chu, J.A., Dill, D.L. (1990) 'Dissociative symptoms in relation to childhood physical and sexual abuse'. *American Journal of Psychiatry*, 147:887–892.

24 Wolfe, V.V., Gentile, C., Wolfe, D.A. (1989) 'The impact of sexual abuse on children: A PTSD formulation'. *Behaviour Therapy*, 20:215–229.

25 Putnam, F.W., Guroff, J.J., Silberman, E.K., Barban, L., Post, R.M. (1986) 'The clinical phenomenology of multiple personality disorder: Review of 100 recent cases'. *Journal of Clinical Psychiatry*, 47:285–293.

26 Ross, C.A., Norton, G.R., Wozney, K. (1989) 'Multiple personality disorder: An analysis of 236 cases'. *Canadian Journal of Psychiatry*, 34:413–418.

27 Zanarini, M.C., Gunderson, J.G., Marino, M.F., Schwartz, E.O., Frankenburg, F.R. (1989) 'Childhood experiences of borderline patients'. *Comparative Psychiatry*, 30:18–25.

28 Ogata, S., Silk, K.R., Goodrich, S., Lohr, N.E., Westen, D. and Hill, E.M. (1990) 'Childhood sexual and physical abuse in adult patients with borderline personality disorder', *American Journal of Psychiatry*, 147:1008–1013.

29 Bryer, J.B., Nelson, B.A., Miller, J.B., Krol, P.A. (1987) 'Childhood sexual and physical abuse as factors in adult psychiatric illness'. *American Journal of Psychiatry*, 144:1426–1430.

30 Westen, D., Ludolph, P., Misle, B., Ruffins, S., Bloch, J. (1990) 'Physical and sexual abuse in adolescent girls with borderline personality disorder'. *American Journal of Orthopsychiatry*, 60:55–66.

31 Waller, G. (1994) 'Childhood sexual abuse and borderline personality disorder in the eating disorders'. *Child Abuse and Neglect*, 18:97–101.

32 Staudenmayer, H., Selner, M.E., Selner, J.C. (1993) 'Adult sequelae of childhood abuse presenting as environmental illness', *Annals of Allergy*, 71:538–546.

33 Burnam, M.A., Stein, J.A., Golding, J.M. (1988) 'Sexual assault and mental disorders in a community population'. *Journal of Consulting and Clinical Psychology*, 56:843–850.

34 Oppenheimer, R., Howells, K., Palmer, R.L., Chaloner, D.A. (1985) 'Adverse sexual experience in childhood and clinical eating disorders: A preliminary description'. *Journal of Psychiatric Research*, 19:357–361.

35 Shearer, S.L., Peters, C.P., Quaytman, M.S., Ogden, R.L. (1990) 'Frequency and correlates of childhood sexual and physical abuse histories in adult female borderline inpatients'. *American Journal of Psychiatry*, 147:214–216.

36 Root, M.P. (1991) 'Persistent, disordered eating as a gender-specific, post-traumatic stress response to sexual assault'. *Psychotherapy*, 28:96–102.

37 Donaldson, M.A., Gardner, R. (1985) 'Diagnosis and treatment of traumatic stress among women after childhood incest'. In C.R. Figley (ed.), *Trauma and Its Wake: The Study and Treatment of Post-traumatic Stress Disorder*, Brunner/Mazel, New York, pp. 356–77.

38 Craine, L.S., Henson, C.E., Colliver, J.A., Maclean, D.G. (1988) 'Prevalence of a history of sexual abuse among female psychiatric

patients in a state hospital system'. *Hospital and Community Psychiatry*, 39:300–304.

39 Rowan, A.B., Foy, D.W., Rodriguez, N., Ryan, S. (1994) 'Posttraumatic stress disorder in a clinical sample of adults sexually abused as children'. *Child Abuse and Neglect*, 18:51–61.

40 Sedney, M.A., Brooks, B. (1984) 'Factors asociated with a history of childhood sexual experience in a nonclinical female population'. *Journal of the American Academy of Child Psychiatry*, 23:215–218.

41 Browne, A., Finkelhor, D. (1986) 'Impact of child sexual abuse: A review of the research'. *Psychological Bulletin*, 99:66–77.

42 Briere, J., Runtz, M. (1986) 'Suicidal thoughts and behaviours in former sexual abuse victims'. *Canadian Journal of Behavioral Science*, 18:413–423.

43 Shearer, S.L., Peters, C.P., Quaytman, M.S., Ogden RL (1990) 'Frequency and correlates of childhood sexual and physical abuse histories in adult female borderline inpatients', *American Journal of Psychiatry*, 147:214–216.

44 Yeo, H.M., Yeo, W.W. (1993) 'Repeat deliberate self-harm: A link with childhood sexual abuse?' *Archives of Emergency Medicine*, 10:161–166.

45 Meiselman, K. (1978) *Incest*. Jossey Bass, San Francisco.

46 Herman, J.L. (1981) *Father-Daughter Incest*, Harvard University Press, Cambridge, Mass.

47 Fromuth, M.E. (1986) 'The relationship of childhood sexual abuse with later psychological and sexual adjustment in a sample of college women'. *Child Abuse and Neglect*, 10:5–15.

48 Simons, R.L., Whitbeck, L.B. (1991) 'Sexual abuse as a precursor to prostitution and victimization among adolescent and adult homeless women'. *Journal of Family Issues*, 12:361–379.

49 Browne, A. (1993) 'Family violence and homelessness: The relevance of trauma histories in the lives of homeless women'. *American Journal of Orthopsychiatry*, 63:370–384.

50 Peters, S.D. (1984) 'The relationship between childhood sexual victimization and adult depression among Afro-American and white women'. Doctoral dissertation, University of California at Los Angeles (University Microfilms No. 84–28, 555).

51 Pribor, E.F., Dinwiddie, S.H. (1992) 'Psychiatric correlates of incest in childhood'. *American Journal of Psychiatry*, 149:52–56.

52 Mullen, P.E., Martin, J.L., Anderson, J.C., Romans, S.E., Herbison, G.P. (1993) 'Childhood sexual abuse and mental health in adult life'. *British Journal of Psychiatry*, 163:721–732.

53 Dempster, H.L., Roberts, J. (1991) 'Child sexual abuse: A methodological quagmire'. *Child Abuse and Neglect*, 15:593–595.

54 Wyatt, G.E., Johnson Powell, G. (1988) *Lasting Effects of Child Sexual Abuse*. Sage Publications, London.

55 Sheldrick, C. (1991) 'Adult sequelae of child sexual abuse'. *British Journal of Psychiatry*, 158 (supplement 10):55–62.

56 Wyatt, G.E., Peters, S.D. (1986) 'Issues in the definition of child sexual abuse in prevalence research'. *Child Abuse and Neglect*, 10:231–240.

57 Finkelhor, D. (1986) *A Sourcebook on Child Sexual Abuse*. Sage Publications, Beverly Hills, Cal.

58 Thomas, P. (1994) *Age*, 24 June 1994.

59 Martin, J., Anderson, J., Romans, S., Mullen, P., O'Shea, M. (1993) 'Asking about child sexual abuse: Methodological implications of a two-stage survey'. *Child Abuse and Neglect*, 17:383–392.

60 Koss, M. (1985) 'The hidden rape victim: Personality, attitudinal and situational characteristics'. *Psychology of Women Quarterly*, 9:193–212.

61 Martin, J., Anderson, J., Romans, S., Mullen, P., O'Shea, M. (1993) 'Asking about child sexual abuse: Methodological implications of a two-stage study'. *Child Abuse and Neglect*, 17:383–392.

62 Mullen, P.E., Romans-Clarkson, S.E., Martin, J.L., Anderson, J.D. (1989) 'The long-term effects of sexual assault on women's mental health', *New Zealand Medical Journal*, 13 December, 633–634.

63 Mazza, D. (1994) quoted in Sweet, M., 'GPs miss sex abuse diagnosis, study finds'. *Sydney Morning Herald*, 15 September.

64 Jacobson, A., Richardson, B. (1987) 'Assault experiences of 100 psychiatric inpatients: Evidence of the need for routine inquiry'. *American Journal of Psychiatry*, 144: 908–913.

65 Kirby, J.S., Chu, J.A., Dill, D.L. (1993) 'Correlates of dissociative symptomatology in patients with physical and sexual abuse histories'. *Comprehensive Psychiatry*, 34:258–263

66 Swett, C., Cohen, C., Surrey, J., Compaine, A., Chavez, R. (1991) 'High rates of alcohol use and history of physical and sexual abuse among women outpatients'. *American Journal of Drug and Alcohol Abuse*, 17:49–60.

67 Yama, M.F., Tovey, S.L., Fogas, B.S. (1993) 'Childhood family environment and sexual abuse as predictors of anxiety and depression in adult women'. *American Journal of Orthopsychiatry*, 63:136–141.

68 Brady, K. (1979) *Father's Days: A True Story of Incest*. Dell, New York.

69 Bass, E., Thornton, L. (eds) (1983) *I Never Told Anyone: Writing by Women Survivors of Child Sexual Abuse*. Harper & Row, New York.

70 Bass, E., Davis, L. (1988) *The Courage to Heal: A Guide for Women Survivors of Child Sexual Abuse*. Harper & Row, New York.

71 Gomes-Schwartz, B., Horowitz, J.M., Cardarelli, A.P. (1990) *Child Sexual Abuse: The Initial Effects*, Sage Publications, Beverley Hills, Cal.

72 Herman, J.L. (1986) 'Histories of violence in an outpatient population: An exploratory study'. *American Journal of Orthopsychiatry*, 56:137–141.

73 Lempert, L.B. (1986) 'Women's health from a woman's point of view: A review of the literature'. *Health Care for Women International*, 7:255–75.

74 Beitchman, J.H., Zucker, K.J., Hood, J.E., DaCosta, G.A., Akman, D., Cassavia, E. (1992) 'A review of the long-term effects of child sexual abuse'. *Child Abuse and Neglect*, 16:101–118.

75 Anderson, G., Yasenik, L., Ross, C.A. (1993) 'Dissociative experiences and disorders among women who identify themselves as sexual abuse survivors'. *Child Abuse and Neglect*, 17:677–686.

76 Nash, M.R., Hulsey, T.L., Sexton, M.C., Harralson, T.L., Lambert, W. (1993) 'Long-term sequelae of childhood sexual abuse: Perceived family environment, psychopathology and dissociation', *Journal of Consulting and Clinical Psychology*, 61:276–283.

77 Saltman, V., Solomon, R.S. (1982) 'Incest and multiple personality'. *Psychological Reports* 50:1127–1141.

78 Stern, C.R. (1984) 'The etiology of multiple personalities'. *Psychiatric Clinics of North America*, 7:149–159.

79 Bliss, E.L. (1980) 'Multiple personalities'. *Archives of General Psychiatry*, 37:1388–1397.

80 Sanders, B., Giolas, M.H. (1991) 'Dissociation and childhood trauma in psychologically disturbed adolescents'. *American Journal of Psychiatry*, 148:50–54.

81 Pribor, E.F., Yutzy, S.H., Dean, J.T., Wetzel, R.D. (1993) 'Briquet's syndrome, dissociation and abuse'. *American Journal of Psychiatry*, 150:1507–1511.

82 Ross, C.A., Ryan, L., Anderson, G., Ross, D., Hardy, L. (1989) 'Dissociative experiences in adolescents and college students'. *Dissociation*, 2:239–242.

83 Ross, C.A., Joshi, S., Currie, R. (1990) 'Dissociative experiences in the general population'. *American Journal of Psychiatry*, 147:1547–1552.

84 Ross, C.A., Miller, S.D., Reagor, P., Bjornson, L., Fraser, G.A., Anderson, G. (1991) 'Abuse histories in 102 cases of multiple personality disorder'. *Canadian Journal of Psychiatry*, 36:97–101.

85 Terr, L.C. (1991) 'Childhood traumas: An outline and overview'. *American Journal of Psychiatry*, 148:10–20.

86 Brown, G. & Harris, T. (1978) *Social Origins of Depression: A Study of Psychiatric Disorder in Women*, Tavistock Publications, London.

87 Roy, A. (1978) 'Vulnerability factors and depression in women'. *British Journal of Psychiatry*. 133:106–110.

88 Roy, A. (1981) 'Specificity of risk factors for depression'. *American Journal of Psychiatry* 138:959–961.

89 Brown, G.W., Prudo, R. (1981) 'Psychiatric disorder in a rural and an urban population: Aetiology of depression'. *Psychological Medicine*, 11:581–599.

90 Paykel, E.S., Emms, E.M., Fletcher, J. and Rassaby, E.S. (1980) 'Life events and social support in puerperal depression'. *British Journal of Psychiatry*, 136:339–346.

91 Campbell, E.A., Cope, S.J., Teasdale, J.D. (1983) 'Social factors and affective disorder: An investigation of Brown and Harris' model'. *British Journal of Psychiatry*, 143:548–553.

92 Parry, G., Shapiro, D.A. (1986) 'Life events and social support in working-class mothers: Stress buffering or independent effects'. *Archives of General Psychiatry* 43:315–323.

93 Cox, J.L., Connor, Y., Kendell, R.E. (1982) 'Prospective study of the psychiatric disorders of childbirth'. *British Journal of Psychiatry*, 140:111–117.

94 Watson, J.P., Elliot, S.A., Rugg, A.J., Brough, D.I. (1984) 'Psychiatric disorder in pregnancy and the first postnatal year'. *British Journal of Psychiatry*, 144:453–462.

95 Astbury, J., Brown, S., Lumley, J., Small, R. (1994) 'Birth events, birth experiences and social differences in postnatal depression'. *Australian Journal of Public Health*, 18:176–184.

96 Wieck, A. (1989) 'Endocrine aspects of postnatal mental disorders'. *Baillière's Clinics in Obstetrics and Gynaecology*, 3:857–877.

97 Brown, S., Lumley, J., Small, R., Astbury, J. (1994) *Missing Voices: The Experience of Motherhood.* Oxford University Press, Melbourne.

98 Dennerstein, L., Lehert, P., Riphagen, F. (1989) 'Postpartum depression — risk factors'. *Journal of Psychosomatic Obstetrics and Gynaecology*, 10:53–67.

99 Kumar, R., Robson, K.M. (1984) 'A prospective study of emotional disorders in childbearing women'. *British Journal of Psychiatry*, 144:35–47.

100 Hilberman, E. (1980) 'Overview: The wife beater's wife reconsidered'. *American Journal of Psychiatry*, 137:1336–1347.

101 Office of the Status of Women, Department of the Prime Minister and Cabinet. *A Say, a Choice, a Fair Go: Report of the Government's National Agenda for Women*, Australian Government Publishing Service, Canberra.

102 Kilpatrick, D.G., Edmunds, C.S., Seymour, A.K. (1992) *Rape in America: A Report to the Nation.* National Victims Center and Medical University of South Carolina, Arlington, Va.

103 Koss, M.P. (1990) 'The women's mental health research agenda: Violence against women', *American Psychologist*, 45:374–380.

104 Rosewater, L.B. (1988) 'Battered or schizophrenic? Psychological tests can't tell'. In K. Yllo & M. Bograd (eds), *Feminist Perspectives on Wife Abuse*, Sage Publications, Newbury Park, Cal, pp. 200–16.

105 Bassuk, E.L., Rubin, L., Lauriat, A. (1986) 'Characteristics of sheltered homeless families'. *American Journal of Public Health*, 76:1097–1101.

106 Dutton, M.A. (1992) *Empowering and Healing the Battered Woman: A Model for Assessment and Intervention.* Springer, New York.

107 Strauss, M.A., Gelles, R.J., Steinmetz, S. (1980) *Behind Closed Doors: Violence in the American Family.* Anchor/Doubleday Press, New York.

108 Commonwealth Department of Community Services and Health (1989) *National Women's Health Policy: Advancing Women's*

Health in Australia, Australian Government Publishing Service, Canberra.

109 Walker, L.E. (1989) 'Psychology and violence against women'. *American Psychologist*, 44:695–702.

110 Frank, E., Turner, S.M., Duffy, B. (1979) 'Depressive symptoms in rape victims'. *Journal of Affective Disorders*, 1:269–277.

111 Atkeson, B.M., Calhoun, K.S., Resick, P.A. (1982) 'Victims of rape: Repeated assessment of depressive symptoms'. *Journal of Consulting and Clinical Psychology*, 50:96–102.

112 Becker, J.V., Skinner, L.J., Abel, G.G. (1984) 'Depressive symptoms associated with sexual assault'. *Journal of Sex and Marital Therapy*, 10:185–192.

113 Winfield, I., George, L.K., Swartz, M., Blazer, E. (1990) 'Sexual assault and psychiatric disorders among a community sample of women'. *American Journal of Psychiatry*, 147:335–341.

114 Symonds, A. (1979) 'Violence against women: The myth of masochism', *American Journal of Psychotherapy*, 33:161–173.

115 Seligman, M.E. (1975) *Helplessness: On Depression, Development and Death*. Wiley, New York.

116 Walker, L.E. (1984) *The Battered Woman Syndrome*, Springer, New York.

117 Eichler, A., Parron, D.L. (1987) *Women's Mental Health: Agenda for Research*, National Institute of Mental Health, Rockville, Md.

118 Lee, S.H. (1988) *Women's Health Data Requirements*, Australian Institute of Health, Australian Government Publishing Service, Canberra.

119 Eaton, W.W., Kessler, L.G. (1985) 'Epidemiologic field methods in psychiatry: The NIMH Epidemiological Catchment Area Program', Academic Press, Orlando, Fla.

120 Harding, S. (1991) *Whose Science? Whose Knowledge?* Open University Press, Buckingham, UK.

BIBLIOGRAPHY

Anderson, G., Yasenik, L., Ross, C.A. (1993) 'Dissociative experiences and disorders among women who identify themselves as sexual abuse survivors'. *Child Abuse and Neglect*, 17:677–686.

Anderson, J., Martin, J., Mullen, P., Romans, S., Herbison, P. (1993) 'Prevalence of childhood sexual abuse experiences in a community sample of women'. *Journal of the American Academy of Child and Adolescent Psychiatry*, 32,5:911–919.

Ardener, E. (1975) 'Belief and the problem of women'. In Ardener, E. (ed.), *Perceiving Women*. Dent, London.

Ardener, S. (1976) *Defining Females: The Nature of Women in Society*. Croom Helm, London.

Arnold, R.P., Rogers, D., Cook, D.A.G. (1990) 'Medical problems of adults who were sexually abused in childhood', *British Medical Journal*, 300:705–708.

Astbury, J., Brown, S., Lumley, J., Small, R. (1994) 'Birth events, experiences and social differences in postnatal depression'. *Australian Journal of Public Health* 18:176–184.

Atkeson, B.M., Calhoun, K.S., Resick, P.A. (1982) 'Victims of rape: Repeated assessment of depressive symptoms'. *Journal of Consulting and Clinical Psychology*, 50:96–102.

Backman, G.A., Moeller, T.P., Bernett, J. (1988) 'Childhood sexual abuse and the consequences in adults'. *Obstetrics and Gynaecology*, 4:631–642.

Bagley, C., Ramsay, R. (1986) 'Sexual abuse in childhood: Psychosocial outcomes and implications for social work practice'. *Journal of Social Work and Human Sexuality*, 4:33–47.

Baker, A.W., Duncan, S.P. (1985) 'Child sexual abuse: A study of prevalence in Great Britain'. *Child Abuse and Neglect*, 9:457–467.

Bass, E., Davis, L. (1988) *The Courage to Heal: A Guide for Women Survivors of Child Sexual Abuse*, Harper & Row, New York.

Bass, E., Thornton L., (eds) (1983) *I Never Told Anyone: Writing by Women Survivors of Child Sexual Abuse*. Harper & Row, New York.

Bassuk, E.L., Rubin, L., Lauriat, A. (1986) 'Characteristics of sheltered homeless families'. *American Journal of Public Health*, 76:1097–1101.

Batchelor, I.R.C. (1969) *Henderson and Gillespie's Textbook of Psychiatry*. Oxford University Press, London.

Beard, G. (1881) *American Nervousness: Its Causes and Consequences*, G.P. Putnam's Sons, New York.

Becker, J.V., Skinner, L.J., Abel, G.G. (1984) 'Depressive symptoms associated with sexual assault'. *Journal of Sex and Marital Therapy*, 10:185–192.

Beitchman, J.H., Zucker, K.J., Hood, J.E., DaCosta, G.A., Akman, D., Cassavia, E. (1992) 'A review of the long-term effects of child sexual abuse'. *Child Abuse and Neglect*, 16:101–118.

Benjamin, M. (ed.) (1992) *Science and Sensibility: Gender and Scientific Enquiry 1780–1945*, Basil Blackwell, Oxford.

Bernheimer, C. & Kahane, C. (eds) (1985) *In Dora's Case: Freud–Hysteria–Feminism*, Virago, London.

Bettelheim, B. (1983; 1991) *Freud and Man's Soul*, Penguin, London.

Bifulco, A., Brown, G.W., Adler, Z. (1991) 'Early sexual abuse and clinical depression in adult life', *British Journal of Psychiatry*, 159:115–122.

Blau, A., Slaff, B., Easton, K., Welkowitz, J., Springarn, J., Cohen, J. (1963) 'The psychogenic aetiology of premature births'. *Psychosomatic Medicine* 25:201–211.

Bliss, E.L. (1980) 'Multiple personalities'. *Archives of General Psychiatry*, 37:1388–1397.

Bloch, S. & Singh, B.S. (1994) *Foundations of Clinical Psychiatry*, Melbourne University Press, Melbourne.

Brady, K. (1979) *Father's Days: A True Story of Incest*, Dell, New York.

Briere, J., Runtz, M. (1986) 'Suicidal thoughts and behaviours in former sexual abuse victims'. *Canadian Journal of Behavioral Science*, 18:413–423.

Broca, P. (1868) 'On anthropology'. *Anthropological Review*, 6.

Broverman, I.K., Vogel, S.R., Broverman, D.M., Clarkson, F.E., Rosencratz, P.S. (1972) 'Sex role stereotypes: A current appraisal'. *Journal of Social Issues* 28:58–78

Brown, G. & Harris, T. (1978) *Social Origins of Depression: A Study of Psychiatric Disorder in Women*, Tavistock Publications, London.

Brown, G.R., Anderson, B. (1991) 'Psychiatric morbidity in adult inpatients with childhood histories of sexual and physical abuse'. *American Journal of Psychiatry*, 148:55–61.

Brown, G.W., Prudo, R. (1981) 'Psychiatric disorder in a rural and an urban population: Aetiology of depression'. *Psychological Medicine*, 11:581–599.

Brown, S., Lumley, J., Small, R., Astbury, J. (1994) *Missing Voices: The Experience of Motherhood*, Oxford University Press, Melbourne.

Browne, A., Finkelhor, D. (1986) 'Impact of child sexual abuse: A review of the research'. *Psychological Bulletin*, 99:66–77.

Browne, A. (1993) 'Family violence and homelessness: The relevance of trauma histories in the lives of homeless women'. *American Journal of Orthopsychiatry*, 63:370–384.

Bryer, J.B., Nelson, B.A., Miller, J.B., Krol, P.A. (1987) 'Childhood sexual and physical abuse as factors in adult psychiatric illness'. *American Journal of Psychiatry*, 144:1426–1430.

Buckley, P. (1989) 'Fifty years after Freud: Dora, the Rat Man and the Wolf Man', *American Journal of Psychiatry*, 146:1394–1403.

Burnam, M.A., Stein, J.A., Golding, J.M. (1988) 'Sexual assault and mental disorders in a community population'. *Journal of Consulting and Clinical Psychology*, 56:843–850.

Campbell, E.A., Cope, S.J., Teasdale, J.D. (1983) 'Social factors and affective disorder: An investigation of Brown and Harris' model'. *British Journal of Psychiatry*, 143:548–553.

Carmen, E.(H.), Rieker, P.P. & Mills, T. (1984) 'Victims of violence and psychiatric illness'. *American Journal of Psychiatry*, 141:378–383.

Chu, J.A., Dill, D.L. (1990) 'Dissociative symptoms in relation to childhood physical and sexual abuse'. *American Journal of Psychiatry*, 147:887–892.

Clouston, T.S. (1884) 'Female education from a medical point of view'. *Popular Science Monthly*.

Commonwealth Department of Community Services and Health (1989) *National Women's Health Policy: Advancing Women's Health in Australia*, Australian Government Printing Service, Canberra.

Comte, A. (1851; 1875–77) *System of Positive Polity*. Longman's Green, London.

Cox, J.L., Connor, Y., Kendell, R.E. (1982) 'Prospective study of the psychiatric disorders of childbirth'. *British Journal of Psychiatry*, 140:111–117.

Craine, L.S., Henson, C.E., Colliver, J.A., Maclean, D.G. (1988) 'Prevalence of a history of sexual abuse among female psychiatric patients in a state hospital system'. *Hospital and Community Psychiatry*, 39:300–304.

Crammond, W.A. (1954) 'Psychological aspects of uterine dysfunction'. *Lancet*, 2:1241–1245.

Darwin, C. (1871; 1900) *The Descent of Man and Selection in Relation to Sex*. 2nd edn, P. F. Collier & Son, New York.

Davids, A., DeVault, S., Talmadge, M. (1961) 'Anxiety, pregnancy and childbirth abnormalities'. *Journal of Consulting Psychology* 25:76–77.

Dempster, H.L., Roberts, J. (1991) 'Child sexual abuse: A methodological quagmire'. *Child Abuse and Neglect*, 15:593–595.

Dennerstein, L., Lehert, P., Riphagen, F. (1989) 'Postpartum depression: Risk factors'. *Journal of Psychosomatic Obstetrics and Gynaecology*, 10:53–65.

Dennerstein, L.D., Astbury, J., Morse, C. (1993) *Psychosocial and Mental Health Aspects of Women's Health*. World Health Organisation, Geneva.

Deutsch, F. (1957; 1985) 'A footnote to Freud's "Fragment of an analysis of a case of hysteria"' in C. Bernheimer & C. Kahane (eds), *In Dora's Case*.

Deutsch, H. (1925) 'The psychology of woman in relation to the functions of reproduction'. Eighth International Psycho-Analytic Congress in Salzburg.

Deutsch, H. (1945; 1973) *The Psychology of Women: A Psychoanalytic Interpretation*. Bantam Books, New York.

Devereux, G. (1954) 'Why Oedipus killed Laius: A note on the complementary Oedipus', *International Journal of Psychoanalysis*, 34:132–141.

Diagnostic and Statistical Manual of Mental Disorders. DSM IV (1994) American Psychiatric Association, Washington.

Dijkstra, B. (1986) *Idols of Perversity: Fantasies of Feminine Evil in Fin-de-siècle Culture*, Oxford University Press, New York and Oxford.

Donaldson, M.A., Gardner, R. (1985) 'Diagnosis and treatment of traumatic stress among women after childhood incest'. In C.R. Figley (ed.), *Trauma and Its Wake: The Study and Treatment of Post-traumatic Stress Disorder*, Brunner/Mazel, New York.

Draijer, N. (1989) 'Long-term psychosomatic consequences of child sexual abuse'. In E. van Hall, W. Everard (eds), *The Free Woman*, Parthenon Publishing, Lancaster, UK.

Dutton, M.A. (1992) *Empowering and Healing the Battered Woman: A Model for Assessment and Intervention*. Springer, New York.

Eaton, W.W., Kessler, L.G. (1985) *Epidemiologic Field Methods in Psychiatry: The NIMH Epidemiological Catchment Area Program*, Academic Press, Orlando, Fla.

Ehrenreich, B., English, D. (1979) *For Her Own Good: 150 Years of the Experts' Advice to Women*, Pluto Press, London.

Eichler, A., Parron, D.L. (1987) *Women's Mental Health: Agenda for Research*, National Institute of Mental Health, Rockville, Md.

Fabrikant, B. (1974) 'The psychotherapist and the female patient: Perceptions, misperceptions and change'. In Franks, V., Burtle, V. (eds), *Women in Therapy*. Brunner/Mazel, New York.

Faludi, S. (1991) *Backlash: The Undeclared War Against Women*, Chatto & Windus, London.

Fee, E. (1978) 'Science and the "woman question", 1860–1920. A study of English scientific periodicals'. Princeton University, PhD dissertation.

Fenichel, O. (1946) *The Psychoanalytic Theory of Neurosis*. Routledge & Kegan Paul, London.

Finkelhor, D. (1979) *Sexually Victimised Children*. Free Press, New York.

Finkelhor, D. (1984) *Child Sexual Abuse: New Theory and Research*. Free Press, New York.

Finkelhor, D. (1986) *A Sourcebook on Child Sexual Abuse*. Sage Publications, Cal.

Finkelhor, D., Browne, A. (1985) 'The traumatic impact of child sexual abuse: A conceptualization'. *American Journal of Orthopsychiatry*, 55:530–541.

Finkelhor, D., Hotaling, G., Lewis, I.A., Smith, C. (1990) 'Sexual abuse in a national survey of adult men and women: Prevalence, characteristics and risk factors'. *Child Abuse and Neglect*, 14:19–28.

Foucault, M. (1992) 'Lecture 1: 7 January 1976'. In Gordon, C. (ed.), *Power/Knowledge: Selected Interviews and Other Writings 1972–1977*. Pantheon Books, New York.

Frank, E., Turner, S.M., Duffy, B. (1979) 'Depressive symptoms in rape victims'. *Journal of Affective Disorders*, 1:269–277.

Freud, E. L. (ed.) (1961) *Letters of Sigmund Freud, 1873–1939* (trans. Stern, T. and J.), Hogarth Press, London.

Freud, S. (1895; 1954) *The Origins of Psychoanalysis: Letters to Wilhelm Fliess, Drafts and Notes* (eds Bonaparte, M., Freud, A., Kris, E.) Imago, London.

Freud, S. (1896; 1962) 'The aetiology of hysteria', SE 3.

Freud, S. (1900) 'The interpretation of dreams', SE 4.

Freud, S. (1905; 1977) 'Fragment of an analysis of a case of hysteria', *Case Histories* (ed. J. Strachey), vol. 8, Pelican, London.

Freud, S. (1905; 1977) *Three Essays on the Theory of Sexuality*, Hogarth Press and the Institute of Psycho-Analysis, London.

Freud, S. (1905; 1991) 'The transformations of puberty', in *On Sexuality*.

Freud, S. (1925) 'Some psychical consequences of the anatomical distinction between the sexes' in *On Sexuality*.

Freud, S. (1925) 'Autobiographical study', SE 20.

Freud, S. (1931) 'Female sexuality' in *On Sexuality*.

Freud, S. (1933; 1964) 'Femininity' in *New Introductory Lectures on Psychoanalysis* (trans. & ed. J. Strachey), Hogarth Press, London.

Freud, S. (1953–74) *The Standard Edition of the Complete Psychological Works of Sigmund Freud* (trans. & ed. Strachey, J.), 24 vols, Hogarth Press and the Institute of Psycho-Analysis, London (referred to as SE followed by volume number).

Freud, S. (1991) *On Sexuality* (trans. & ed. Strachey, J.), Penguin Freud Library, vol. 7 (ed. Richards, A.), Penguin Books, London.

Fromuth, M.E. (1986) 'The relationship of childhood sexual abuse with later psychological and sexual adjustment in a sample of college women'. *Child Abuse and Neglect*, 10:5–15.

Gallop, J. (1982) *The Daughter's Seduction: Feminism and Psychoanalysis*, Cornell University Press, Ithaca, NY.

Gay, P. (1988) *Freud: A Life for Our Time*, J.M. Dent & Sons, London.

Geddes, P., Thomson, J.A. (1889; 1901) *The Evolution of Sex*. Revised ed. Walter Scott, London.

Gellner, E. (1985) *The Psychoanalytic Movement*, Paladin, London.

Gilbert, S.M., Gubar, S. (1979) *The Madwoman in the Attic: The Woman Writer and the Nineteenth Century Literary Imagination*. Yale University Press, New Haven, Conn. and London.

Gilman, C. Perkins (1981), *The Yellow Wallpaper*, Virago, London.

Gilman, S. (1991) *Inscribing the Other*. University of Nebraska Press, Lincoln.

Gilman, S. (1989) *Sexuality: An Illustrated History*, John Wiley, New York.

Gilman, S. (1991) *The Jew's Body*, Routledge, New York.

Gitlin, M.J., Pasnau, R.O. (1989) 'Psychiatric syndromes linked to reproductive function in women: A review of current knowledge'. *American Journal of Psychiatry*, 146:1413–1422.

Gomes-Schwartz, B., Horowitz, J.M., Cardarelli, A.P. (1990) *Child Sexual Abuse: The Initial Effects*, Sage, Beverley Hills, Cal.

Gould, S.J. (1989) *Wonderful Life: The Burgess Shale and the Nature of History*. Penguin Books, London.

Greenstein, B. (1993) *The Fragile Male*. Boxtree, London.

Gregory, I. (1968) *Fundamentals of Psychiatry*, W.B. Saunders Company, Philadelphia.

Hall, G. Stanley (1904) *Adolescence: Its Psychology and Its Relation to Physiology, Anthropology, Sociology, Sex, Crime, Religion and Education*. 2 vols. Sidney Appleton, London, D. Appleton & Co., New York.

Harding, S. (1991) *Whose Science? Whose Knowledge?* Open University Press, Buckingham, UK.

Harding, S. (ed.) (1987) *Feminism and Methodology*, Indiana University Press, Bloomington.

Hardman, C. (1973) 'Can there be an anthropology of children?' *Journal of the Anthropological Society of Oxford*, 4:85–99.

Harrop-Griffiths, J., Katon, W., Walker, E. (1988) 'The association between chronic pelvic pain, psychiatric diagnosis and childhood sexual abuse'. *Obstetrics and Gynaecology*, 71:589–594.

Herman, J.L. (1981) *Father-Daughter Incest*, Harvard University Press, Cambridge, Mass.

Herman, J.L. (1986) 'Histories of violence in an outpatient population: An exploratory study'. *American Journal of Orthopsychiatry*, 56:137–141.

Hilberman, E. (1980) 'Overview: The wife beater's wife reconsidered'. *American Journal of Psychiatry*, 137:1336–1347.

Horney, K. (1967) 'The flight from womanhood', in K. Horney, *Feminine Psychology* (ed. Harold Kelman), W.W. Norton & Company, New York.

Howells, J.G. (1968) *Theory and Practice of Family Psychiatry*, Oliver & Boyd, Edinburgh.

Jack, D.C. (1991) *Silencing the Self: Women and Depression*. Harvard University Press, Cambridge, Mass.

Jacobson, A., Richardson, B. (1987) 'Assault experiences of 100 psychiatric inpatients: Evidence of the need for routine inquiry'. *American Journal of Psychiatry*, 144:908–913.

James, A. (1982) *The Diary of Alice James* (ed. Edel, L.) Penguin Books, New York.

Jordanova, L. (1989) *Sexual Visions: Images of Gender in Science and Medicine between the Eighteenth and Twentieth Centuries*. Harvester Wheatsheaf, Hemel Hempstead, UK.

Kanner, L. (1957) *Child Psychiatry*, 3rd edn. Blackwell Scientific Publications, Oxford.

Kempe, C.H. (1978) 'Sexual abuse: Another hidden pediatric problem'. *Pediatrics*, 62:382–389.

Kempe, C.H., Silverman, F.N., Steele, B.F. (1962) 'The battered child syndrome'. *Journal of the American Medical Association*, 181:17–24.

Kerr, J. (1994) *A Most Dangerous Method: The Story of Jung, Freud and Sabina Spielrin*, Vintage Books, New York.

Kilpatrick, A. (1986) 'Some correlates of women's childhood sexual experiences: A retrospective study'. *Journal of Sex Research*, 22:221–242.

Kilpatrick, D.G., Edmunds, C.S., Seymour, A.K. (1992) *Rape in America: A Report to the Nation*. National Victims Center and Medical University of South Carolina, Arlington, Va.

Kirby, J.S., Chu, J.A., Dill, D.L. (1993) 'Correlates of dissociative symptomatology in patients with physical and sexual abuse histories'. *Comprehensive Psychiatry*, 34:258–263.

Kleinman, D.l., Cohen, L.J. (1991) 'The decontextualization of mental illness: The portrayal of work in psychiatric drug advertisements'. *Social Science and Medicine*, 32:867–874

Koss, M. (1985) 'The hidden rape victim: Personality, attitudinal and situational characteristics'. *Psychology of Women Quarterly*, 9:193–212.

Koss, M.P. (1990) 'The women's mental health research agenda: Violence against women', *American Psychologist*, 45:374–380.

Koutroulis, G. (1990) 'The orifice revisited: Women in gynaecological texts'. *Community Health Studies*, 14:73–84.

Kumar, R. and Robson, K.M. (1984) 'A prospective study of emotional disorders in childbearing women'. *British Journal of Psychiatry*, 144:35–47.

La Barbera, J.D., Dozier, J.E. (1980) 'Hysterical seizures: The role of sexual exploitation'. *Psychosomatics*, 21:890–897.

Lee, S.H. (1988) *Women's Health Data Requirements*, Australian Institute of Health, Australian Government Publishing Service, Canberra.

Lempert, L.B. (1986) 'Women's health from a woman's point of view: A review of the literature'. *Health Care for Women International*, 7:255–75.

Leventhal, J.M. (1990) 'Epidemiology of child sexual abuse' in R.K. Oates (ed.), *Understanding and Managing Child Sexual Abuse*, Harcourt Brace Jovanovich, Sydney.

Lewis, R.W.B. (1991) *The Jameses: A Family Narrative*, Farrar, Strauss & Giroux, New York.

Linton, E.L. (1891) 'The wild women: As politicians'. *Nineteenth Century*, 30.

Malcolm, J. (1982) *Psychoanalysis: The Impossible Profession*, Picador, London.

Margo, J. (1994) 'Gaslighting snuffs the flame', *Sydney Morning Herald*, 15 September.

Margolin, L. (1992) 'Sexual abuse by grandparents'. *Child Abuse and Neglect*, 16:735–742.

Martin, J., Anderson, J., Romans, S., Mullen, P., O'Shea, M. (1993) 'Asking about child sexual abuse: Methodological implications of a two-stage survey'. *Child Abuse and Neglect*, 17:383–392.

Masson J. (1984; 1992) *The Assault on Truth*, Fontana, London.

Masson, J. (1988) *Against Therapy*, Collins, London.

Mazza, D. (1994) quoted in Sweet, M., 'GPs miss sex abuse diagnosis, study finds'. *Sydney Morning Herald*, 15 September.

McDonald, R.L., Gynther, M.D., Christakos, A.C. (1965) 'Relations between self and parental perceptions of unwed mothers and obstetric complications'. *Psychosomatic Medicine*, 27:31–38.

McGrigor, Allan J. (1869) 'On the real differences in the minds of men and women'. *Journal of the Anthropological Society*, 7.

Mead, M. (1928; 1971) *Coming of Age in Samoa*, Penguin Books, London.

Meiselman, K. (1978) *Incest*. Jossey Bass, San Francisco.

Mill, J.S. (1869; 1965) *On the Subjection of Women*, Dent, London.

Mitchell, J. (1975) *Psychoanalysis and Feminism*, Penguin, Harmondsworth.

Monk, R. (1991) *Ludwig Wittgenstein: The Duty of Genius*, Vintage, London.

Morrison, J. (1989) 'Childhood sexual histories of women with somatization disorder.' *American Journal of Psychiatry*, 146:239–241.

Morrison, T, (1993) Interview with David Streitfeld, *Washington Post*, reproduced in the *Age*, 23 October.

Mullen, P.E., Romans-Clarkson, S.E., Walton, V.A. & Herbison, P. (1988) 'Impact of sexual and physical abuse on women's mental health.' *Lancet*, 16:841–845.

Mullen, P.E., Romans-Clarkson S.E., Martin, J.L., Anderson, J.D. (1989) 'The long-term effects of sexual assault on women's mental health,' *New Zealand Medical Journal* (December) 13:633–634.

Mullen, P.E., Martin, J.L., Anderson, J.C., Romans, S.E., Herbison, G.P. (1993) 'Childhood sexual abuse and mental health in adult life.' *British Journal of Psychiatry*, 163:721–732.

Murphy, S.M., Kilpatrick, D.G., Amick-McMullan, A., Veronen, L.J., Paduhovich, J., Best, C.L., Villeponteauz, L.A. and Saunders, B.E. (1988) 'Current psychological functioning of child sexual assault survivors.' *Journal of Interpersonal Violence*, 3:55–79.

Nash, M.R., Hulsey, T.L., Sexton, M.C., Harralson, T.L., Lambert, W. (1993) 'Long term sequelae of childhood sexual abuse: Perceived family environment, psychopathology and dissociation,' *Journal of Consulting and Clinical Psychology*, 61, 276–283.

Office of the Status of Women, Commonwealth Department of the Prime Minister and Cabinet (1988) *A Say, a Choice, a Fair Go: Report of the Government's National Agenda for Women*, Australian Government Publishing Service, Canberra.

Ogata, S., Silk, K.R., Goodrich, S., Lohr, N.E., Westen, D. and Hill, E.M. (1990) 'Childhood sexual and physical abuse in adult patients with borderline personality disorder,' *American Journal of Psychiatry*, 147:1008–1013.

Oppenheimer, R., Howells, K., Palmer, R.L., Chaloner, D.A. (1985) 'Adverse sexual experience in childhood and clinical eating disorders: A preliminary description.' *Journal of Psychiatric Research*, 19:357–361.

Palmer, R.L., Evans, D. (1971) 'Psychoneurotic status, hostility and complications of pregnancy.' In *Proceedings of the Third Interna-*

tional Congress of Psychosomatic Medicine in Obstetrics and Gynae-cology. London.

Parry, G., Shapiro, D.A. (1986) 'Life events and social support in working-class mothers: Stress buffering or independent effects'. *Archives of General Psychiatry* 43:315–323.

Paykel, E.S., Emms, E.M., Fletcher, J., Rassaby, E.S. (1980) 'Life events and social support in puerperal depression'. *British Journal of Psychiatry*, 136:339–346.

Peters, S.D. (1984) 'The relationship between childhood sexual victimisation and adult depression among Afro-American and white women'. Doctoral dissertation, University of California at Los Angeles (University Microfilms No 84-28, 555).

Pribor, E.F., Dinwiddie, S.H. (1992) 'Psychiatric correlates of incest in childhood'. *American Journal of Psychiatry*, 149:52–56.

Pribor, E.F., Yutzy, S.H., Dean, J.T., Wetzel, R.D. (1993) 'Briquet's syndrome, dissociation and abuse'. *American Journal of Psychiatry*, 150:1507–1511.

Putnam, F.W., Guroff, J.J., Silberman, E.K., Barban, L., Post, R.M. (1986) 'The clinical phenomenology of multiple personality disorder: Review of 100 recent cases'. *Journal of Clinical Psychiatry*, 47:285–293.

Ratcliffe, J.W. (1976) 'Analyst biases in KAP surveys: A cross-cultural comparison'. *Studies in Family Planning*, 7:322–330.

Rees, J.R. (ed.) (1949) *Modern Practice in Psychological Medicine*. Butterworth & Co., London.

Richards, T.W. (1946) *Modern Clinical Psychology*, McGraw-Hill, New York.

Rieker, P.P., Carmen, E. (H) (1986) 'The victim-to-patient process: The disconfirmation and transformation of abuse'. *American Journal of Orthopsychiatry*, 56:360–370.

Ringrose, C.A.D. (1961) 'Psychosomatic influences in the genesis of toxaemia of pregnancy'. *Canadian Medical Journal*, 84:647–651.

Ritvo, L.B. (1990) *Darwin's Influence on Freud: A Tale of Two Sciences*. Yale University Press, New Haven, Conn.

Root, M.P. (1991) 'Persistent disordered eating as a gender-specific, post-traumatic stress response to sexual assault'. *Psychotherapy*, 28:96–102.

Rosewater, L.B. (1988) 'Battered or schizophrenic? Psychological tests can't tell'. In K. Yllo & M. Bograd (eds), *Feminist Perspectives on Wife Abuse*, Sage, Newbury Park, Cal.

Ross, C.A., Joshi, S., Currie, R. (1990) 'Dissociative experiences in the general population.' *American Journal of Psychiatry*, 147:1547–1552.

Ross, C.A., Miller, S.D., Reagor, P., Bjornson, L., Fraser, G.A., Anderson, G. (1991) 'Abuse histories in 102 cases of multiple personality disorder.' *Canadian Journal of Psychiatry*, 36:97–101.

Ross, C.A., Norton, G.R., Wozney, K. (1989) 'Multiple personality disorder: An analysis of 236 cases.' *Canadian Journal of Psychiatry*, 34:413–418.

Ross, C.A., Ryan, L., Anderson, G., Ross, D., Hardy, L. (1989), 'Disso-ciative experiences in adolescents and college students.' *Dissociation*, 2:239–242.

Ross, T.A. (1941) *The Common Neuroses: Their Treatment by Psy-chotherapy.* 2nd edn, Edward Arnold & Co., London.

Rowan, A.B., Foy, D.W., Rodriguez, N., Ryan, S. (1994) 'Posttraumatic stress disorder in a clinical sample of adults sexually abused as chil-dren.' *Child Abuse and Neglect*, 18:51–61.

Roy, A. (1978) 'Vulnerability factors and depression in women.' *British Journal of Psychiatry.* 133:106–110.

Roy, A. (1981) 'Specificity of risk factors for depression.' *American Jour-nal of Psychiatry* 138:959–961.

Ruskin, J. (1865) *Sesame and Lilies*, Blackie & Son, London.

Russell Davis, D. (1957) *An Introduction to Psychopathology*, Oxford University Press, London.

Russell, D.E. (1983) 'The incidence and prevalence of intrafamilial and extrafamilial sexual abuse of female children.' *Child Abuse and Neglect*, 7:133–146.

Russell, D.E. (1986) *The Secret Trauma: Incest in the Lives of Girls and Women*, Basic Books, New York.

Russett Eagle, C. (1989) *Sexual Science: The Victorian Construction of Womanhood*, Harvard University Press, Cambridge, Mass.

Saltman, V., Solomon, R.S. (1982) 'Incest and multiple personality.' *Psy-chological Reports* 50:1127–1141.

Sanders, B., Giolas, M.H. (1991) 'Dissociation and childhood trauma in psychologically disturbed adolescents.' *American Journal of Psychia-try*, 148:50–54.

Schur, M. (1972) *Freud: Living and Dying*, International Universities Press, New York.

Scully, D., Bart, P. (1973) 'A funny thing happened on the way to the ori-fice: Women in gynecology textbooks.' *American Journal of Sociol-ogy*, 78:1045–1050.

Sedney, M.A., Brooks, B. (1984) 'Factors associated with a history of childhood sexual experience in a nonclinical female population.' *Jour-nal of the American Academy of Child Psychiatry*, 23:215–218.

Seligman, M.E. (1975) *Helplessness: On Depression, Development and Death.* Wiley, New York.

Shearer, S.L., Peters, C.P., Quaytman, M.S., Ogden, R.L. (1990) 'Fre-quency and correlates of childhood sexual and physical abuse histo-ries in adult female borderline inpatients.' *American Journal of Psychiatry*, 147:214–216.

Sheldrick, C. (1991) 'Adult sequelae of child sexual abuse.' *British Jour-nal of Psychiatry*, 158 (supplement 10) 55–62.

Shirley, H.F. (1963) *Pediatric Psychiatry*, Harvard University Press, Cambridge, Mass.

Shorter, E. (1989) 'Women and Jews in a private nervous clinic in late nineteenth century Vienna.' *Medical History*, 33:149–183.

Shorter, E. (1992) *From Paralysis to Fatigue: A History of Psychosomatic Illness in the Modern Era*, Free Press, New York.

Showalter, E. (1987) *The Female Malady: Women, Madness and English Culture, 1830–1980*. Virago Press, London.

Showalter, E. (1989) 'A historical overview: Opening up the woman's case.' In E. Van Hall and W. Everard (eds) *The Free Woman: Women's Health in the 1990s*, Parthenon, Carnforth, UK and New Jersey, 1989.

Sim, M. (1968) *Guide to Psychiatry*, 2nd edn, E. & S. Livingstone, Edinburgh.

Simmel, G. (1967) *Philosophische Kultur*, quoted in K Horney, 'The flight from womanhood', *Feminine Psychology*, pp. 54–70.

Simons, R.L., Whitbeck, L.B. (1991) 'Sexual abuse as a precursor to prostitution and victimization among adolescent and adult homeless women.' *Journal of Family Issues*, 12:361–379.

Skottowe, I. (1953) *Clinical Psychiatry for Practitioners and Students*, Eyre & Spottiswoode, London.

Sprengnether, M. (1985) 'Enforcing Oedipus: Freud and Dora', in Bernheimer and Kahane (eds), *In Dora's Case*.

Staudenmayer, H., Selner, M.E., Selner, J.C. (1993) 'Adult sequelae of childhood abuse presenting as environmental illness,' *Annals of Allergy*, 71:538–546.

Stein, J.A., Golding, J.M., Siegel, J.M., Burnam, M.A. & Sorenson, S.B. (1988) 'Long term psychological sequalae of child sexual abuse: The Los Angeles Epidemiologic Catchment Area study.' In G.E. Wyatt and G.J. Powell (eds), *Lasting Effects of Child Sexual Abuse*, Sage, Newbury Park, Cal.

Steinhauer, P.D., Rae-Grant, Q. (eds) (1983) *Psychological Problems of the Child in the Family*. Basic Books, New York.

Stephen, L. (1883) 'Remarks on the influence of science'. *Popular Science Monthly*, 24:82.

Stern, C.R. (1984) 'The etiology of multiple personalities'. *Psychiatric Clinics of North America*, 7:149–159.

Strauss, M.A., Gelles, R.J., Steinmetz, S. (1980) *Behind Closed Doors: Violence in the American Family*. Anchor/Doubleday Press, New York.

Swett, C., Cohen, C., Surrey, J., Compaine, A., Chavez, R. (1991) 'High rates of alcohol use and history of physical and sexual abuse among women outpatients'. *American Journal of Drug and Alcohol Abuse*, 17:49–60.

Symonds, A. (1979) 'Violence against women: The myth of masochism', *American Journal of Psychotherapy*, 33:161–173.

Tan, A. (1989) *The Joy Luck Club*, William Heinemann, London.

Terr, L.C. (1991) 'Childhood traumas: An outline and overview'. *American Journal of Psychiatry*, 148:10–20.

Thomas, P. (1994) *Washington Post* article reprinted in the *Age*, 24 June.

Topinard, P. (1878) *Anthropology*, Chapman & Hall, London.

Uddenburg, N., Fagerstrom, C.F. (1976) 'The deliveries of daughters of reproductively maladjusted mothers'. *Journal of Psychosomatic Research* 20:223–230.

Vertinsky, P. (1990) *The Eternally Wounded Woman: Women, Doctors and Exercise in the Nineteenth Century*. Manchester University Press, Manchester and New York.

Walker, L.E. (1984) *The Battered Woman Syndrome*, Springer, New York.

Walker, L.E. (1989) 'Psychology and violence against women'. *American Psychologist*, 44:695–702.

Waller, G. (1994) 'Childhood sexual abuse and borderline personality disorder in the eating disorders'. *Child Abuse and Neglect*, 18:97–101.

Ware, N.C., Kleinman, A. (1992) 'Culture and somatic experience: The social course of illness in neurasthenia and chronic fatigue syndrome', *Psychosomatic Medicine*, 54:546–560.

Watkins, S.C. (1993) 'If all we knew about women was what we read in *Demography*, what would we know?' *Demography* 30, 551–574.

Watson, J.P., Elliot, S.A., Rugg, A.J., Brough, D.I. (1984) 'Psychiatric disorder in pregnancy and the first postnatal year'. *British Journal of Psychiatry*, 144:453–462.

Weedon, C. (1987) *Feminist Practice and Poststructuralist Theory*. Basil Blackwell, Oxford.

Weininger, O. (1904; 1906) *Sex and Character*, William Heinemann, London.

Westen, D., Ludolph, P., Misle, B., Ruffins, S., Bloch, J. (1990) 'Physical and sexual abuse in adolescent girls with borderline personality disorder'. *American Journal of Orthopsychiatry*, 60:55–66.

Wieck, A. (1989) 'Endocrine aspects of postnatal mental disorders'. *Baillière's Clinics in Obstetrics and Gynaecology*, 3:857–877.

Wilkerson, I. (1989) 'Charges against doctor bring ire and questions'. *New York Times*, 11 December.

Winfield, I., George, L.K., Swartz, M., Blazer, E. (1990) 'Sexual assault and psychiatric disorders among a community sample of women'. *American Journal of Psychiatry*, 147:335–341.

Wolfe, V.V., Gentile, C., Wolfe, D.A. (1989) 'The impact of sexual abuse on children: A PTSD formulation'. *Behaviour Therapy*, 20:215–229.

Wyatt, G.E. (1985) 'The sexual abuse of Afro-American and white American women in childhood'. *Child Abuse and Neglect*, 9:507–519.

Wyatt, G.E., Peters, S.D. (1986) 'Issues in the definition of child sexual abuse in prevalence research'. *Child Abuse and Neglect*, 10:231–240.

Wyatt, G.E., Johnson Powell, G. (1988) *Lasting Effects of Child Sexual Abuse*. Sage Publications, London, 1988.

Yama, M.F., Tovey, S.L., Fogas, B.S. (1993) 'Childhood family environment and sexual abuse as predictors of anxiety and depression in adult women'. *American Journal of Orthopsychiatry*, 63:136–141.

Yeo, H.M., Yeo, W.W. (1993) 'Repeat deliberate self harm: A link with childhood sexual abuse?' *Archives of Emergency Medicine*, 10:161–166.

Zanarini, M.C., Gunderson, J.G., Marino, M.F., Schwartz, E.O., Frankenburg, F.R. (1989) 'Childhood experiences of borderline patients'. *Comparative Psychiatry*, 30:18–25.

Zilboorg, G. (1928) 'Malignant psychoses related to childbirth'. *American Journal of Obstetrics and Gynecology*, 15:145.

Zilboorg, G. (1929) 'The dynamics of schizophrenic reactions related to parenthood'. *American Journal of Psychiatry* 8:733–767.

INDEX